IMAGES
of America

AROUND CAMBRIDGE, WHITE CREEK, AND JACKSON

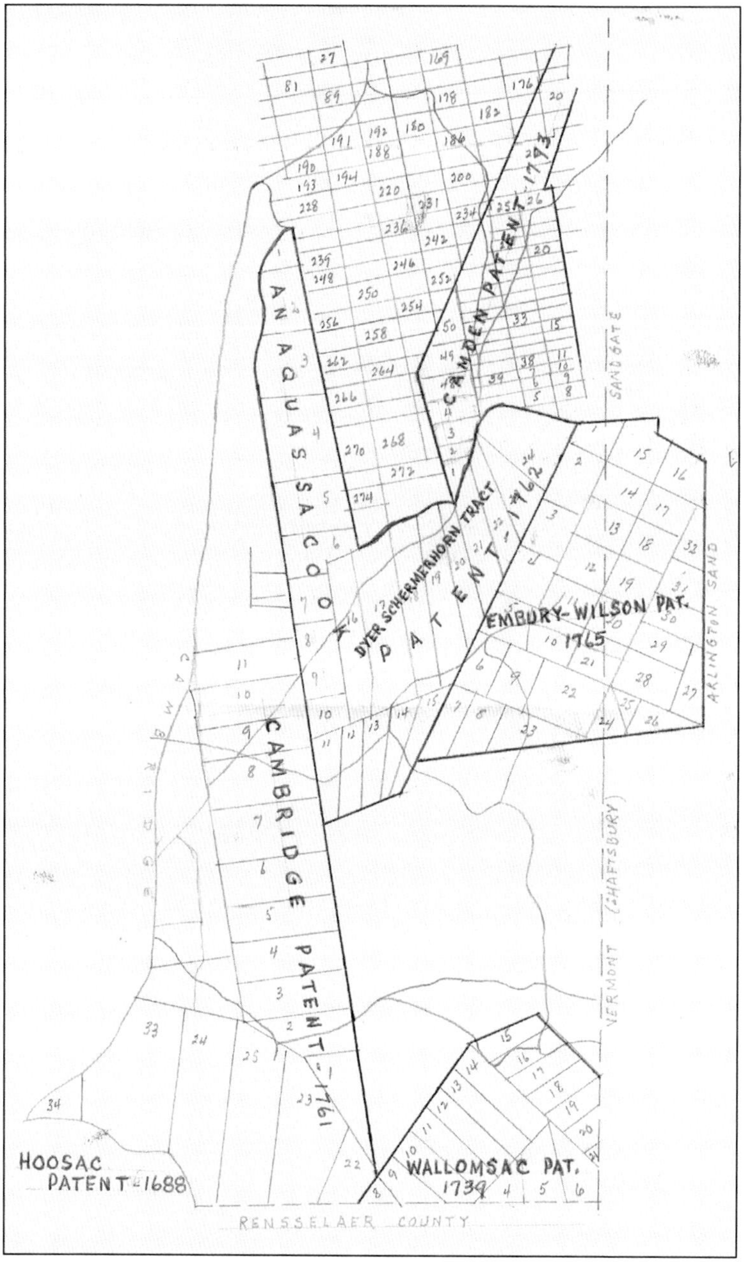

The Cambridge Valley was settled in the mid- to late 1700s through the issuance of land grants known as patents. Many of today's property deeds trace back to the lot number on one of these patents. For many years, the boundaries of these patents, not the district or town boundaries drawn by governments, identified the communities. (Map drawn by Ken Gottry Sr.)

ON THE COVER: Cambridge developed as two separate communities only three-quarters of a mile apart. In the late 1800s, Jerome B. Rice filled in the intervening swamp and built his seed house, seen here decorated for the 1916 Old Home Week. However, it was not until 1924 that the village reincorporated, finally eliminating the terms East District and West District. (Courtesy of Cambridge Public Library.)

IMAGES
of America

AROUND CAMBRIDGE, WHITE CREEK, AND JACKSON

Ken Gottry

ARCADIA
PUBLISHING

ISBN 978-0-7385-7372-4

Published by Arcadia Publishing
Charleston, South Carolina

Printed in the United States of America

Library of Congress Control Number: 2010925884

For all general information, please contact Arcadia Publishing:
Telephone 843-853-2070
Fax 843-853-0044
E-mail sales@arcadiapublishing.com
For customer service and orders:
Toll-Free 1-888-313-2665

Visit us on the Internet at www.arcadiapublishing.com

To Ken Gottry Sr., whose life and accomplishments I'm only now beginning to fully appreciate.

Contents

ACKNOWLEDGMENTS

Thanks to my father, Ken Gottry Sr., who spent thousands of hours collecting and organizing local history. His collection formed the starting point of my collection. I used his record of village board meetings to add the facts around which I love to weave my stories.

Thanks to my mother, Charlotte Hitchcock Gottry, who spent years writing for local newspapers. I used her articles to recall and clarify everyday life in the mid- to late 1900s.

Thanks to Dave Thornton, my high school English teacher and local historian. Everywhere I turned during my research, I saw evidence of Dave having been there before me. Dave enlightened and entertained a generation with his "Tales of Old Cambridge" series in the local newspaper.

Finally, thanks to you, the reader and the collector. I am sure my stories will elicit corrections and additions that will enhance my understanding of our history.

Unless otherwise noted, all images appear courtesy of the author. Other major contributions came from the Cambridge Village Archives (CVA), under the direction of Mary Anne McAvoy, and the Cambridge Public Library (CPL), under the direction of Judy Center.

INTRODUCTION

When the New York colony was divided into counties in 1683, Albany County was established, extending north to Canada and encompassing all of the current towns of Cambridge, White Creek, and Jackson. The division of this land occurred over the next 80 years through the issuance of land grants by representatives of King George III.

The first division occurred in 1688 with the issuance of the Hoosic patent. Today this land along the Hoosick River is in the town of Cambridge. The next division occurred in 1739, when Stephen Van Rensselaer procured the Wallomsac patent whose 12,000 acres covered the White Creek Valley.

The next portion of the valley to be settled was the 31,500 acres north of the Hoosic patent. This 1761 Cambridge patent included the current village and, as such, is used as the establishment date of the community. The original six land speculators (Isaac Sawyer, Edmond Wells, Jacob Lansing, Alexander Colden, William Smith, and Goldsboro Banyer) subdivided the land into 100-acre lots for the first 30 families to settle in Cambridge.

Between 1761 and 1764, the first families to settle in Cambridge included John McClung, James and Robert Cowan, Samuel Bell, Col Blair, George Gilmore, George Duncan, David Harrow, William Clark, John Scott, and Thomas Morrison. Morrison's lot No. 9 became the center of today's village, and his son was the first child born in Cambridge.

Many of today's residents of the Cambridge Valley can trace their ancestry to other early settlers of the Cambridge patent, including Ephram Cowan, Robert Gilmore, Austin Wells, Samuel Clark, Jonathan Morrison, Edmond Wells, John Allen, David Sprague, Seth Chase, John Harroun, Thomas McCool, Thomas Ashton, Simeon Fowler, John Young, Josiah Dewey, Ruel Beebe, William Eager, William Selfridge, John Younglove, and John Corey.

The areas to the north and east were the next to be settled. To the north, 10,000 acres became the Annaquassacoke patent granted to Schermerhorn. Early settlers to this portion of Jackson included James Irvine, Peter McGill, Jonathan Conger, and Eben Billings. To the east, 8,000 acres became the Embury patent. This is often referred to as the Embury-Wilson patent, as a second patent for the same land appears to have been granted to Wilson. Early settlers to this portion of White Creek included James McKie and John, Francis, and William Nicholson.

The people who settled each patent usually had much in common. Often they were from the same families. Sometimes they came from the same area, either in the colonies or in the British Isles. Also, they often had similar religious beliefs.

However, when the British colonial government began mapping the new territories, lines were drawn without respect for the ties within a patent. In 1772, the Colonial Assembly passed an act that declared Cambridge a district (districts were, by colonial law, similar to towns today). When the act went into law the following year, the Cambridge District covered all or part of seven different patents—land that today includes the towns of Cambridge, White Creek, and Jackson, as well as Shaftsbury in present-day Vermont.

The first Cambridge District meeting was held on the first Tuesday of May 1773. Thomas Morrison served as moderator. From the start, the residents of the district let it be known that boundaries drawn on a map did not necessarily mean cohesiveness. On February 1, 1775, the White Creek portion of the district unsuccessfully petitioned the assembly to be set off from Cambridge.

The issuance of the patents brought many settlers to the Cambridge Valley. The increased population prompted changes in the government alignment. In 1772, the northern portion of Albany County was set off and called Charlotte County, named for King George's queen. The Battenkill River served as the boundary between the counties, thus, Cambridge, located south of the river, remained part of Albany County.

For many years, the eastern boundary of the state was indefinite. New Hampshire and New York both claimed the land between the Connecticut River and the Hudson River. The British government originally settled the issue by declaring that the Cambridge District was in New York State. However, as the war for independence progressed, the issue became muddy once again.

Buoyed by the colonies' success at the Battle of Bennington in 1777, the Green Mountain Boys of Vermont declared themselves independent of both New York and New Hampshire. In fact, this led some to conclude that Vermont was not at war with England since it was not part of the 13 colonies. In 1781, Vermont, not yet a state, declared it owned all the land west to the Hudson River, including Charlotte County and the northern portion of Albany County.

Representatives of the districts in Albany and Charlotte Counties held the Union Convention in Cambridge on May 9, 1781, to decide their allegiance. Those faithful to New York ignored the convention, so the secessionists had their way at the convention. They produced the Articles of Union, signed by the Cambridge representatives, which resolved that they were no longer part of New York State but rather under the jurisdiction of Vermont.

On June 16, 1781, Phineas Whiteside and Joseph Caldwell took seats in the Vermont Legislature as representatives of the Cambridge District. One year later, on March 1, 1782, a second convention was held in Cambridge, at which time a petition was sent to New York State, asking to restore the districts to their former status in the state.

Following the Revolutionary War, the new American government renamed the territories but did not initially adjust any boundaries. In 1784, Charlotte County was renamed Washington County in honor of the great general. In 1788, the district was declared the Town of Cambridge, still encompassing all of Jackson, White Creek, and Cambridge.

The population of the Cambridge Valley grew rapidly following the war. The first national census in 1790 lists Cambridge under Albany County with a population of 4,996, forty-five of whom were slaves. By the 1800 census, the population of Cambridge had risen to 6,108.

With the growing population, it was again necessary to adjust boundaries, though these lines drawn on a map by governments often meant little to the residents. In 1791, Albany County was split again. The town of Cambridge, whose business and social relations were closely tied to Lansingburgh, desired to be part of the new county of Rensselaer to the south. However, Salem, which had considerable influence in Albany, desired the county line to be placed as far south as possible. As a result, the Hoosick River was chosen as the dividing line between Washington and Rensselaer counties, moving Cambridge into Washington County.

By an Act of the New York State Legislature in 1815, effective April 1, 1816, the town of Cambridge was subdivided into the present towns of Cambridge, White Creek, and Jackson. The reason for the division is not clear; however, it may go back as far as White Creek's 1775 petition to separate from Cambridge. The first town supervisors were James Stevenson (Cambridge), William Richards (White Creek), and James Irvine (Jackson).

While the town boundaries were being addressed by the government, the village began to take shape as settlers coalesced into four distinct communities at the corners along the current Main Street. Moving from east to west, these communities were Dorr's Corners (Gilbert Street), North White Creek (Park Street), Cambridge Corners (Union Street), and Stephenson's Corners, later known as Coila (Center Cambridge Road).

Cambridge Corners (today known as the West End) and North White Creek (today known as the East End) were separated by half a mile. In between, Blair's Brook (today known as the Owl Kill) and the Cambridge Creek converged south of Main Street to form the Cambridge swamp.

Following storms, the swamp made Main Street impassable, adding to the separation between the East End and West End that shaped the development of the village of Cambridge.

Cambridge Corners (West End) was the first to develop, thanks to the Northern Turnpike. In 1799, a superhighway was built from Lansingburgh to Granville. Traffic from New York City to Canada went by boat to Albany, then took the turnpike through Cambridge to Granville where another road took the traveler to Montreal. Cambridge Corners prospered as the stage traffic led to the creation of hotels and liveries at the intersection of the current Main and Union Streets.

Soon after, North White Creek (East End) found a way to divert the lucrative turnpike traffic. A shunpike heading to the east was built south of Cambridge Corners. This road circumvented the turnpike toll booths in Cambridge Corners, routing stage traffic through the East End. North White Creek began to prosper as hotels and liveries grew up at the intersection of the current Main and Park Streets.

In the 1820s, the Champlain Canal was built 20 miles west of Cambridge, shifting some traffic to the new water route to Canada. Although turnpike traffic decreased, it remained a vital component of Cambridge's economic development for the first half of the 1800s, although the two ends of the community maintained their separate identities and development.

Many prominent citizens envisioned a united Cambridge in the mid-1800s. In 1850, when a plan was devised for a railroad from Troy to Rutland, Coila was the obvious location because of its flat, dry land. The residents there said "no thanks," so in 1852, the railroad was built through the Cambridge swamp halfway between the West End and East End. Commercial expansion driven by the railroad began the convergence of "The Corners."

In the early 1860s, the communities began talking seriously about merging into a single village. This was partly driven by the desire for a unified fire department following two devastating fires: one on the East End and one on the West End. The swamp separating the East and the West Ends was so muddy that a pumper transported by railroad car from Salem 10 miles away arrived at the East End fire before the fire department from the West End.

After five years of debates, petitions, and votes, The Corners finally agreed on a plan. On April 20, 1866, the New York State Legislature passed an act incorporating the Village of Cambridge. However, mixed with the force of unity was the century-old desire for separation, as evidenced by the incorporation's provision for an East District and a West District. The lack of total unity is further evidenced by three amendments to the incorporation over the first two years: on April 10, 1867, on April 22, 1868, and again on May 9, 1868. Two generations later, the village was reincorporated in 1924, finally eliminating the two districts.

The separation and unity of the community can also be seen in the history of local schools. In 1799, a private school was created on the far west side of the West End, which angered the East Enders, who, unable to regularly navigate the swamp, withdrew their support for the school. This school became the Cambridge Washington Academy in 1815.

In addition to this private school, the East End and West End each had a one-room schoolhouse. The East End brick schoolhouse on North Park Street stands today, being the oldest schoolhouse in Cambridge. The East End (school district No. 10) and the West End (school district No. 1) held heated debates 150 years later when trying to name the newly centralized school district.

Throughout the latter half of the 1800s and the first half of the 1900s, the East End and West End chose to maintain their separation rather than unite to take advantage of financial aid offered by New York State to consolidate schools. In 1853, Cambridge did not participate in New York State's Union School Act. Twenty years later, they voted to unite but could not agree on a plan, so they ended up starting two schools. The old Cambridge Washington Academy was reopened as the Cambridge Union School of the West District, while the Putnam estate was opened as the Cambridge Union School of the East District.

In 1891, almost 100 years after the first school vote highlighted the community's division, the residents of the village finally agreed to build one school. The Cambridge Union School was built in the reclaimed swamp, halfway between the West End and the East End. The land was sold by Jerome Rice so that the school could be built next to his seed house.

However, outside the village in the towns of Cambridge, White Creek, and Jackson, the residents wanted to preserve their independence and their rural, one-room schoolhouses. In 1927, New York State's Central School Act encouraged the 276 rural schools in Washington County to consolidate into 11 centralized schools. The state offered money to help with the construction and transportation costs. The voters of the Cambridge Central School District said "no thanks."

Around 1940, the voters in the school district began discussing building a new school, one large enough to consolidate all the rural schools and the current Union School. In 1946, the Hitchcock farm on South Park Street was purchased for a new centralized school. However, throughout the next year, the East Enders and West Enders had bitter debates and votes over the plans for the new school.

The issue became forced when the old school burned in August 1947 (some still call the fire mysterious). For four years, students attended classes in churches and businesses throughout the village as voters debated the plans and costs of a new school. The plans had not even been completely finalized when the cornerstone of the new school was laid in September 1950. The desire for separation and the desire for unity lingered.

One more microcosm of the unity and separation that has existed since the late 1700s can be seen in the paving of Main Street with yellow bricks in 1913. Paving began in March 1913 but was delayed due to numerous problems. Beneath much of the problem lay the century-old feud between the East End and the West End.

By July 1913, bricklaying on the East End had proceeded from Dorr's Corners (Gilbert Street) to Park Street, but on the West End, no bricks had been laid. The ongoing feud between the East End and West End resulted in a construction plan to lay some bricks on one end of the village then move the entire operation to the other end of the village. All of this to ensure neither end would have an advantage.

As 1913 drew to a close, two sections of the completed yellow-brick road on the West End cracked from curb to curb, which was met with howls of laughter from the East Enders. Yet in April 1914, villagers from East and West held a joint impromptu street dance to celebrate their dry, paved street following a late snowstorm.

Cambridge, White Creek, and Jackson celebrate many dates of unity and separation in their history. There was the 1873 town centennial, the 1916 Old Home Week, and the 1966 village centennial. The nation's 1976 bicentennial celebration included the planting of trees throughout the village, just as had been done 100 years earlier. The 200th anniversary of the Old Cambridge District in 1988 produced a 300-page compilation of history and family genealogy.

One motivation for this book is the 250th anniversary of the Cambridge patent (1761–2011), another opportunity for Cambridge, White Creek, and Jackson to celebrate their unity and their separation.

One

East End

The East End of the village of Cambridge, originally known as North White Creek, centered at the intersection of Main and Park Streets. The shunpike diverted stage traffic around tollbooths on the Northern Turnpike (Union Street) and through the East End. This probably helped in the creation of the numerous hotels, liveries, and taverns at that intersection.

Another, longer shunpike went along New York Route 313, across Plains Road, reconnecting to the turnpike near Long Pond (Lake Lauderdale). This shunpike probably helped the formation of Dorr's Corners at the intersection of Main and Gilbert Streets.

What is today called the East End was officially designated the East District when the village incorporated in 1866. The brick house on North Park Street just north of the United Presbyterian Church served the original school district No. 10, for which the Union School and, later, the Central School were named.

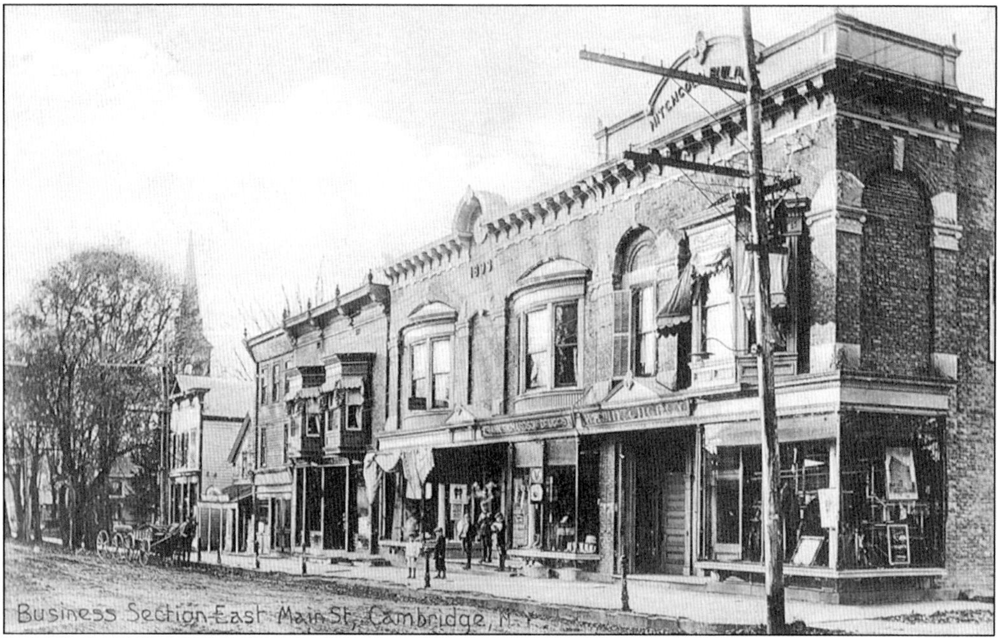

The main business district of the East End has not changed much since the Hitchcock building was erected in 1899. The clothing store on the corner was run by the Hitchcock family for over 60 years. The children are standing in front of the drugstore run by Frank Richardson, later Walter LeGrys, and then Walter Kinnan.

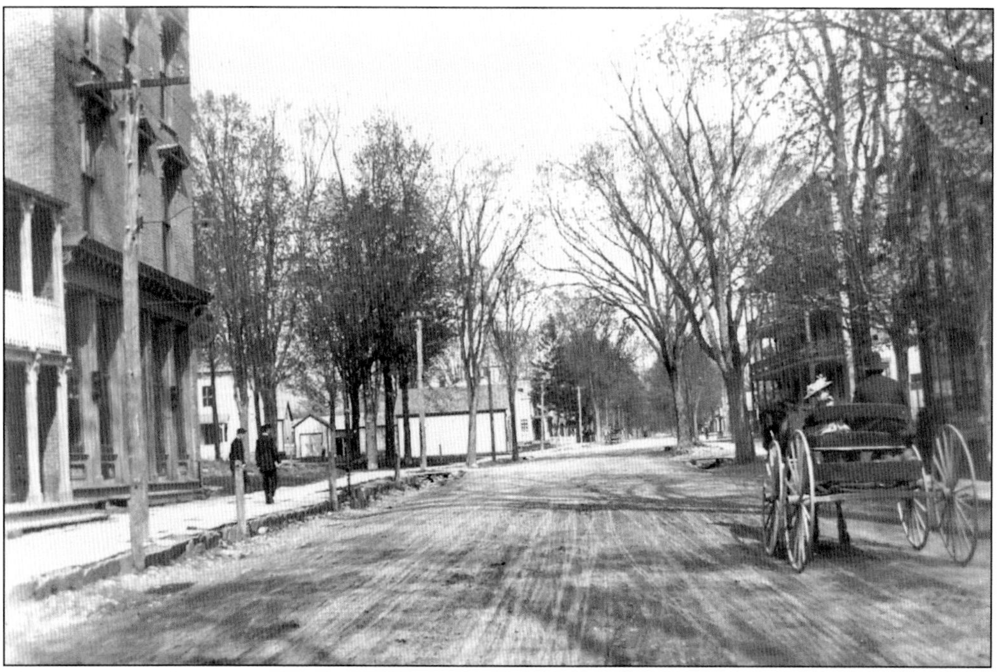

The three-story brick building on the left is Nicholson Hardware. It stood just west of where the Hitchcock block would be built in 1899. Just past that is Park Place, where the United Presbyterian Church stands today. The old United Presbyterian Church, later the Grange Hall, on the east side of North Park Street can be seen peeking out past Nicholson's.

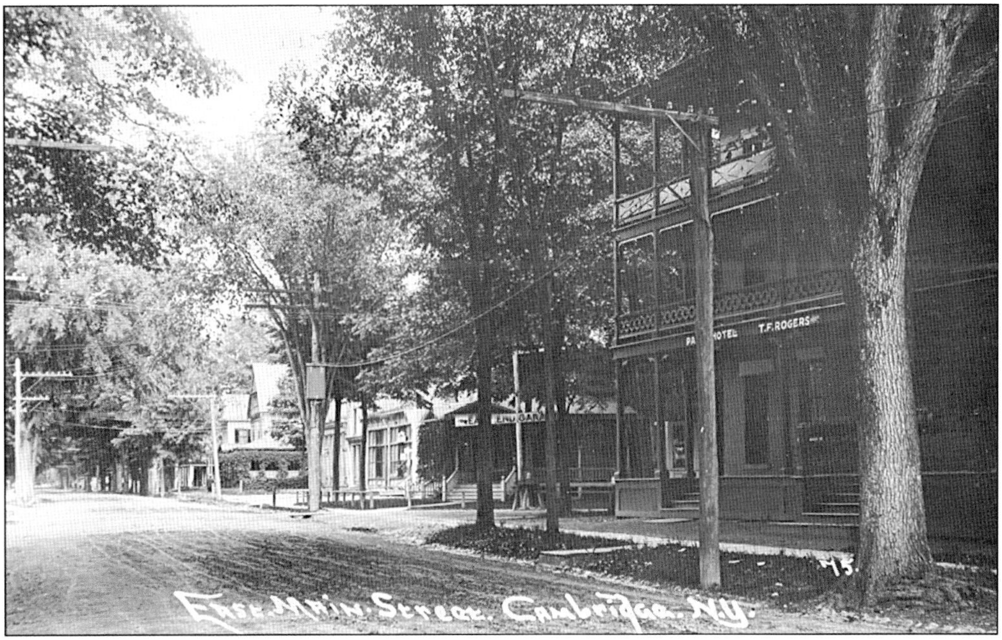

The Park Hotel stood on the southwest corner of Main and Park Streets. Across South Park Street was the East End Garage. Beyond that was the Fuller block. This photograph was taken after February 6, 1900, when permission was granted to Granville Telephone Company to install service in the village.

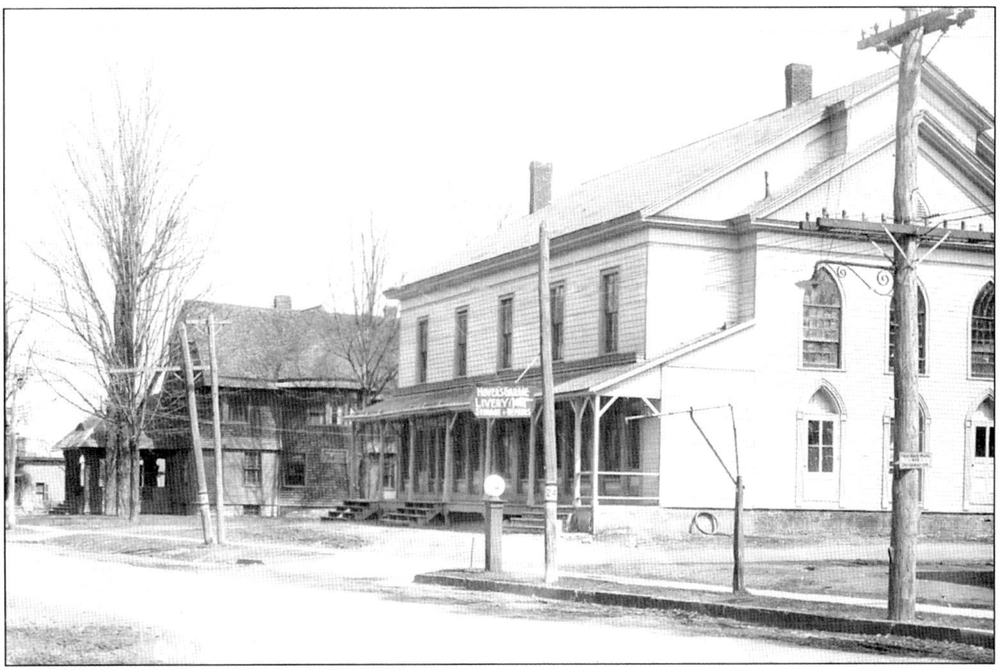

The sign on the pole by Grange Hall reads 24, which was the road number before it became its current New York State Route 22. When the hall was torn down in the early 1960s to make way for the new A&P grocery store, Frank Plunkett's livery stable in the rear was also removed. Plunkett's was likely the same as Hover's Garage and Livery advertised on the pole.

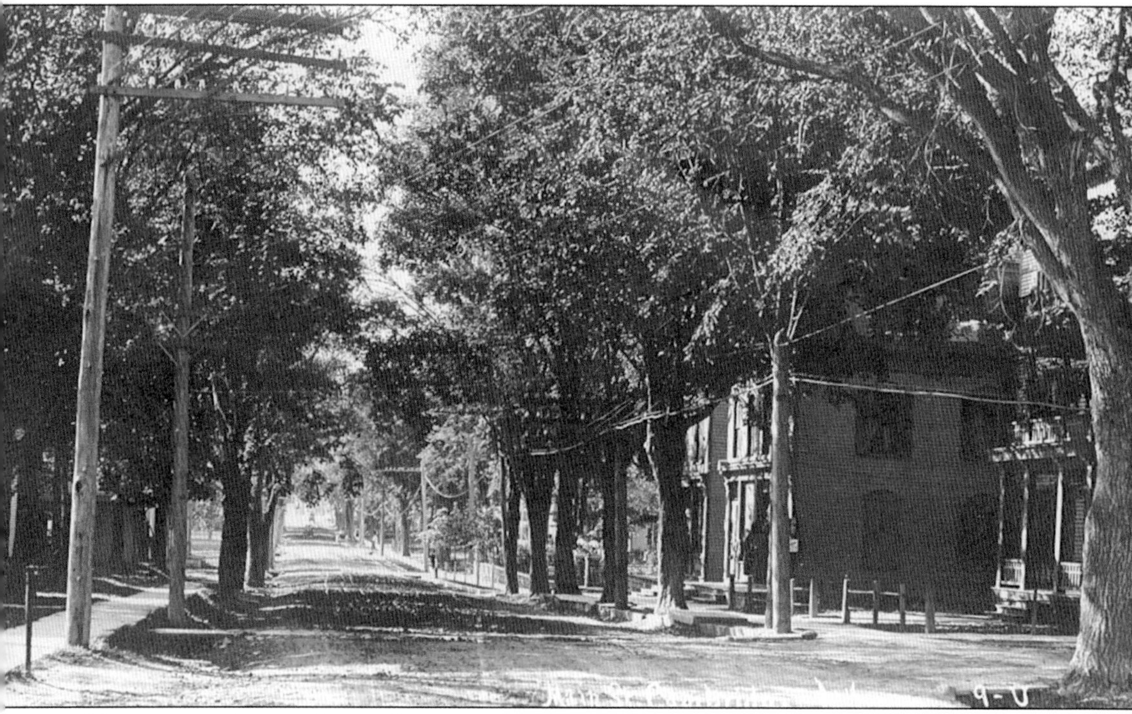

This westward view of Main Street is taken from the intersection with Broad Street. The front porch of the Cambridge Hotel is just visible at the right. From the 1790s, the Cambridge area post office was located at the intersection of Main and Park Streets. About 1829, Matthew Stephenson became postmaster and moved the office westward three-quarters of a mile to Cambridge Corners at the intersection of Main and Union Streets. A new post office was created for the East End. It was named North White Creek and located on the northwest corner of Main and Broad Streets. In the 1870s, A. Jay Tefft published the *Enterprise* newspaper from his office above the post office. In 1885, when the Cambridge Hotel was built on that corner, the post office moved westward two places to the second building on the right in this photograph (partially hidden by trees). The post office was moved to its current location on East Main Street in the late 1950s. (Courtesy CVA.)

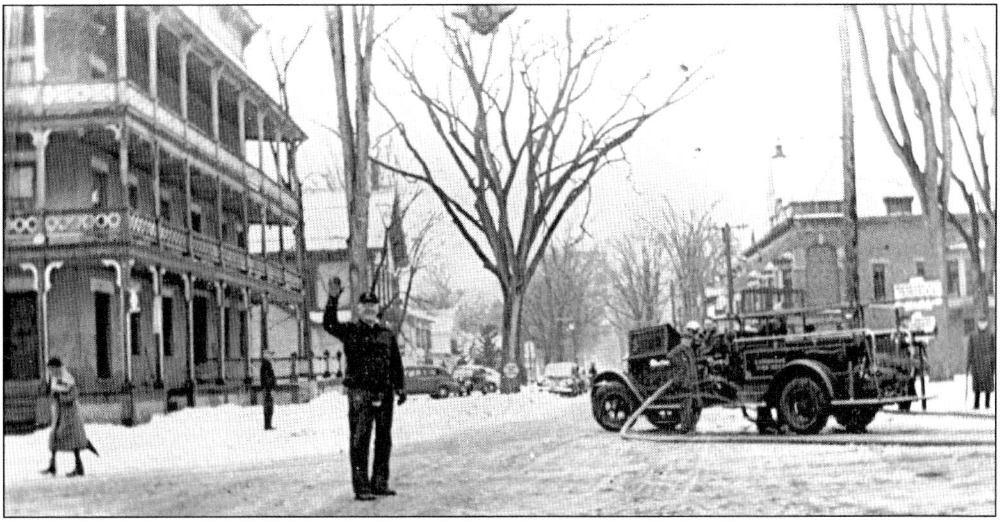

Percy Morse waves as they fight a small 1943 fire at the Grange Hall (not visible on right). Bill Wells, standing by truck, talks to Bob McWhorter. In 1916, Cambridge installed three "silent policemen" along Main Street at Park Street, Union Street, and Tannery Pond in Coila. In 1929, the silent policeman at Main and Park Streets was replaced by the traffic light in this photograph. (Courtesy CVA.)

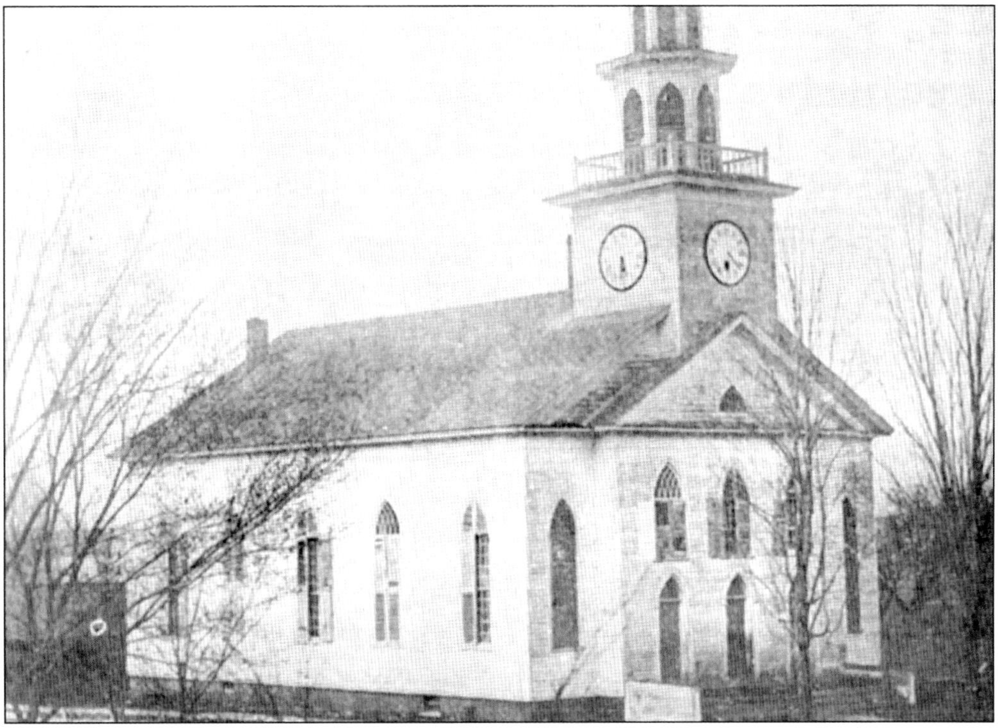

The old white church was built in 1832 to replace the 1792 old white meetinghouse on the northeast corner of Main and Park Streets. This church faced south toward East Main Street. The current United Presbyterian Church was built across the street on the northwest corner in 1872. Later the pictured building served as home to the Cambridge Valley Grange, with a side entrance along North Park Street.

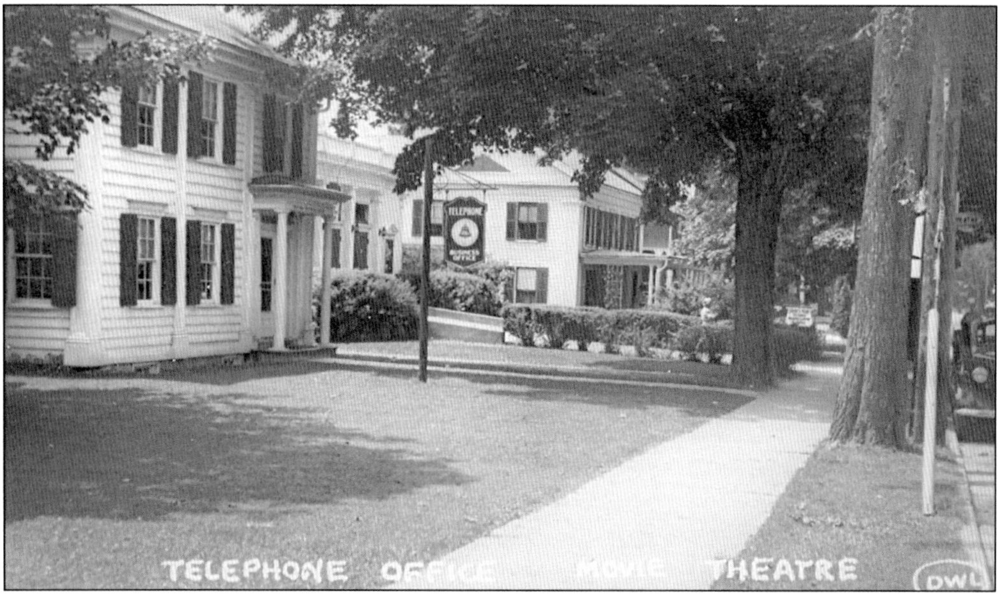

The Bell Systems telephone office on East Main is now a private residence with the Verizon switching station in the rear. At the time of the photograph, the recessed building next to the telephone office was a movie theater. In 1932, when it was the Fischer Playhouse, the village board approved its request to show motion pictures on Sunday evening. Today it is the home of A and M Printers.

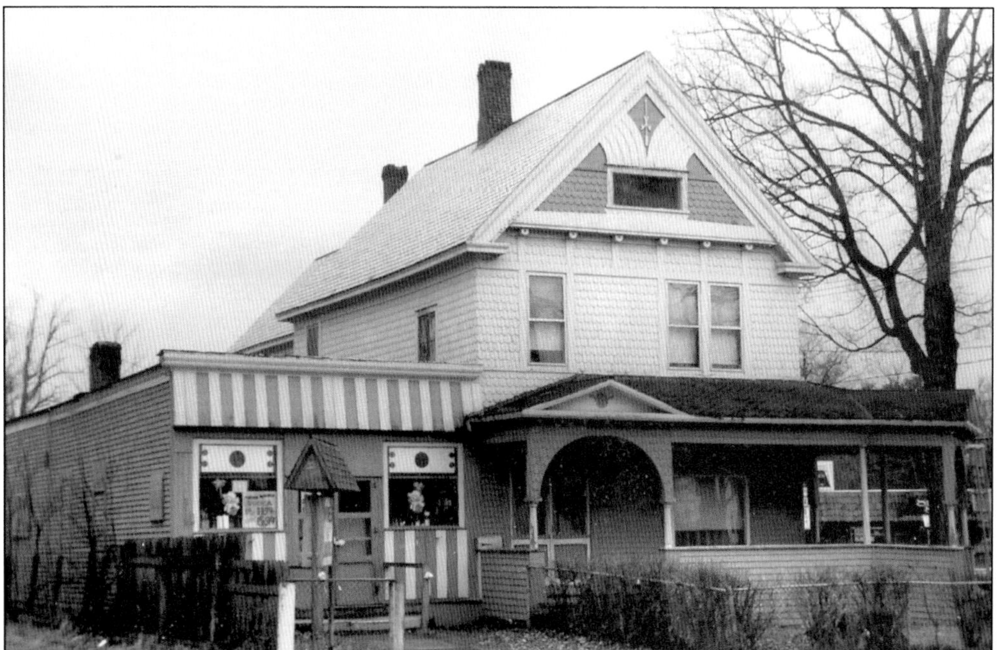

This building stands on the southeast corner of Main and Park Streets. In the late 1790s, Adonijah Skinner, Cambridge's first postmaster, operated a tavern on this corner. He added a second story to his tavern for use by the Masonic Order. In the early 1800s, other owners were Maj. John Porter and Paul Dennis. Later in the 1800s, this was the site of Comstocks and Fenton House.

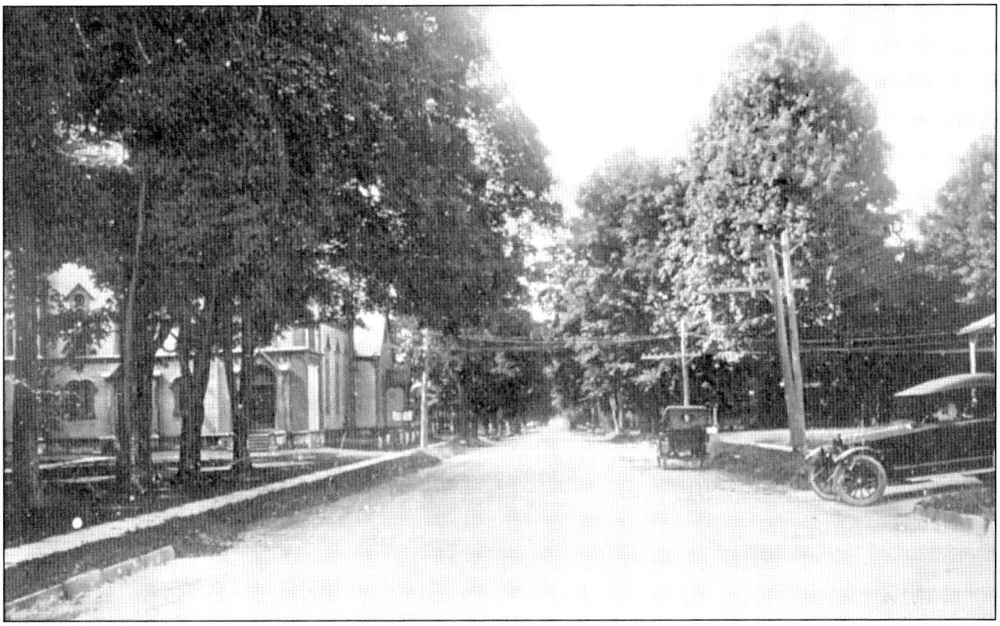

Cambridge seems to have been fond of naming its churches and meetinghouses based on their color. When the current United Presbyterian Church (left) was built in 1872, it was painted light tan with dark tan trim. This may have been done to avoid confusion with the old white church across the street. It was not until the 1930s that the present-day church was painted its current white color.

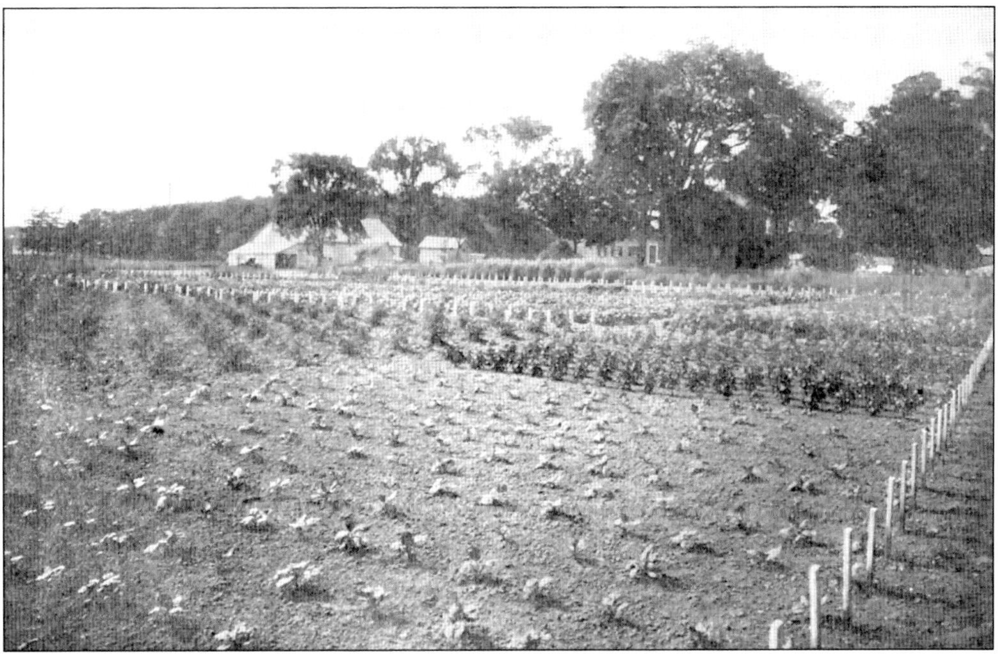

The Rice Seed Company planted its annual trial gardens on Park Street at the southern entrance to the village. According to folklore, Franklin Delano Roosevelt, then governor of New York, stopped his automobile and asked to be wheeled through the beautiful garden. The Hitchcock farm in the background was torn down in 1948 to make room for the new Cambridge Central School.

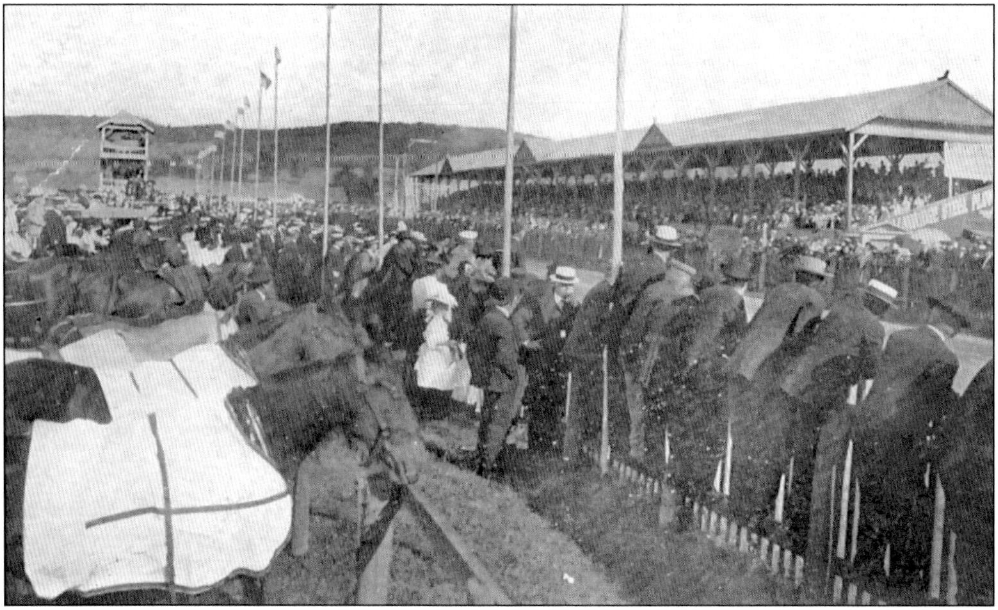

The great Cambridge Fair was a mainstay of Cambridge from 1891 to 1943. The Cambridge Valley Agricultural Society, headed by Jerome B. Rice, moved the Lauderdale Fair to the northeast edge of the village in 1891. At the left in the infield is the bandstand. An awning on the west side shielded the band from the late afternoon sun.

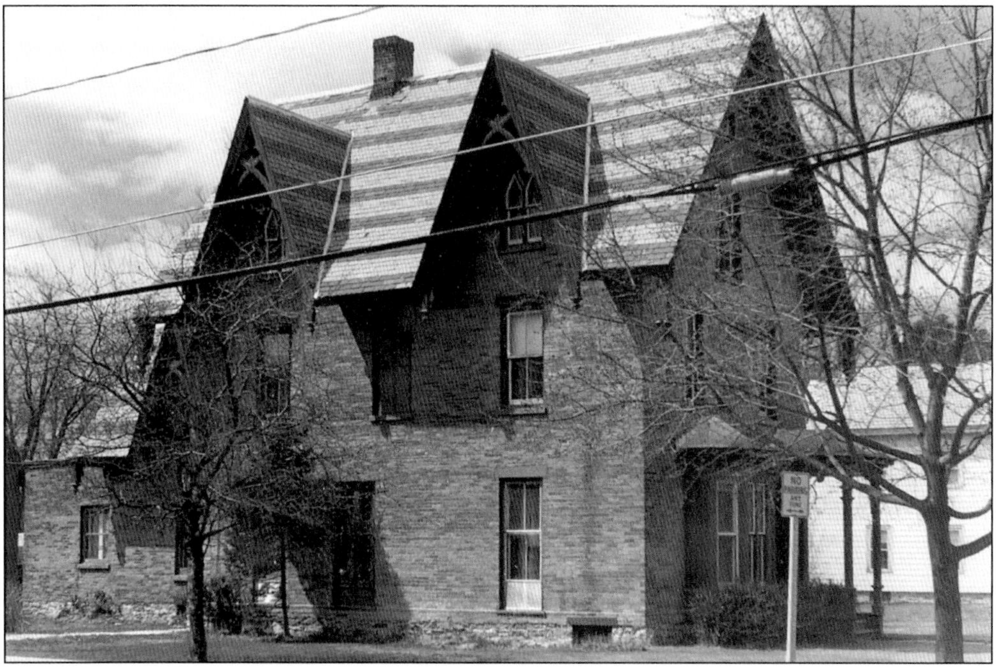

In 1869, Benjamin Porter Crocker purchased the land on the west side of South Park Street. Crocker cut down the huge pines in Putnam's Grove, selling them as ship masts. Crocker developed the land between South Park Street and the railroad tracks through the creation of Avenue A, Avenue B, and Grove Street. His house still stands on the southwest corner of Park Street and Avenue A.

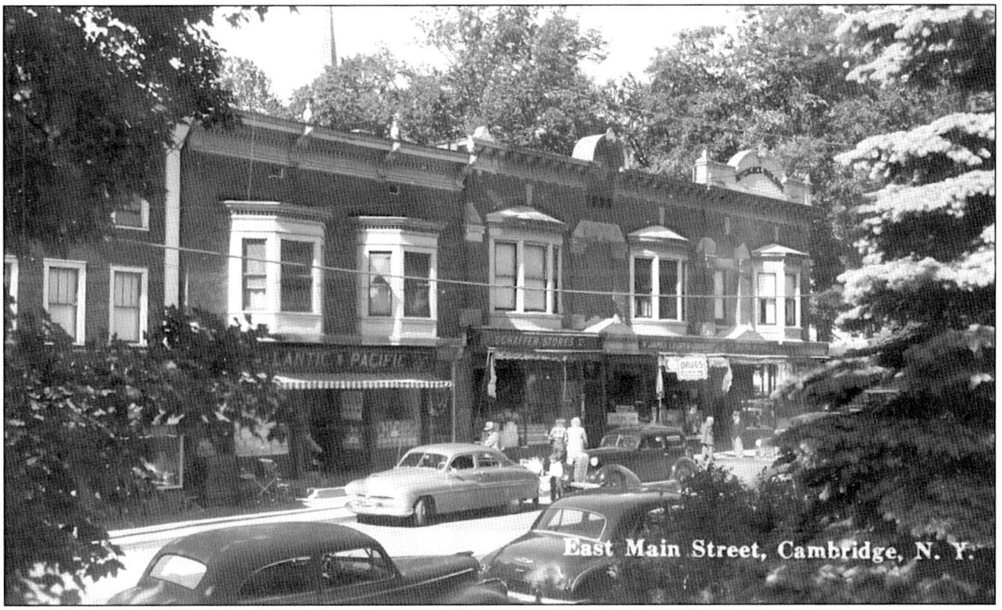

The Great Atlantic and Pacific Tea Company (A&P) moved from this location to the old movie theater. In the early 1960s, it moved to the northeast corner of Main and Park Streets. Josephine Hartford Bryce, granddaughter of George Huntington Hartford (founder of A&P), owned many houses, one of which was Black Hole Hollow Farm at the east end of Ash Grove.

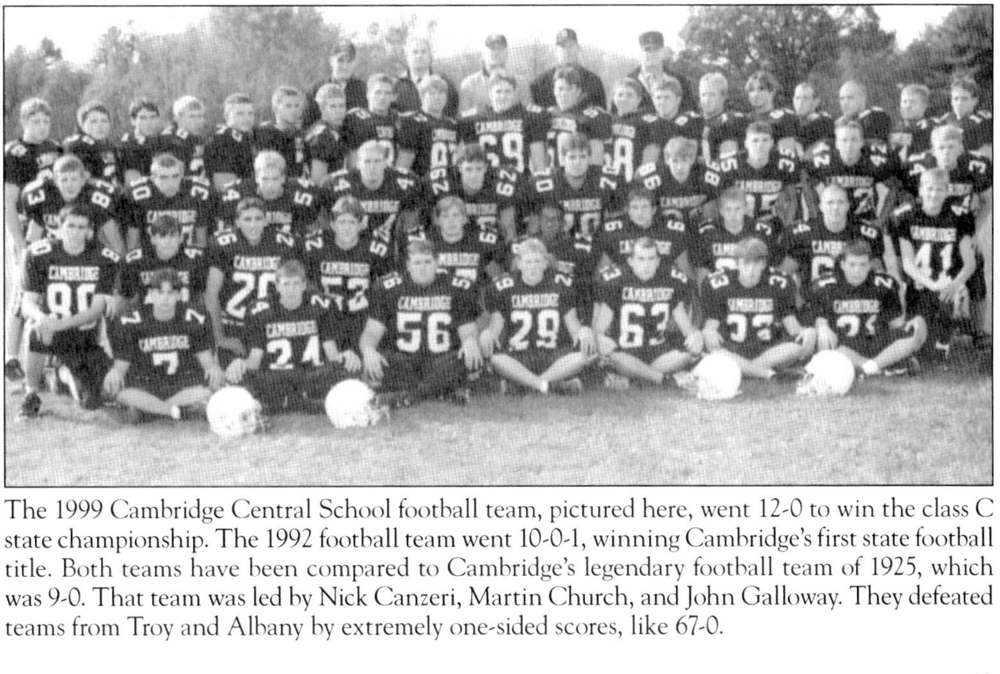

The 1999 Cambridge Central School football team, pictured here, went 12-0 to win the class C state championship. The 1992 football team went 10-0-1, winning Cambridge's first state football title. Both teams have been compared to Cambridge's legendary football team of 1925, which was 9-0. That team was led by Nick Canzeri, Martin Church, and John Galloway. They defeated teams from Troy and Albany by extremely one-sided scores, like 67-0.

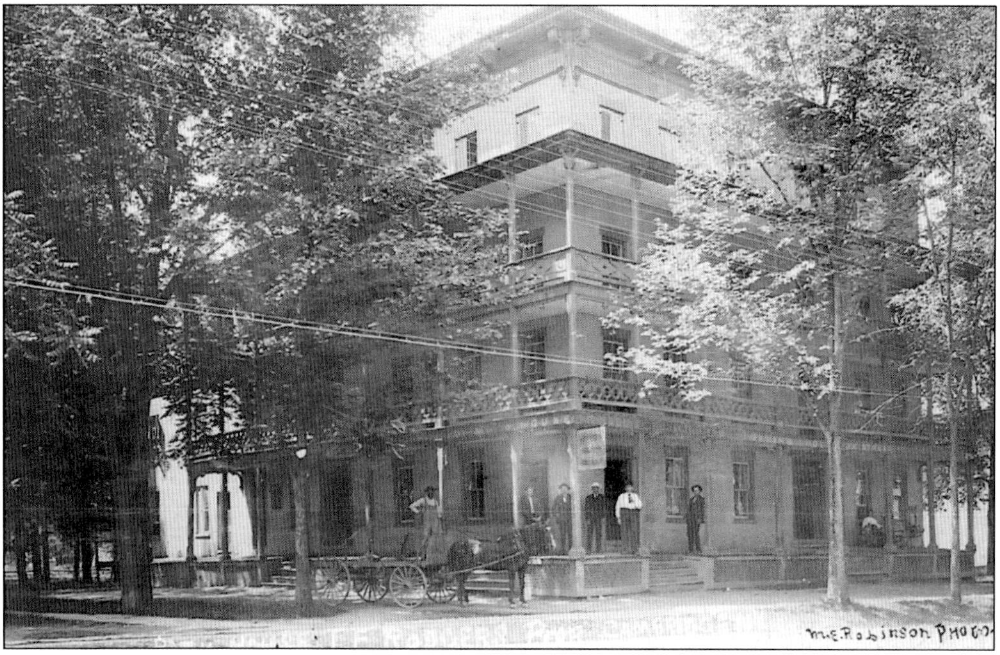

The hotel at the intersection of Main and Park Streets has had many names. Here the postcard calls it Park House, but the sign over the door still reads Irving House. In 1899, the village board discussed complaints about slot machines in hotels and saloons. That same year, the board heard complaints about oyster shells in the road, which were damaging horses' feet.

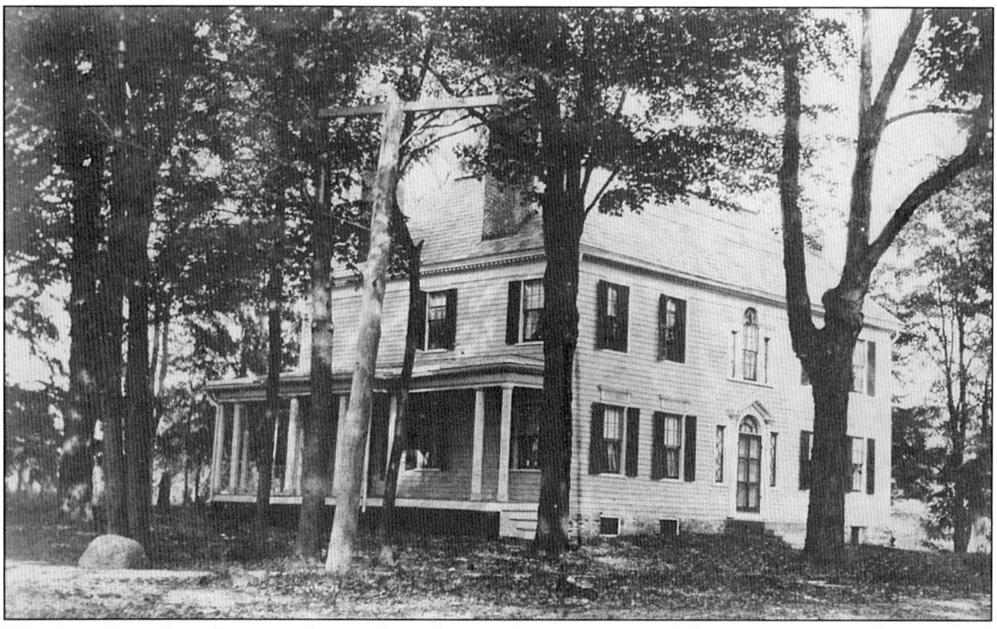

The Jonathan Dorr house is located on the northeast corner of the intersection of Main and Gilbert Streets, known then as Dorr's Corners. Built in 1799, the Georgian-style house has Palladian windows and nine fireplaces. Elizabeth, the daughter of the prominent doctor, married lawyer John Pope Putnam in 1813. In the mid-1800s, Dr. Henry Gray, brother of J. J. Gray, lived here. (Courtesy CVA.)

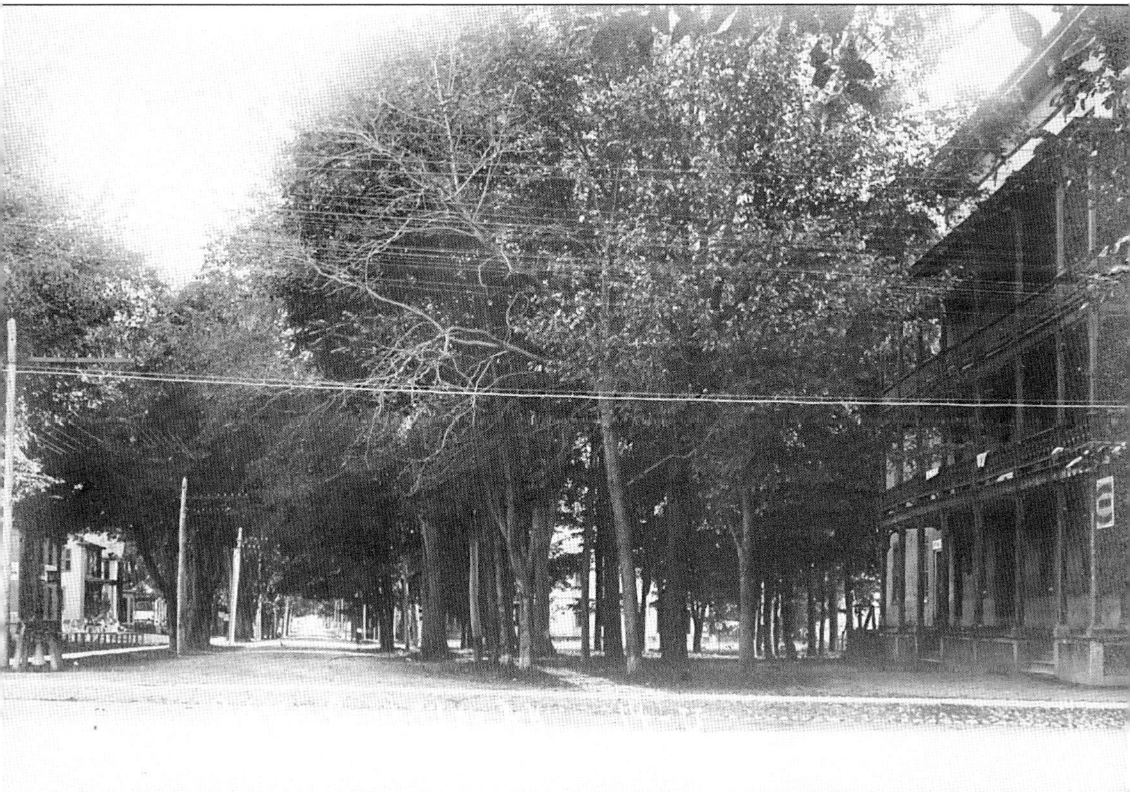

This southward view on Park Street was taken from the intersection with East Main Street. In the late 1800s, just south of the Park Hotel on the right, set back from the road at the end of a long tree-lined driveway, was the estate of John Putnam. The estate was called Putnam Institute when it served as Union School of the East District from 1872 to 1891. Until Avenue A was built in the late 1800s, there were no streets and no houses on the west side of South Park Street between the Putnam estate and the southern edge of the village. The large pines between South Park Street and the railroad tracks were known as Baker's Grove, Putnam's Grove, and later as Fuller's Grove. In the mid- to late 1800s, this was the site of many major community events featuring swing sets and a dance floor. Grove Street, at the back (west) edge of the Putnam estate, probably received its name in honor of the grove.

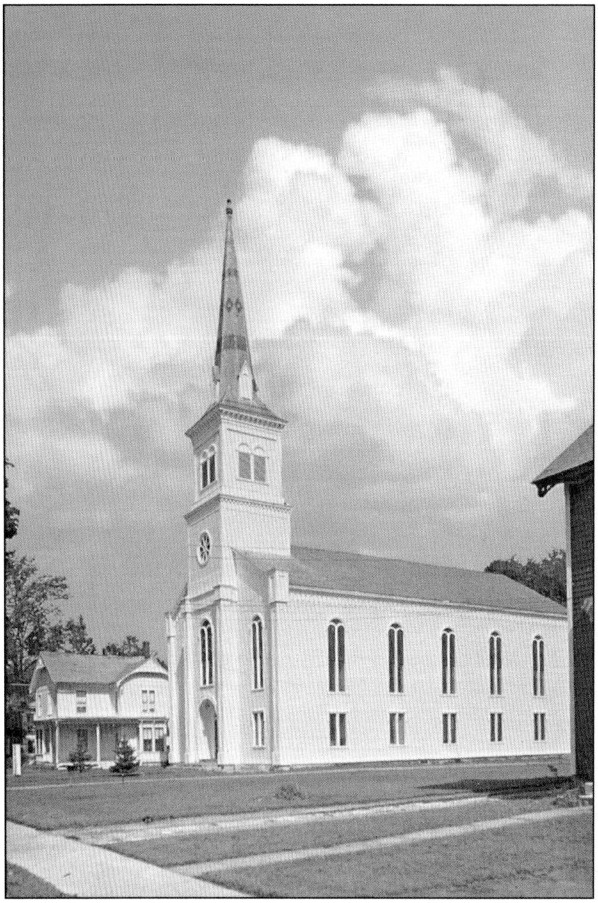

In 1770, Philip Embury, along with Thomas Ashton, formed the second Methodist church in America. A house of worship was built in Ash Grove in 1788 and enlarged in 1803. A new, larger church, built just west of the original one in 1831, was destroyed by arson in 1835. The current Methodist church, pictured here, was built between 1836 and 1838 in North White Creek.

Clockwise, from top left: at the Cambridge Fair in 1909, there were often four races each day with purses around $300. Daily attendance was about 8,000, many arriving from Troy via the railroad. The midway featured a Ferris wheel. The Stroebel airship, which won first prize at the 1907 International Race in St Louis, was a big draw at the 1908 Cambridge Fair, even though it never launched.

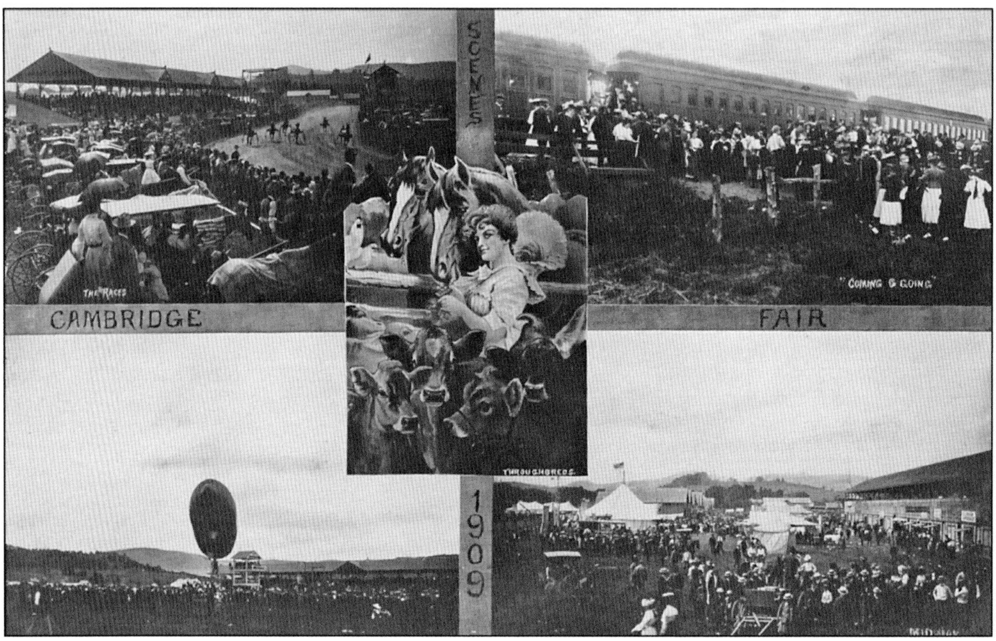

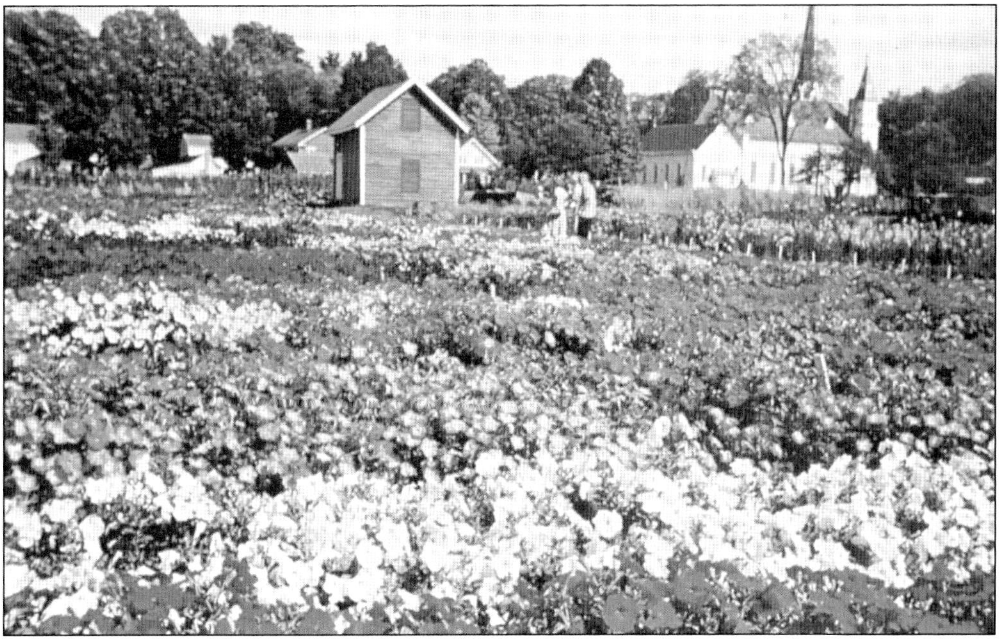

Asgrow (Associated Seed Growers), which took over the Cambridge seed business from Rice, had a trial garden on the east side of Washington Street. The United Presbyterian Church can be seen in the background. The man in the middle of the photograph is believed to be Lyman White, former Asgrow president. This field now serves as the community garden.

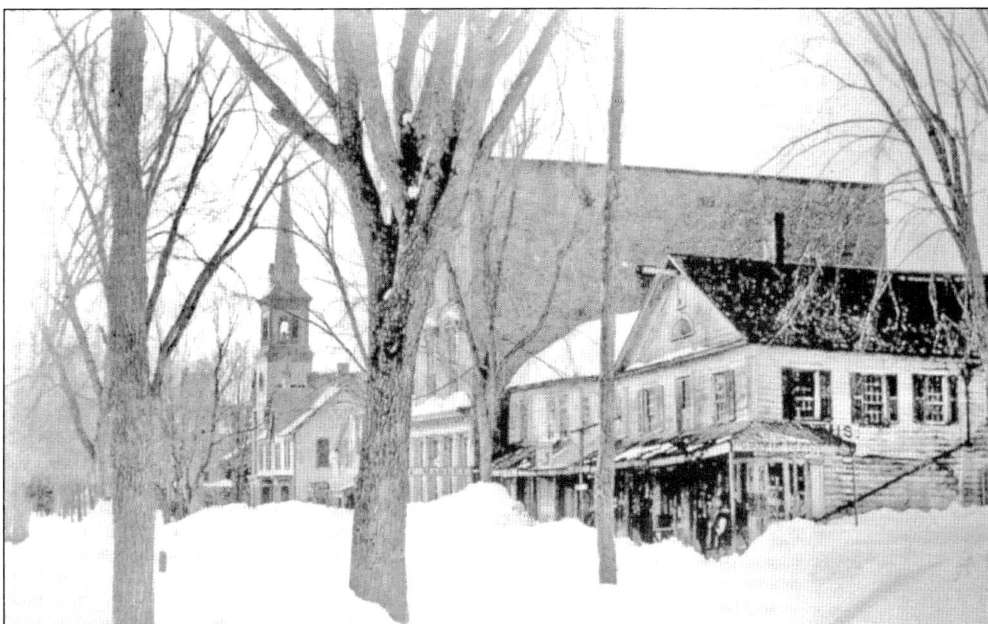

The blizzard of 1888 is the worst in modern history, surpassing the 1993 "Superstorm." Between March 11 and March 14, snowfall of 58 inches was recorded in nearby Saratoga. Snow drifts over 50 feet were reported in New York. The three-story brick Nicholson Hardware store is in the center. The other East End buildings to the right were removed when the Hitchcock building was erected in 1899.

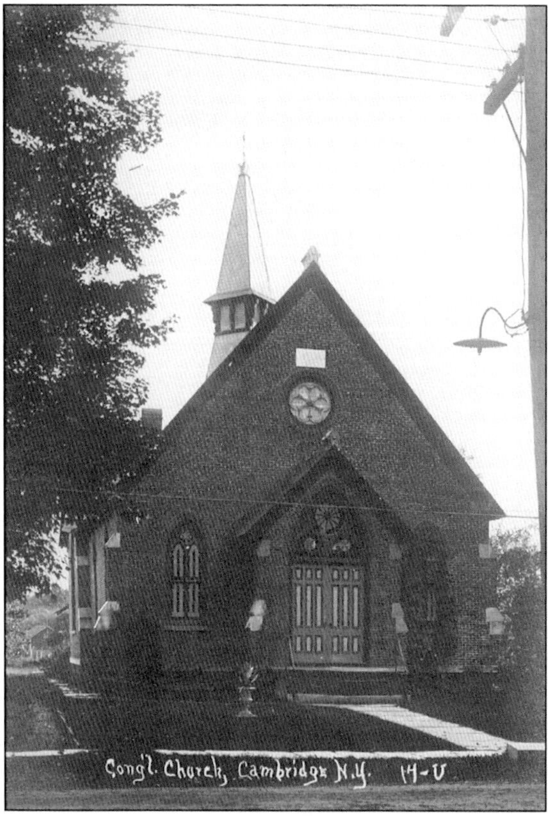

Shortly after the current United Presbyterian Church was opened in 1872, a splinter group broke off. By 1875, they had built the Congregational Church. It was located across the street from the present-day post office on the lot that held the movie theater, the A&P store, and today's A and M Printers. The church was active until the early 1900s.

On February 6, 1900, the Granville Telephone Company was granted permission to put service in the village. In 1906, a movement to put electric and telephone wires underground was defeated. Elizabeth Ford is shown at the Cambridge switchboard. If a party was not at home when someone called, Ford was known to call around the village trying to locate the party in other places he or she was known to frequent.

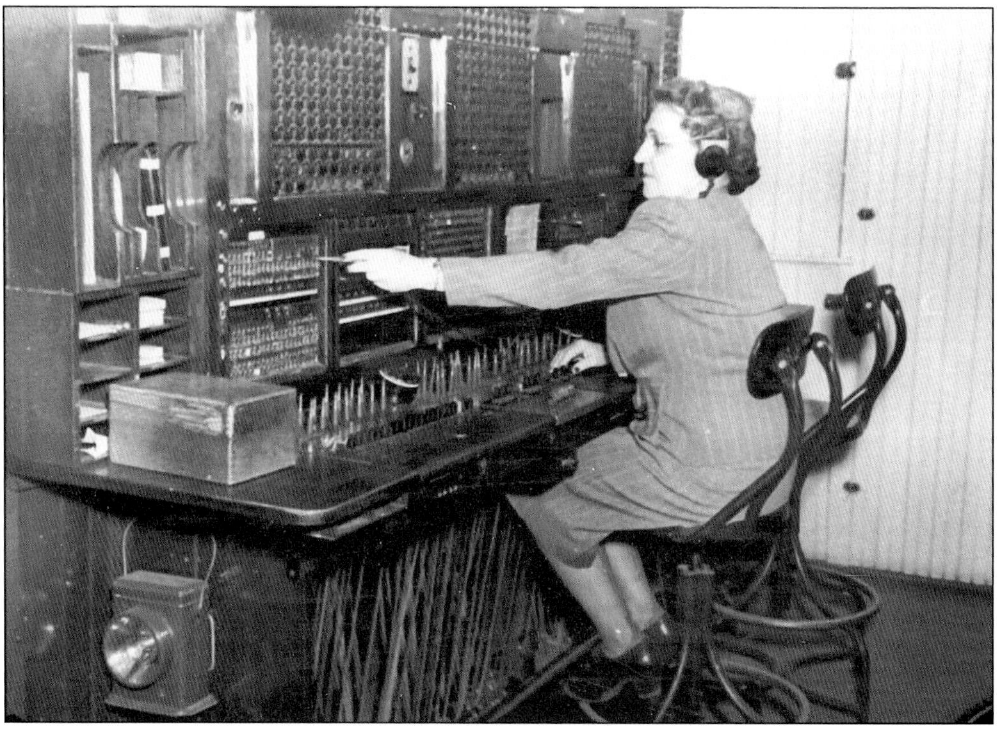

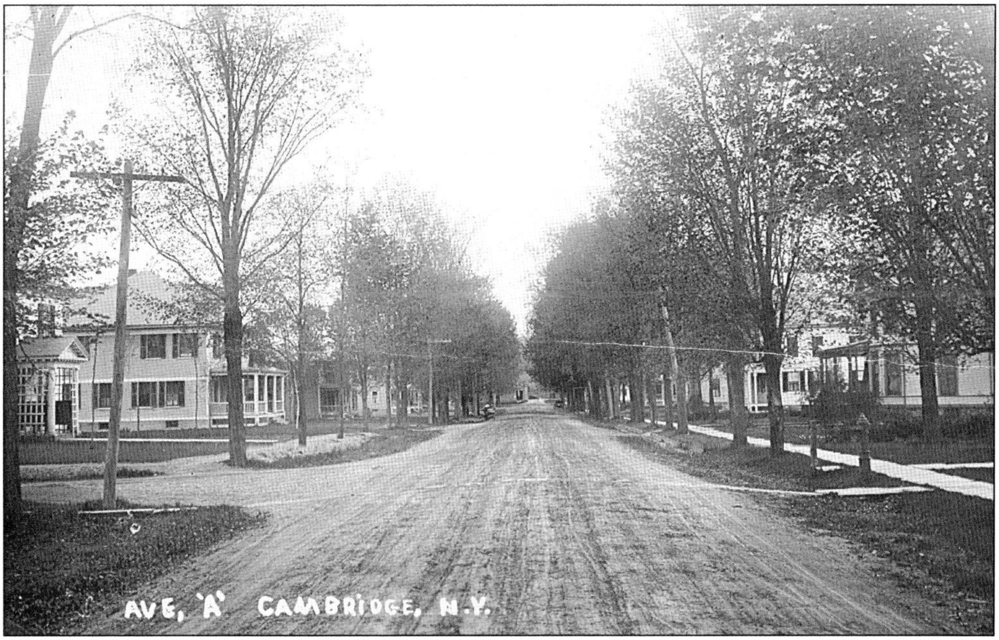

In 1855, an estimated crowd of 30,000 attended the 15th annual Washington County Fair held in the meadow that is now Avenue A. At that time, the Putnam estate occupied all land between South Park Street and the railroad tracks. The new, nearby railroad provided easy access to the fair. The fair raised controversy because, for the first time, it included an equestrian competition for female riders.

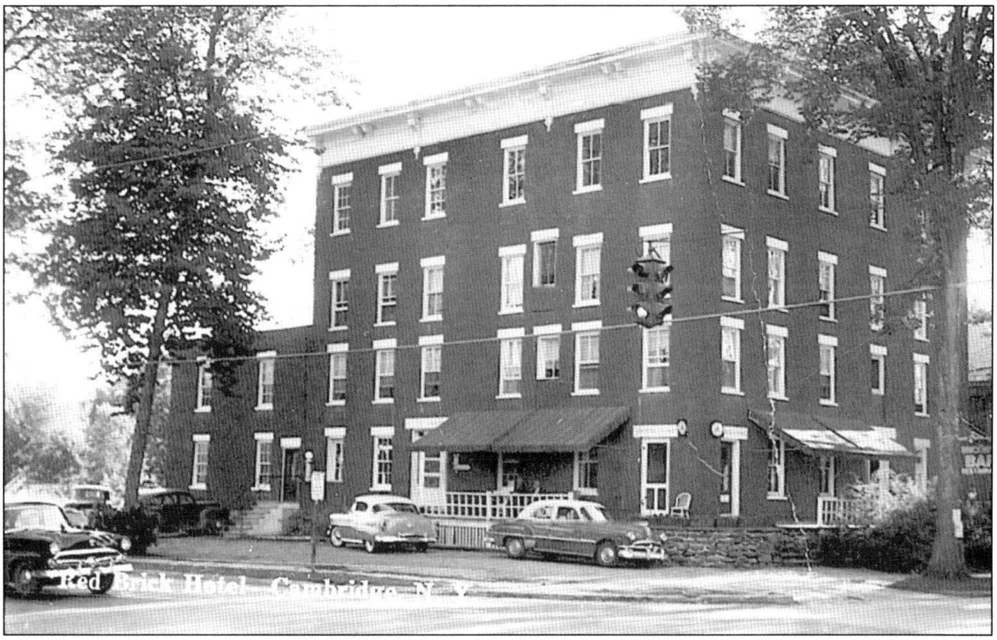

In the 1950s, Joe Powers ran the barbershop in the addition of the Red Brick Hotel (left). Note the upper of the two small windows above the dark awning in the middle of the photograph. Unlike the other windows, this one is dark. According to local folklore, it was a fake window disguising a hidden passage at the end of the hallway.

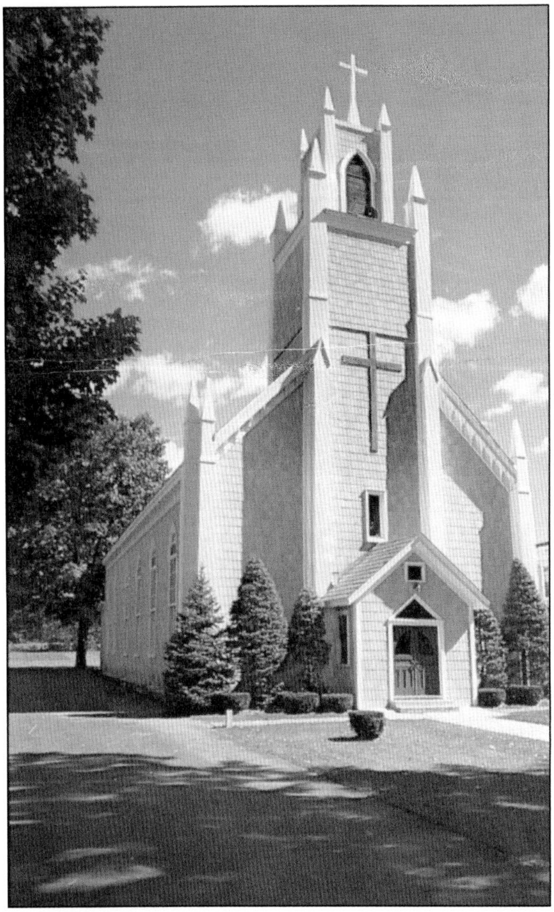

The St. Patrick's Church was erected in 1853, about the time of the construction of the Rutland and Washington Railroad. The original church (pictured here) was torn down in the early 1980s and replaced with the current structure that was dedicated in 1984.

In 1878, Martin Hubbard built an opera house for the East End. One hundred years later, the Hubbard Hall organization was founded in the same building as a not-for-profit community arts center. In 1865, Hubbard sold the lot on the corner to the Cambridge Valley National Bank, replacing the bank across the street. In the early 1960s, the bank was moved to its current location on West Main Street.

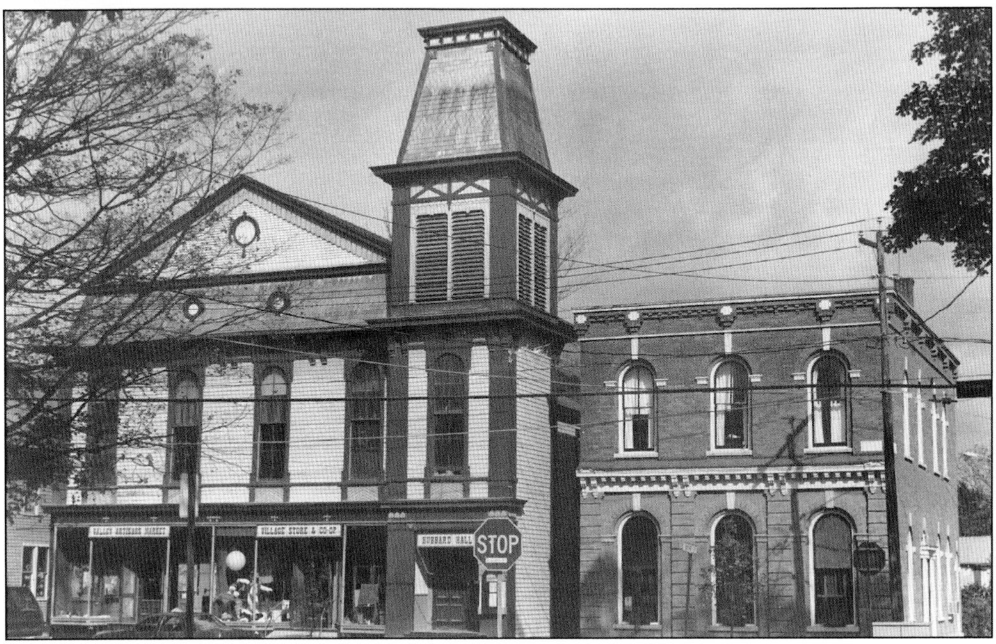

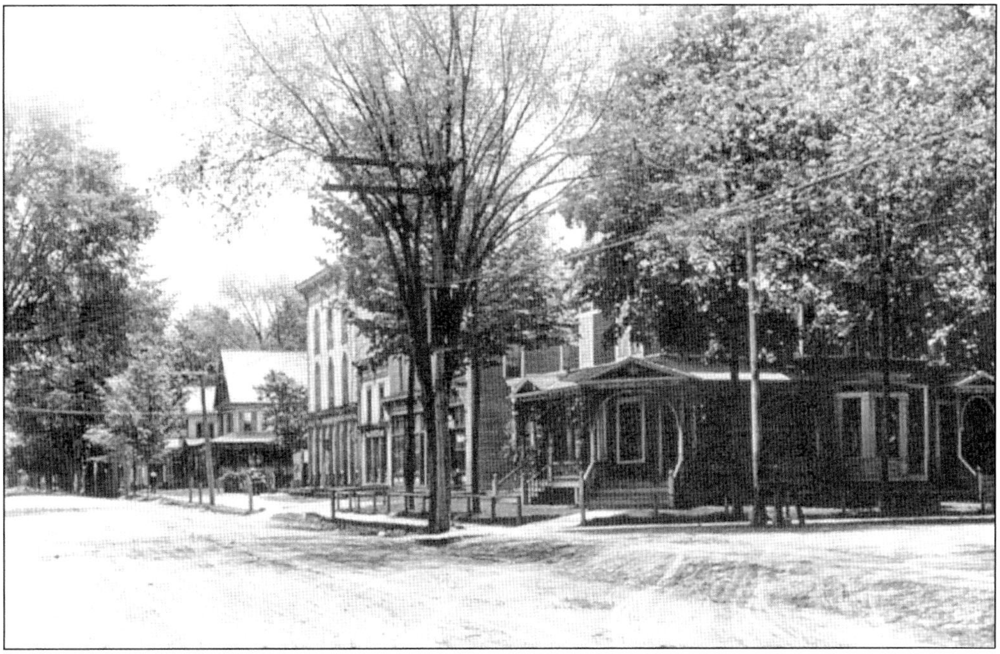

Electricity was installed on Main Street in 1891. The building on the southeast corner of Main and Park Streets, which stands today, was Comstock Hotel and the Fenton House in the late 1800s. The three-story structure in the distance is the Fuller building, a meeting place for the Grand Army of the Republic and the Masons. The Fuller block burned in the early 1900s.

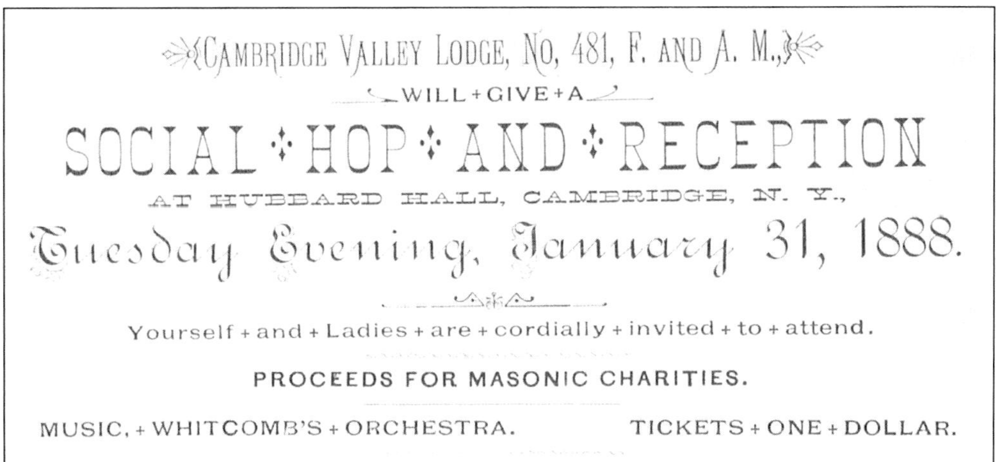

Cambridge Valley Lodge, No, 481, F. and A. M.,

Will + Give + A

SOCIAL ✣ HOP ✣ AND ✣ RECEPTION

AT HUBBARD HALL, CAMBRIDGE, N. Y.,

Tuesday Evening, January 31, 1888.

Yourself + and + Ladies + are + cordially + invited + to + attend.

PROCEEDS FOR MASONIC CHARITIES.

MUSIC, + WHITCOMB'S + ORCHESTRA. TICKETS + ONE + DOLLAR.

COMMITTEE :

John Larmon. A. G. Taylor. D. Morris Pratt.
D. C. Brownell Romain Bennett. D. E. Whitcomb.

The Cambridge Valley Lodge No. 481 of Free and Accepted Masons celebrates its 150th anniversary in 2010. A prior organization formed in 1793, Rural Lodge No. 32, met alternately in the towns of Cambridge, Easton, and Salem. The $1 ticket price for the social equates to about $50 in today's currency.

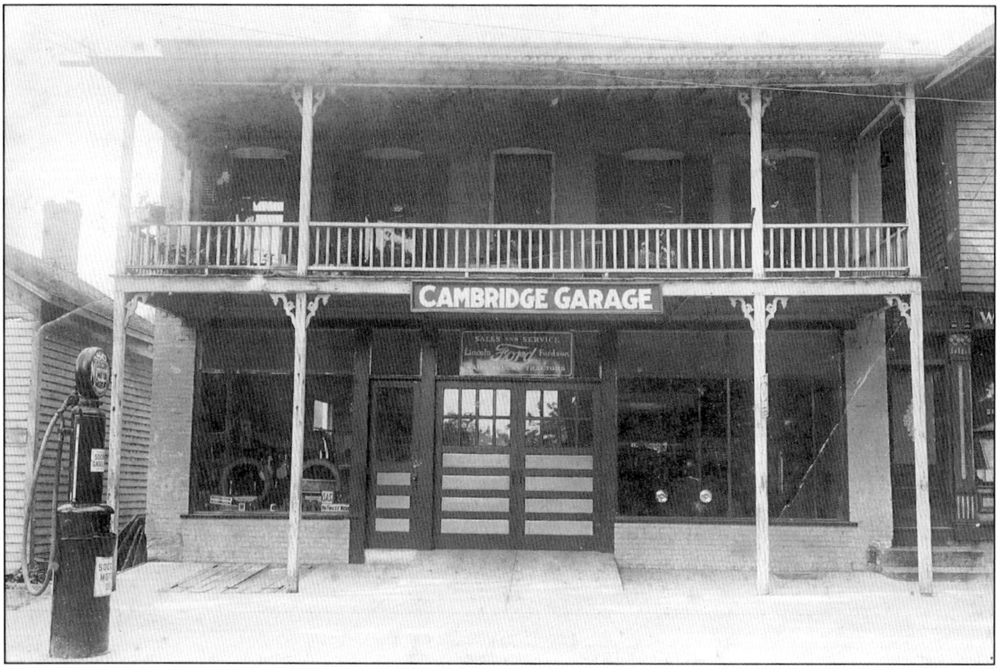

This building now houses Battenkill Books on East Main Street, just west of Hubbard Hall. The Model T in the window was manufactured around 1916–1917. The sign over the door lists the Ford, Fordson, and Lincoln brands. There is a sign for Firestone tires. Cash was required, as a sign in the window states "No Credit." Socony gas, priced at 25¢ per gallon, was pumped right at the curb.

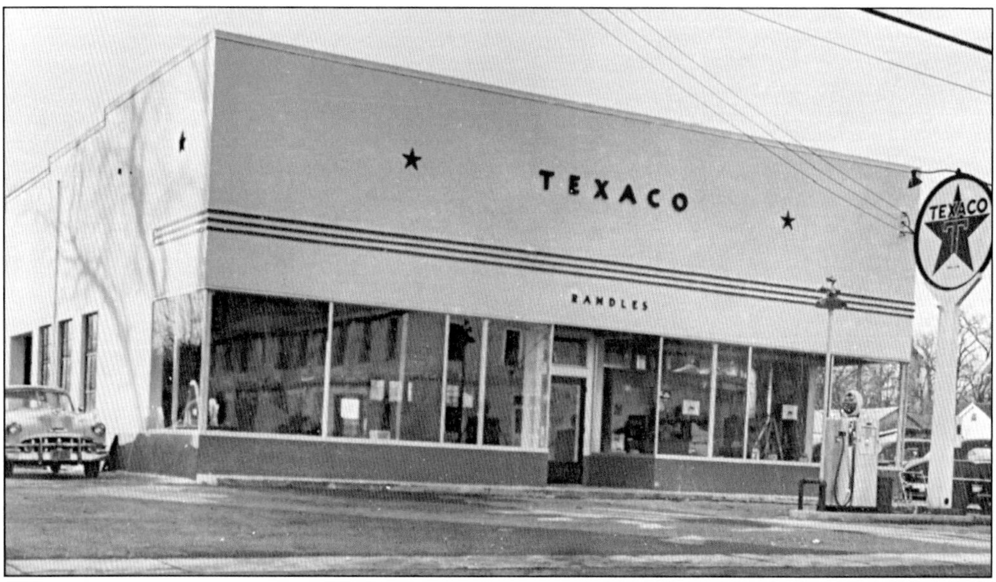

In the late 1920s or early 1930s, the Park Garage was erected on site of the Brick Hotel's livery stable. In 1951, it was destroyed by fire. The owner, Ken Randles, constructed this building, which was later owned by George MacArthur. Gordon Lockrow sold Dodge cars here and may have been the last new automobile dealership in Cambridge. Today this building houses a sub shop and a pizza restaurant.

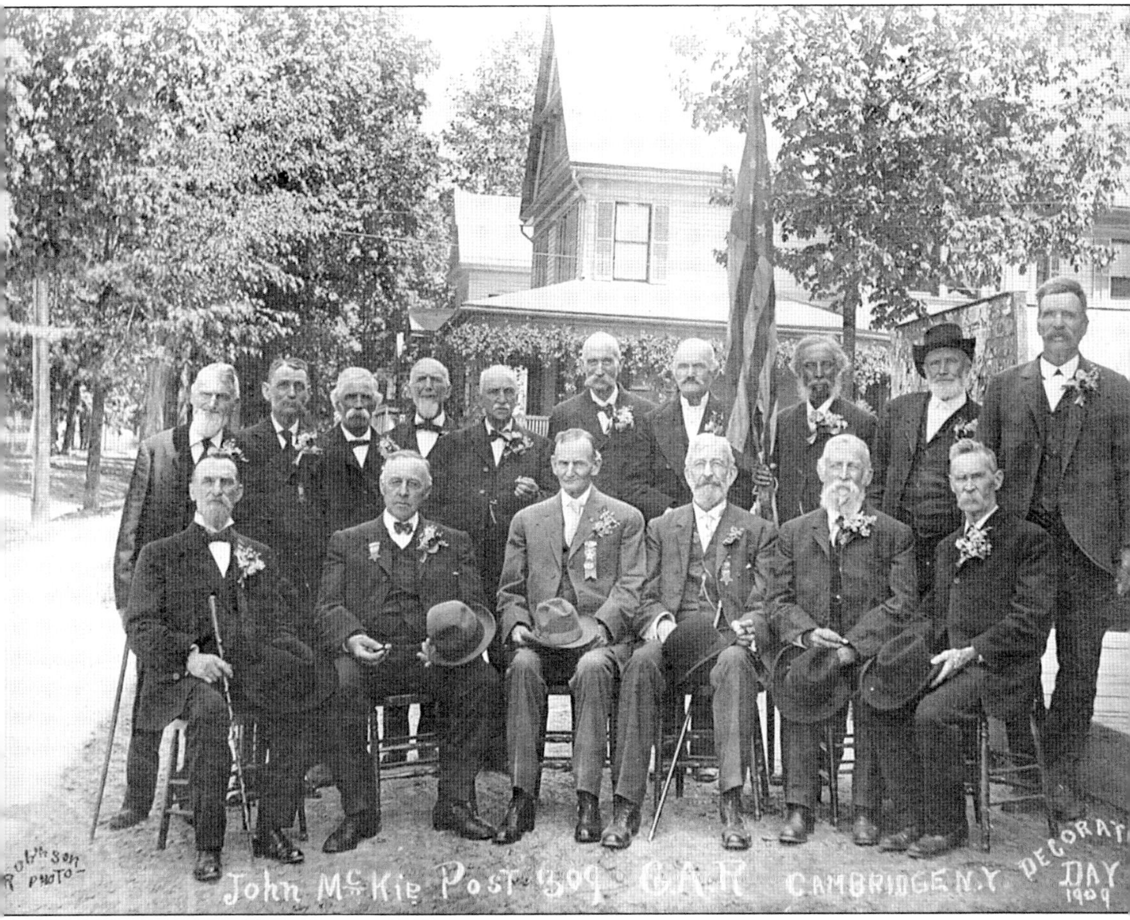

Cambridge Post 309 of the Grand Army of the Republic (GAR) was formed on November 3, 1882. There were 12 veterans listed on the original application, including Mitchell McFarland (seated fourth from left). The GAR was a large multifaceted organization founded in 1866 in Decatur, Illinois. The organization was a brotherhood of Civil War veterans dedicated to helping other veterans. The Cambridge post was named in honor of James McKie, who was honorably discharged with the rank of lieutenant colonel in 1863 as the result of a physical disability. In 1864, he was tragically killed on his family farm in Ash Grove when he fell from a wagon because the team of horses was startled. GAR post commander Willard Lawton, seated second from left, disbanded the post on February 12, 1924. The post members pose in front of Fuller block on Decoration Day in 1909. The GAR hall was on the second story of the Fuller building.

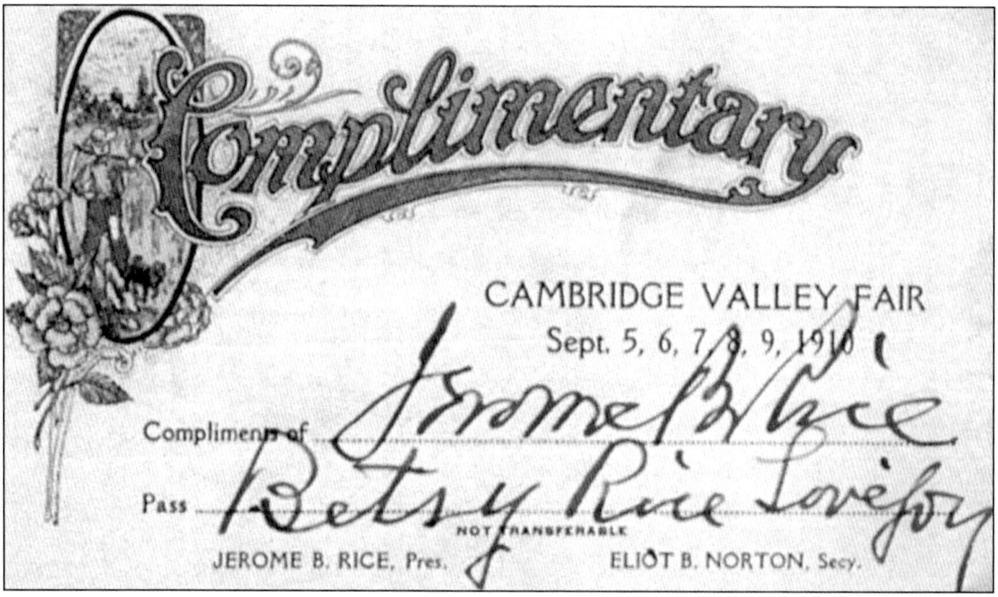

Jerome B. Rice was behind many successful endeavors in Cambridge. For many years, Rice served as president of the Cambridge Valley Agricultural Society. In his role as president of the great Cambridge Fair in 1910, he issued this complimentary pass to his niece, Betsy Lovejoy.

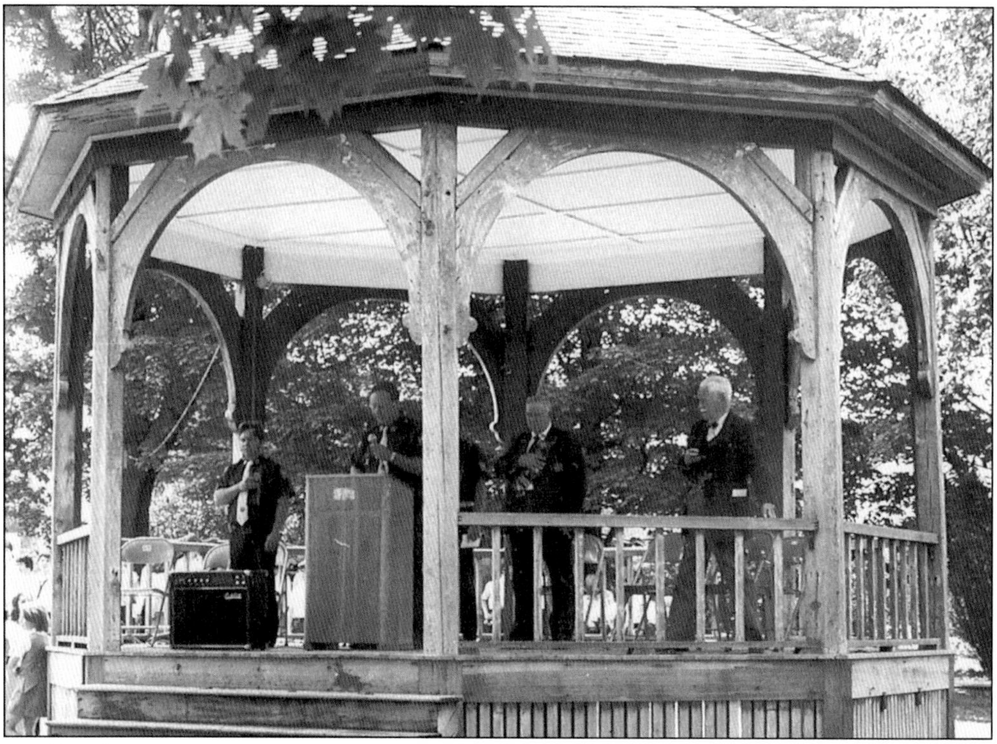

In 1976, this structure was moved from the Cambridge Fairgrounds at the northeast edge of the village to the school grounds. It is commonly referred to as the bandstand, although the band at Cambridge Fairgrounds actually sat in a different, three-story, rectangular building. This photograph is from the dedication ceremony held during the 1976 bicentennial celebration.

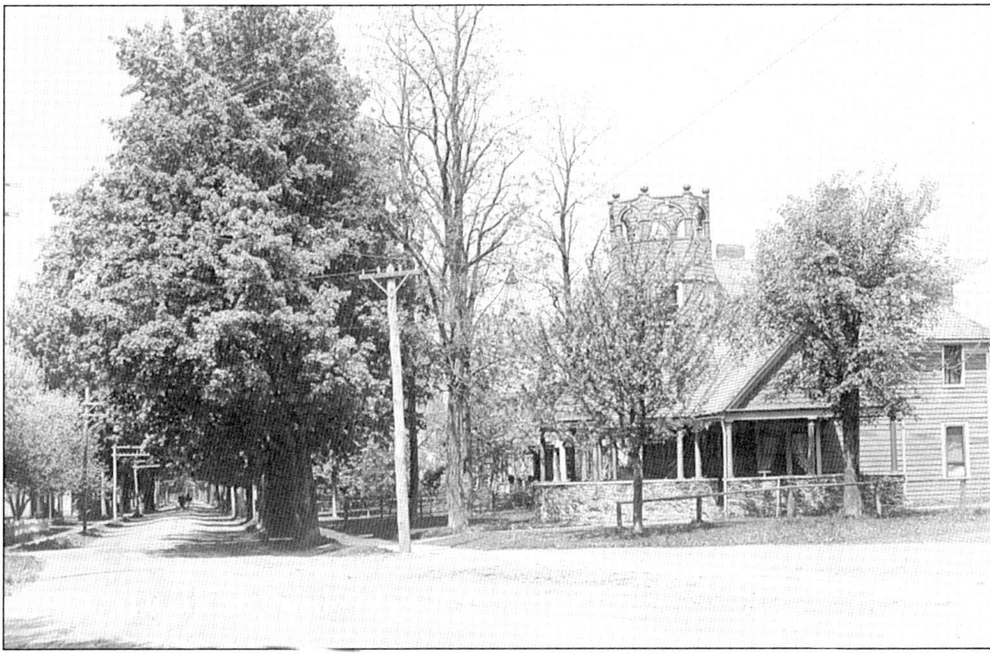

Dorr's Corners was at the intersection of Main and Gilbert Streets. An early merchant, Jeremiah Stillwell, was succeeded by Rice and Billings and, later, Eddy and Brown. In 1866, Dorr's Corners joined North White Creek and Cambridge Corners to form the village of Cambridge. In 1913, when Main Street was paved with yellow bricks, Pres. Charles Tingue placed a time capsule under the first brick here. The village leader was called "president" until 1924 when the title was changed to "mayor."

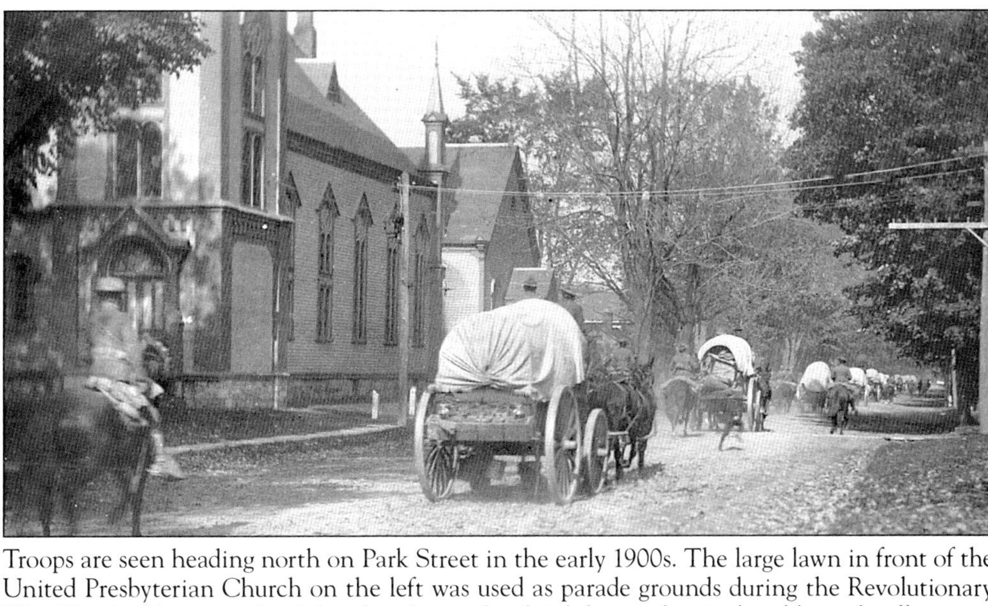

Troops are seen heading north on Park Street in the early 1900s. The large lawn in front of the United Presbyterian Church on the left was used as parade grounds during the Revolutionary War. Two buildings north of the church stands a brick house that is the oldest schoolhouse in Cambridge. (Courtesy CVA.)

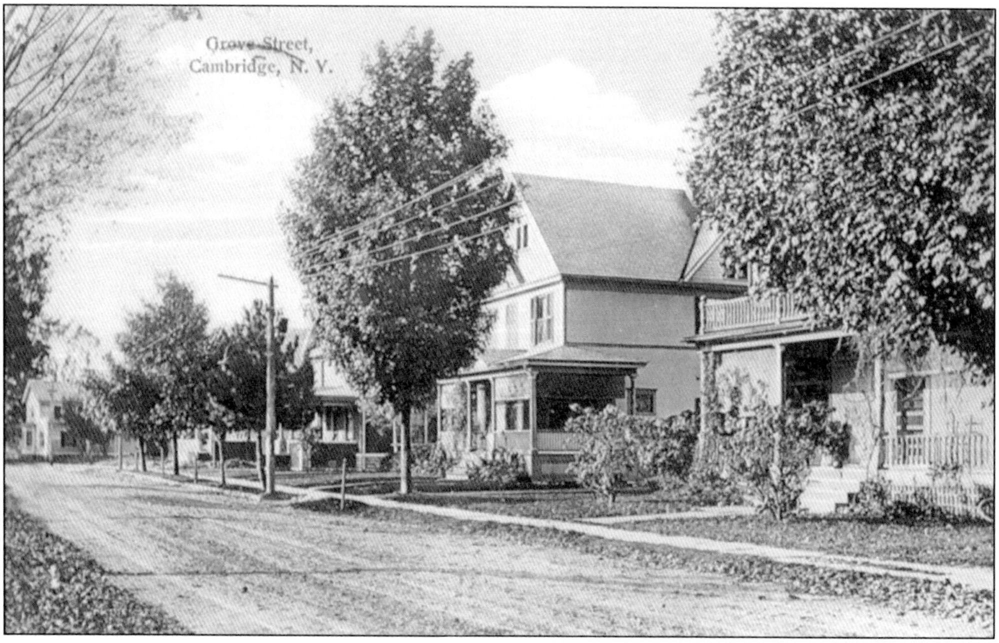

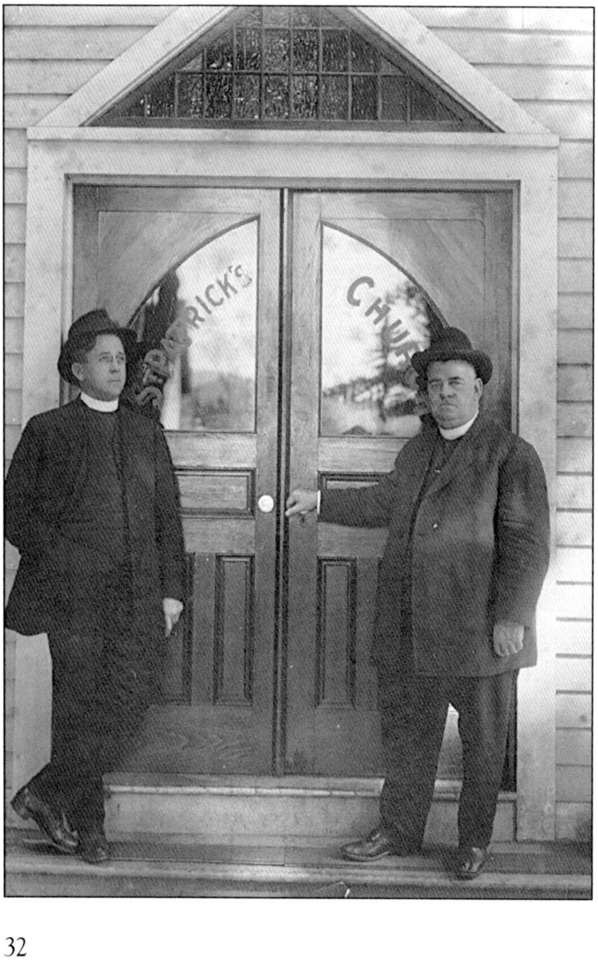

In 1947, the village board approved street dances on Broad Street in front of the hotel. That same year, they voted to allow public sports on Sunday afternoon. In 1956, the village board approved a street dance on Grove Street. Only a handful of the famous Cambridge pines, from which Grove Street probably derived its name, still stand.

The first Catholic mass in the town of Cambridge was celebrated in the house of James Connaughty in the fall of 1839. Prior to 1853, when the church was built, mass was held in the brick schoolhouse on the west side of North Park Street and in the Porter building, just east of the intersection of Main and Park Streets.

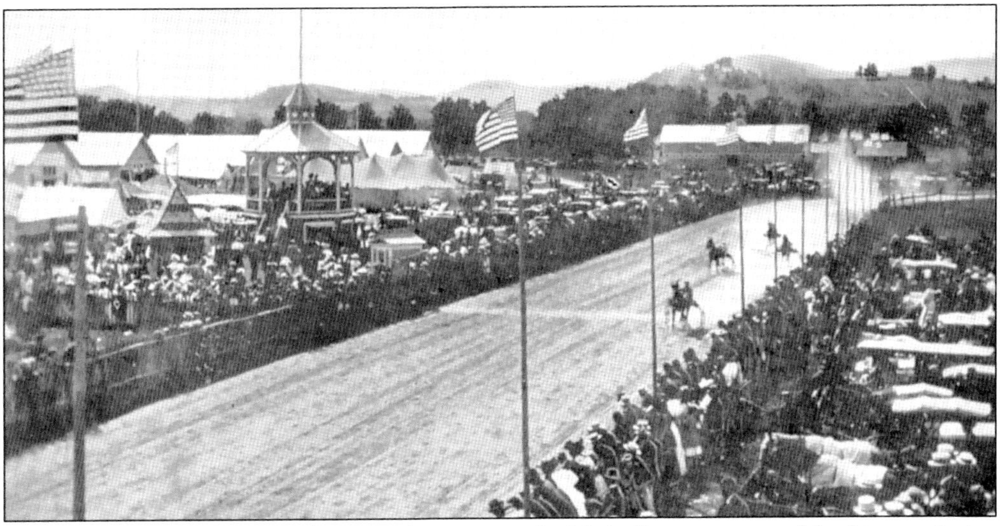

This photograph accompanied a 1910 advertisement by H. A. Qua, treasurer of the fair association for the great Cambridge Fair. The Delaware and Hudson Railroad, just out of sight in the upper right of the photograph, brought tens of thousands of people to the fair each year.

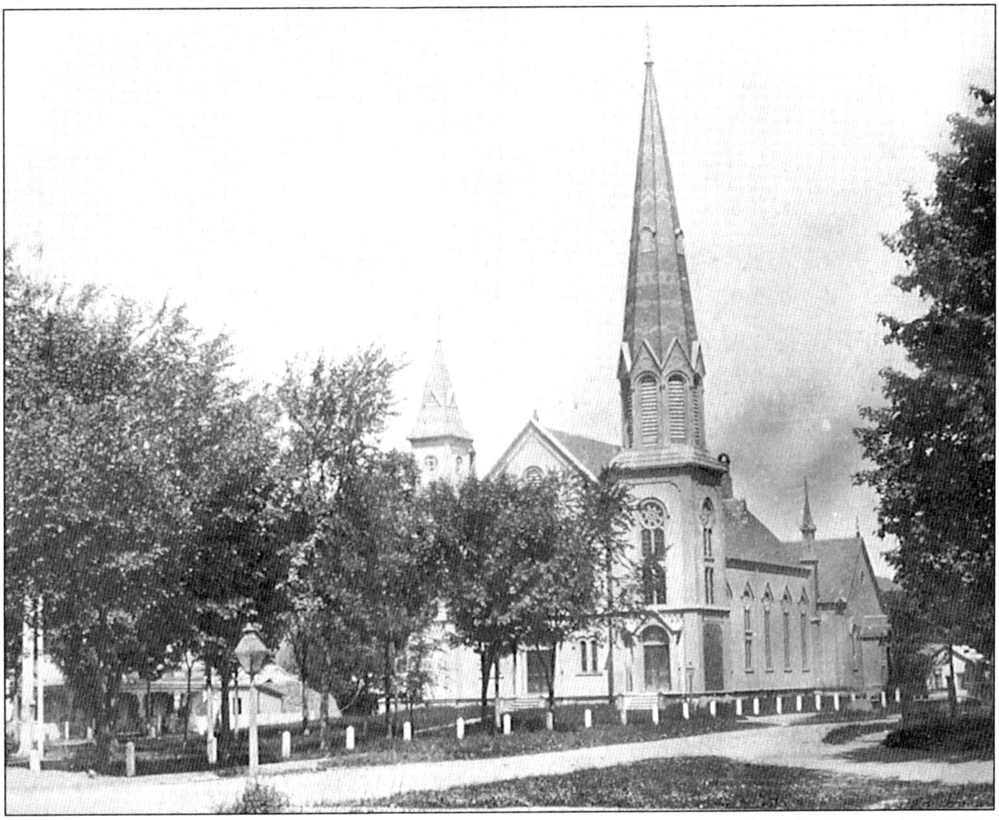

This is the third house of worship built for the United Presbyterian Church. Erected in 1872, it is still in use today. All churches in Cambridge were built to hold large congregations, with this building capable of seating 700. In the foreground is a gas streetlamp. Village lamplighters maintained these lamps until 1891 when electric lights were installed on Main Street.

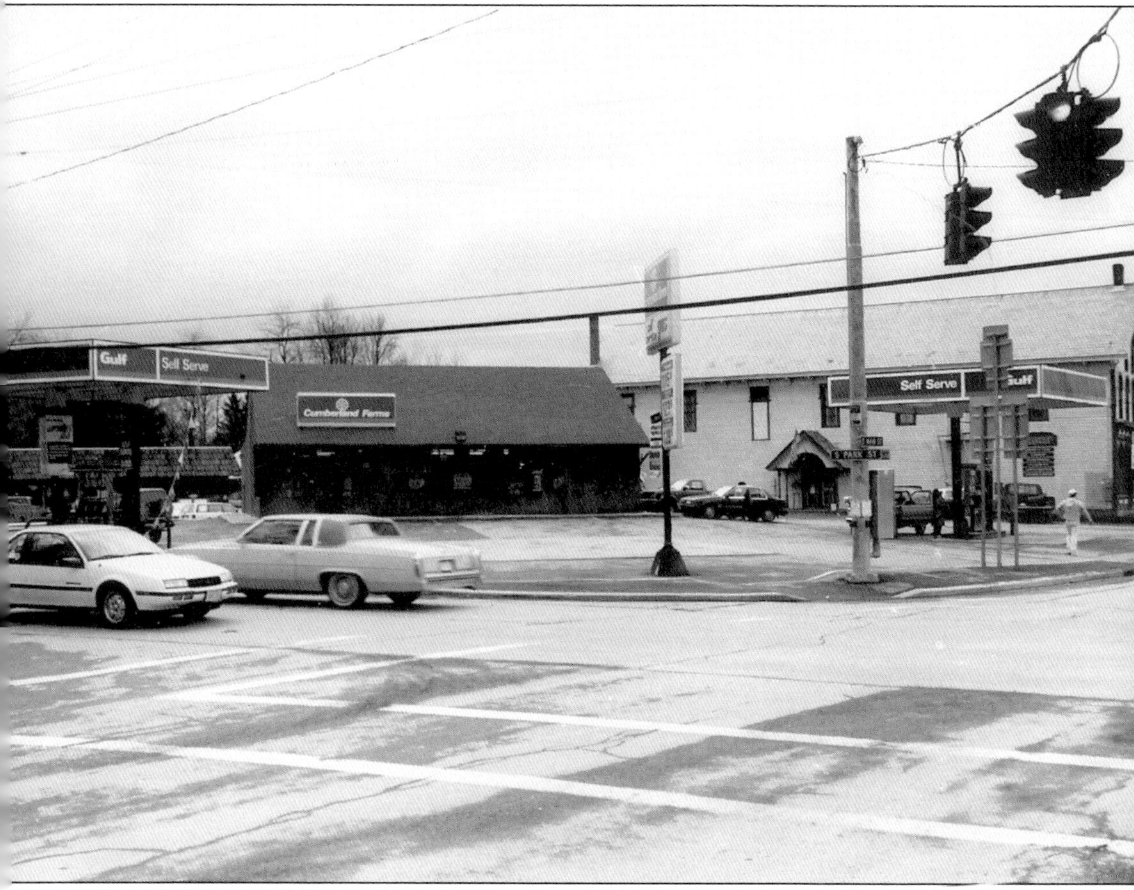

This 1990s view of the southwest corner Main and Park Streets shows the Cumberland Farms convenience store. In the 1800s, the Putnam estate stood to the left and rear of this building. There was no Avenue A, as the estate occupied all the land from South Park Street to the railroad tracks. Putnam was the grandson of Gen. Israel Pope, a hero of the Revolutionary War. On April 19, 1775, at Lexington, General Pope captured the pistols that had fired the "Shot Heard Round the World" from British major John Pitcairn. General Pope allegedly carried these pistols on June 17, 1775, at the Battle of Bunker Hill. In 1812, his grandson, Putnam, started up his law practice in Cambridge following his graduation from Williams College and Albany Law School. The famous Pitcairn Pistols, located in Putnam's Cambridge estate for many years, were lent to the Town of Lexington for the 1876 Centennial Celebration exhibition. In 1879, Putnam's widow donated the pistols to the Lexington Historical Society, where they are now on display.

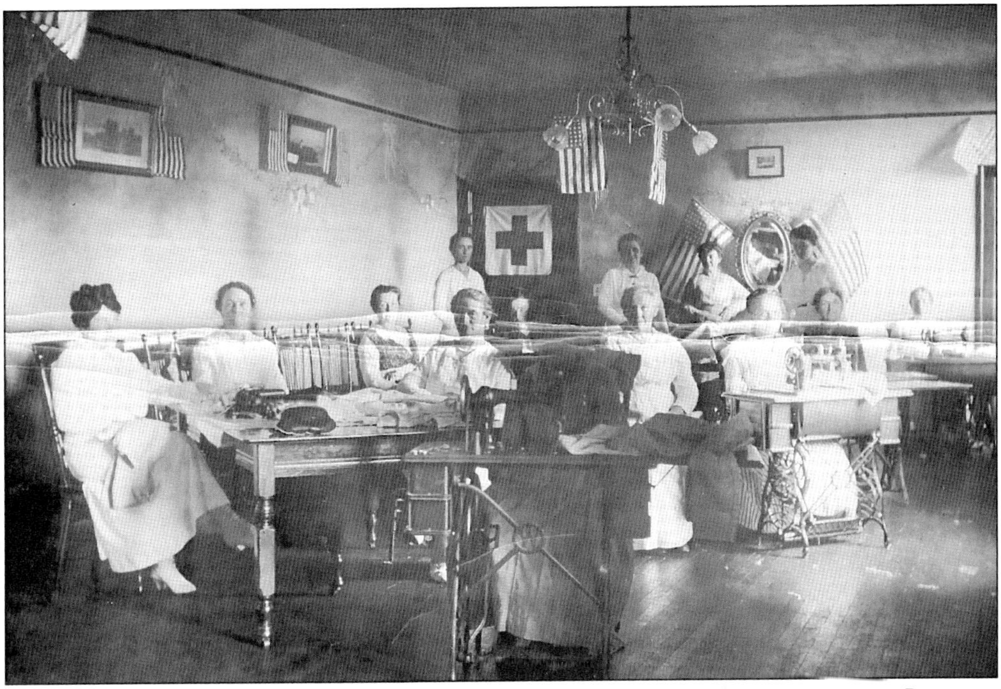

During World War I, the American Red Cross established an East End sewing center at Patrician Hall on the northwest corner of Park Street and Avenue B. The sewing hours were Tuesday and Friday from 1:00 p.m. to 5:00 p.m. Mrs. Donovan and Mrs. Loomis were in charge of the operation that included four machines. Later Patrician Hall hosted traveling theater troupes, with local residents serving in cameo roles. (Courtesy CPL.)

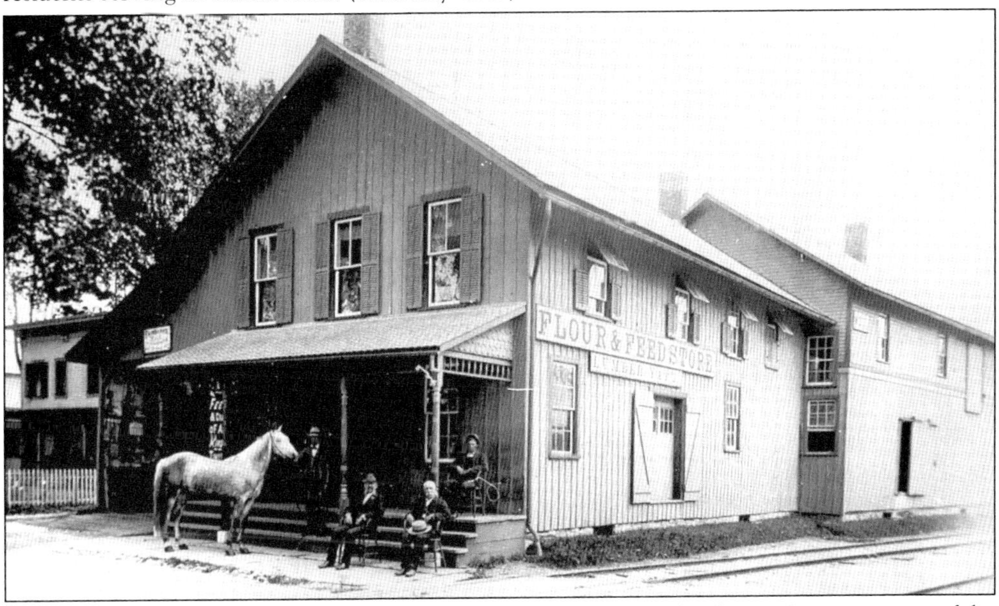

John Hubbard ran a lumberyard from the building on the south side of Main Street just east of the railroad tracks. In 1863, the train brought a circus to town. Hubbard, upset by the circus, created a ruckus. The circus people became upset, a fight ensued, Hubbard was killed, and several circus members slipped out of town during the night.

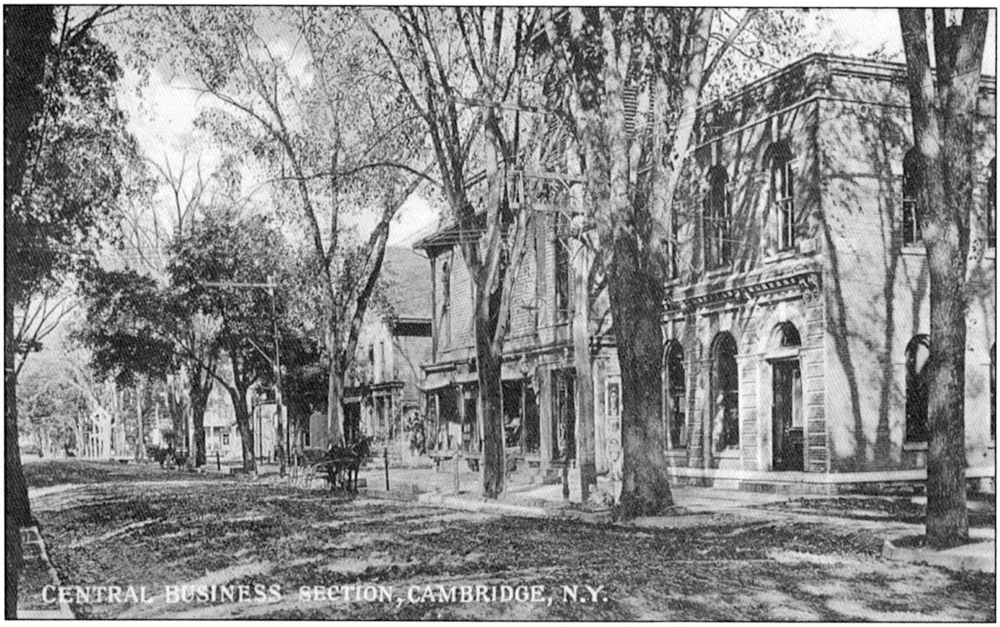

In 1958, fourteen diseased elms were taken down on Main Street. In 1959, another 16 were taken down. That year, the village board voted to plant a new tree for anyone desiring one. During the 1976 bicentennial celebration, a committee planted new trees throughout the village, especially on Main Street.

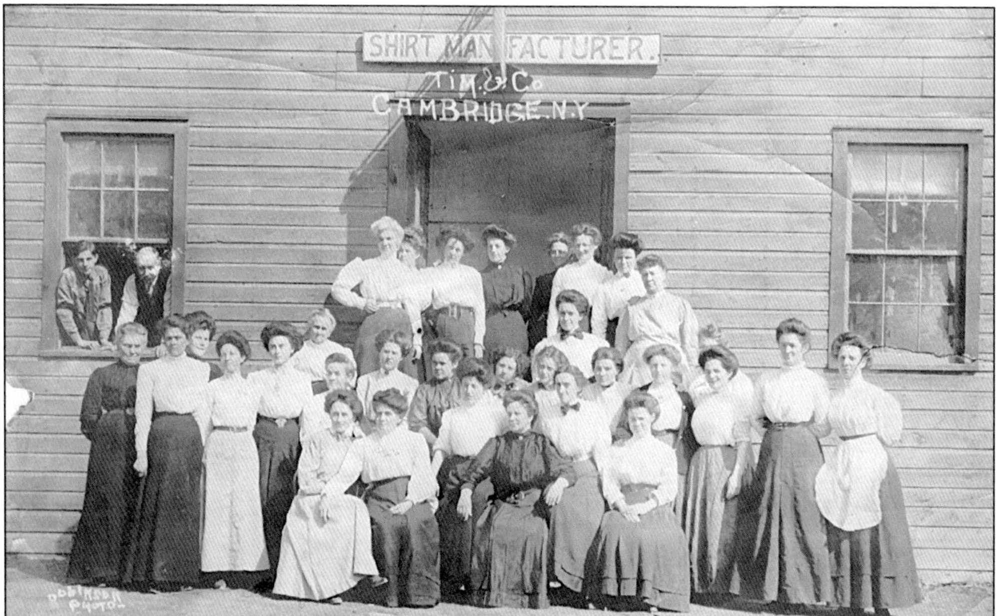

In 1910, the Tim and Company shirt factory occupied the building on the east side of South Park Street across from the present-day Stewart's Shop. In 1904, it had been run by George Smith. By 1925, the building had been converted into the Cambridge Hinge Tube and Chaplet Factory. In 2009, the building was converted into apartments, retaining much of the original flooring and wainscoting.

Two

West End

The West End of the village of Cambridge, originally known as Cambridge or Cambridge Corners, centered around the intersection of Main and Union Streets. In the very early 1800s, the Northern Turnpike (present-day Union Street) was part of the only major route between New York City and Canada. The daily stage traffic through the West End probably aided the creation of the numerous hotels, liveries, and taverns at the intersection.

An early church and cemetery were built half a mile south of the intersection. This flat land preceded the steep hill as the turnpike rose to the corner intersection. This hill on South Union Street remains steep today, in spite of numerous loads of fill being dumped there over the years.

In 1816, when the town of Cambridge was divided into the three current towns, the turnpike was used as the dividing line between the town of White Creek and the town of Cambridge. However, when the village first numbered houses in 1921, the railroad tracks were used as the dividing line between East Main and West Main Streets.

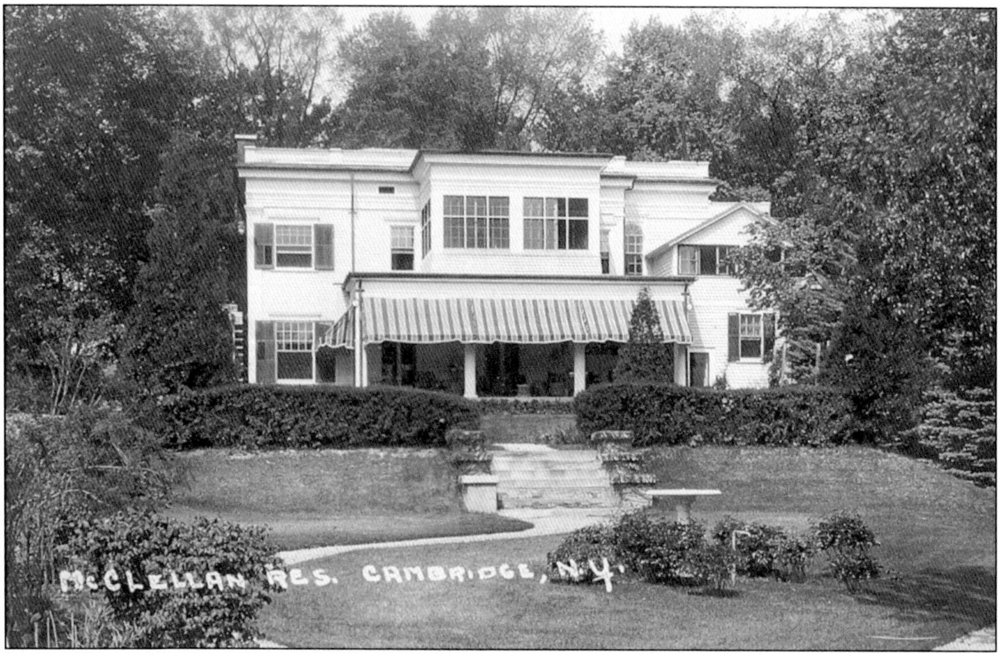

After the widow of J. J. Gray sold him the house on South Union Street, Edwin McClellan renovated it and named it Meikleknox. His brother, Robert, built the magnificent Northwoods estate on North Union Street just south of Woodlands Cemetery. Robert died in December 1924, only a few months after Northwoods was completed.

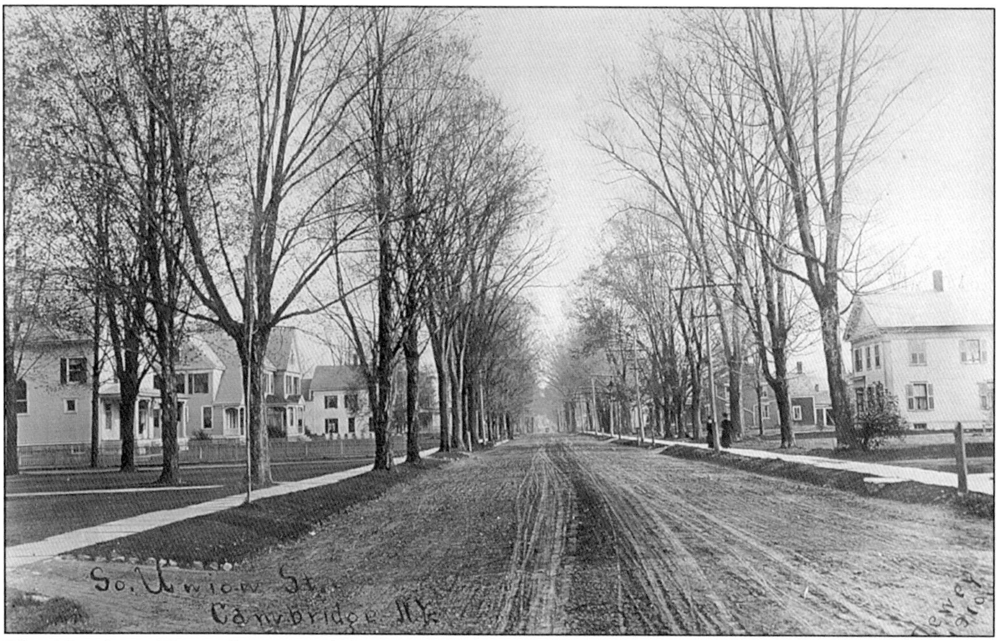

The Northern Turnpike entered the town of Cambridge at the north end of the Buskirk Bridge, climbed the steep Oak Hill, passing through Cambridge Corners as what is now Union Street. From there it roughly followed the current New York State Route 22 to Granville. This was a major route from New York to Montreal until the railroad in the early 1850s.

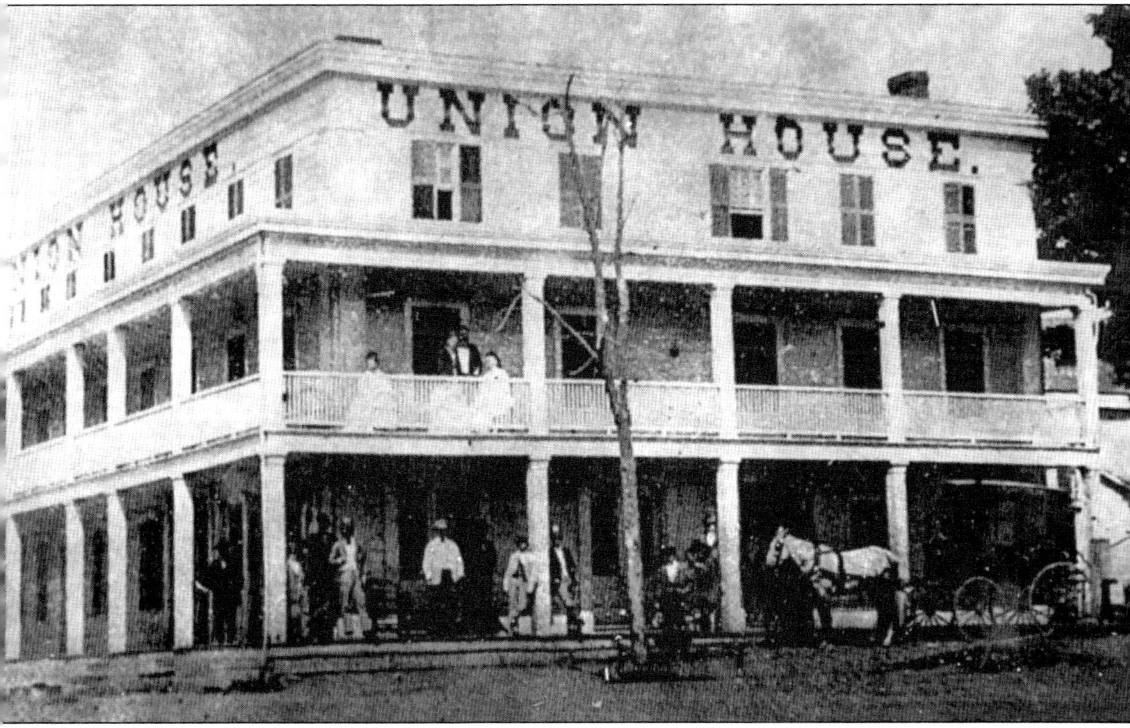

The Union House building has been a mainstay on the West End for over 150 years. When the Northern Turnpike was built between 1799 and 1804, it was the main route from New York City, through Albany, north to Canada. The turnpike passed through Cambridge on what is now Union Street, making the intersection of Main and Union a perfect location for hotels and livery stables. There were three buildings at the turnpike crossing that have been referred to as the Union Hotel or Union House. The first, believed to be the one in the photograph, was destroyed by fire in 1875. The second one was damaged by the December 1884 fire that destroyed Ackley Hall across the street. In early 1885, the remains of the second hotel were torn down to make room for a magnificent new Union Hotel. At the same time, the Cambridge Hotel was started near the railroad tracks. The Union House lost the "Great Hotel Race of 1885," opening in November a few weeks after the Cambridge Hotel. (Courtesy CVA.)

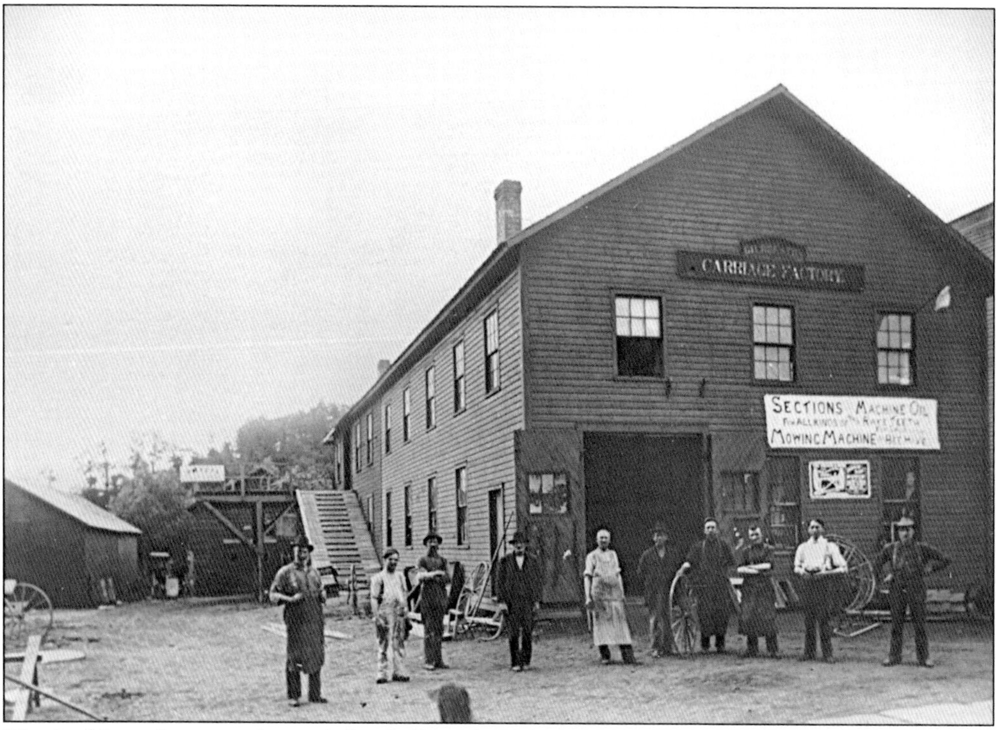

The building that once housed the Galbraith Carriage Factory burned in 1927. The ramp on the left side was used to take wagons to the second story. Bell and Costello automobile sales and service later occupied this location.

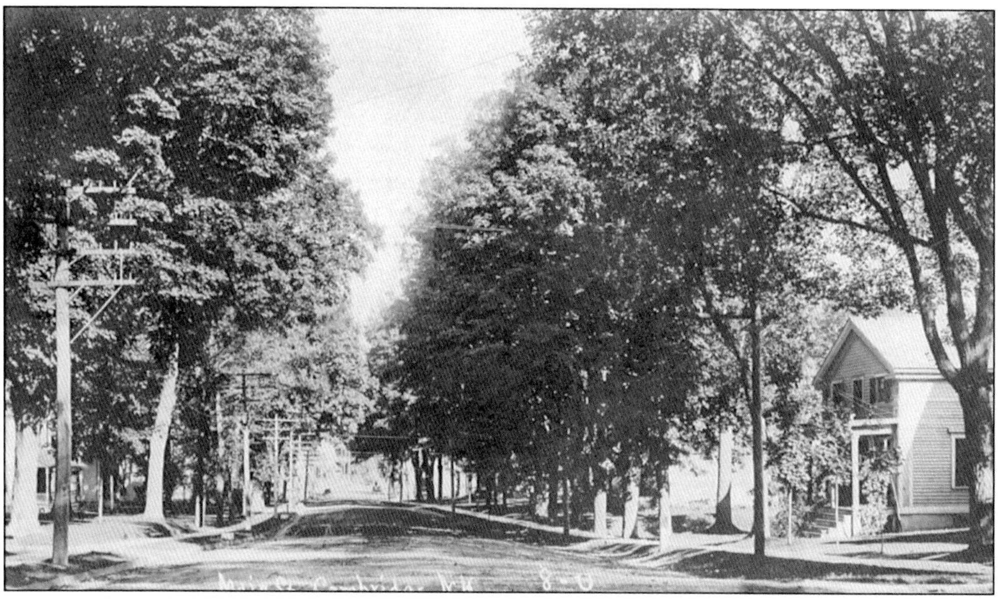

In 1921, the village board voted to number the houses for the first time. In October 1954, the U.S. Post Office renumbered all houses in the village. Confusion with property deeds ensued. For example, on East Main Street, not only did the numbers change, but the odd/even designations switched sides of the street—26 East Main Street became 39 East Main Street.

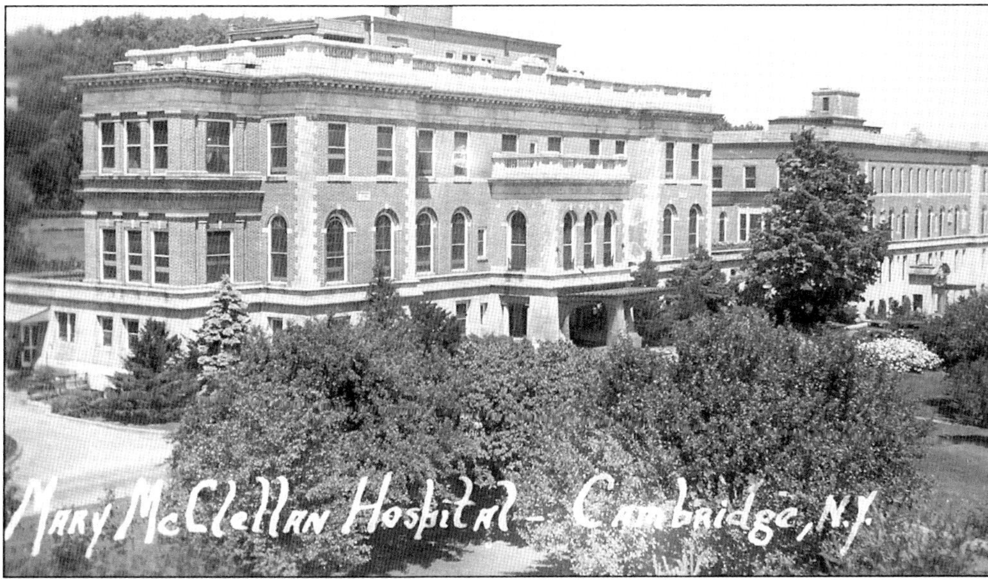

In 1928, the village board voted to blow the fire siren each day at noon for test purposes. In 1952, shortly after the new fire station was completed, the village made an arrangement with the hospital for a system of blowing the fire siren. In 1964, the village board put a base station at the hospital for fire alarms.

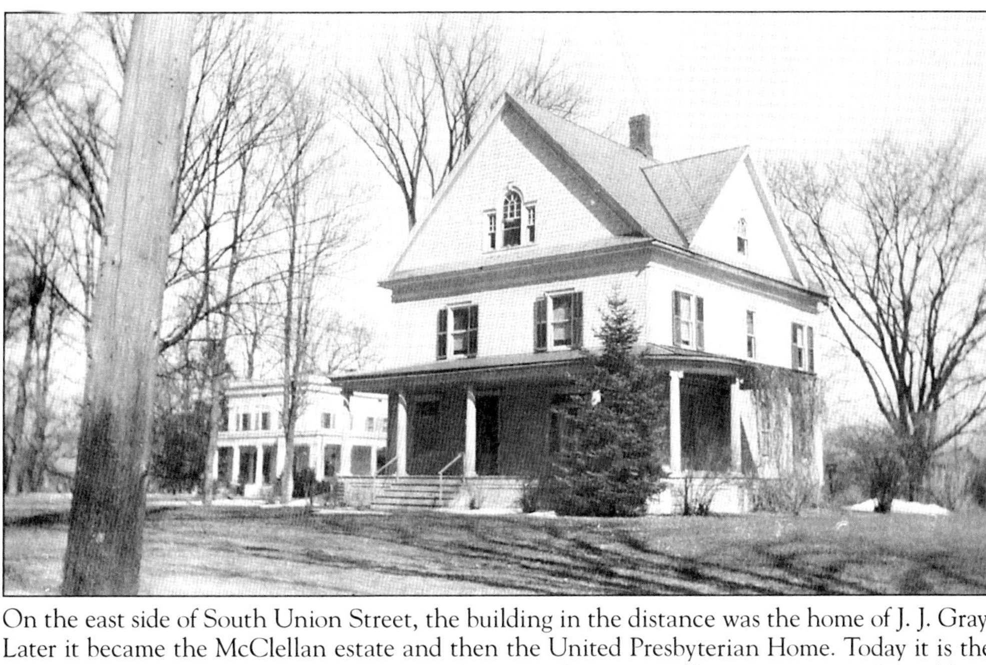

On the east side of South Union Street, the building in the distance was the home of J. J. Gray. Later it became the McClellan estate and then the United Presbyterian Home. Today it is the Cambridge Guest Home. The home in the foreground was owned by M. Gray in 1859 and later passed on to his descendants, the Art Center family.

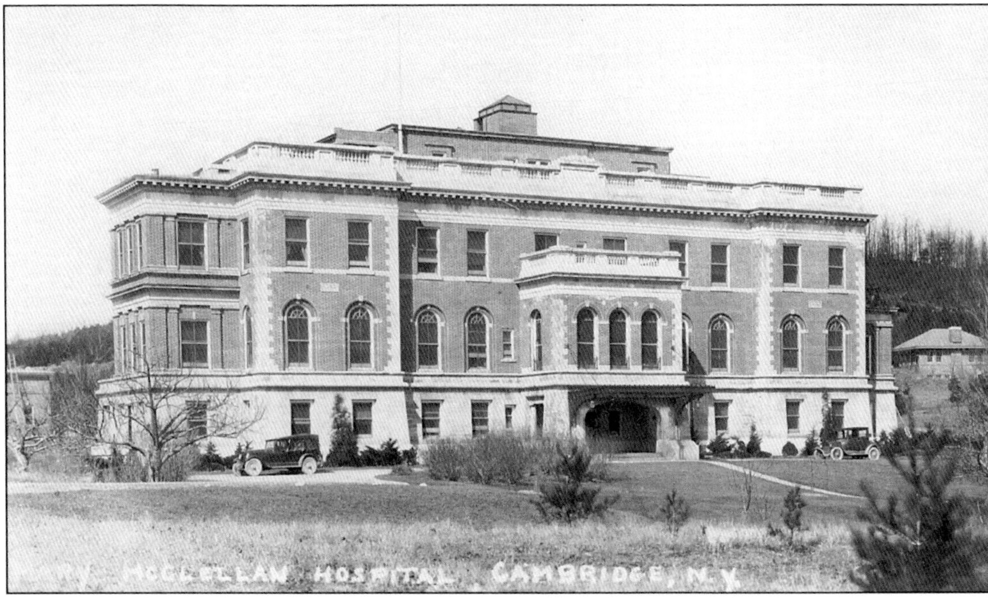

Edwin McClellan had his brother-in-law, William Mynderse, design the Mary McClellan Memorial Hospital in memory of Edwin's mother. The hospital, though named "Memorial," was in honor of Edwin's mother while she was still alive. In fact, Mary did not die until 1927, three years after Edwin.

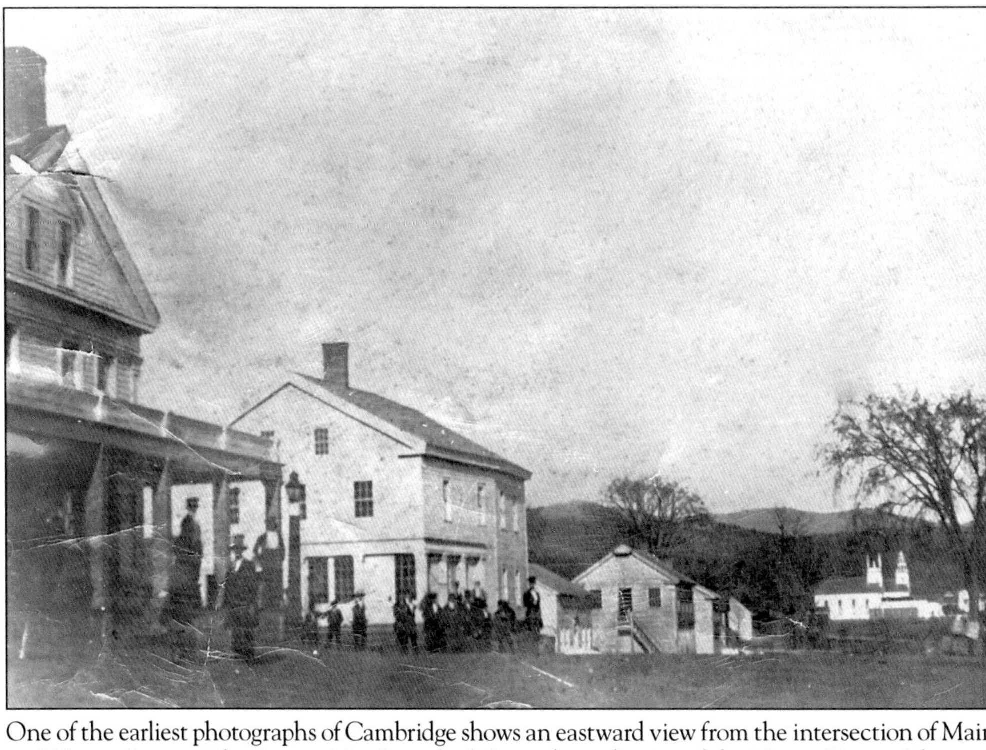

One of the earliest photographs of Cambridge shows an eastward view from the intersection of Main and Union Streets. The Fenton Hotel on the left was later the site of the Union House. The road has a steep grade down, heading east (right) to North White Creek. A swamp, separating the West End and East End, formed where the road crossed Blair's Brook (later Owl Kill). (Courtesy CVA.)

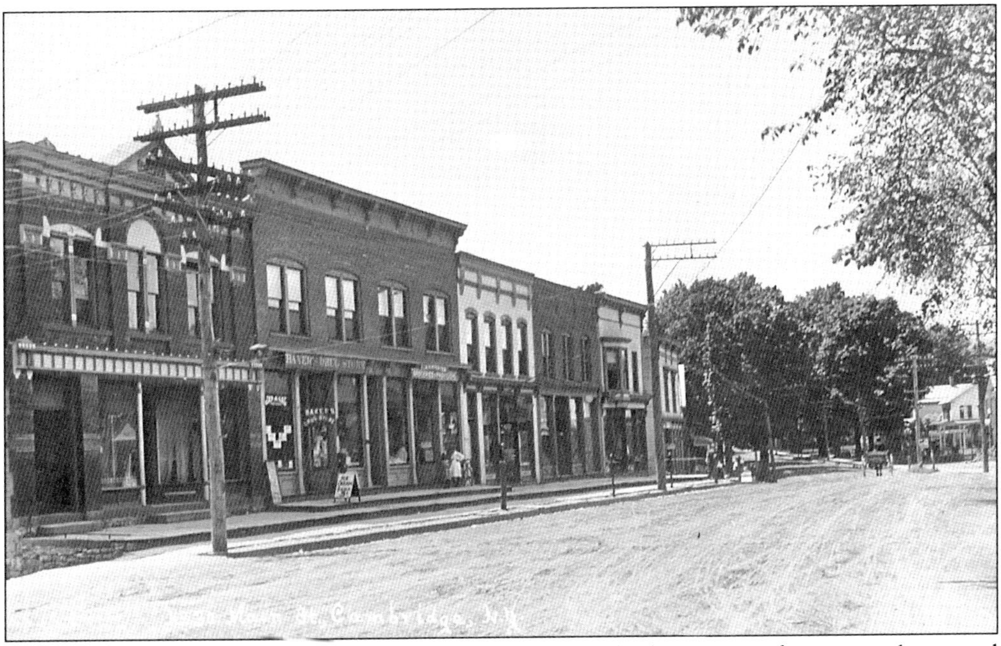

The first four buildings on the left still stand on the West End. This section of stores was devastated repeatedly by fire during the late 1800s. One of the worst fires was in December 1884 when the great Ackley Hall was destroyed. This photograph was taken after 1891 when electricity was installed on Main Street and before 1913 when Main Street was paved with yellow bricks.

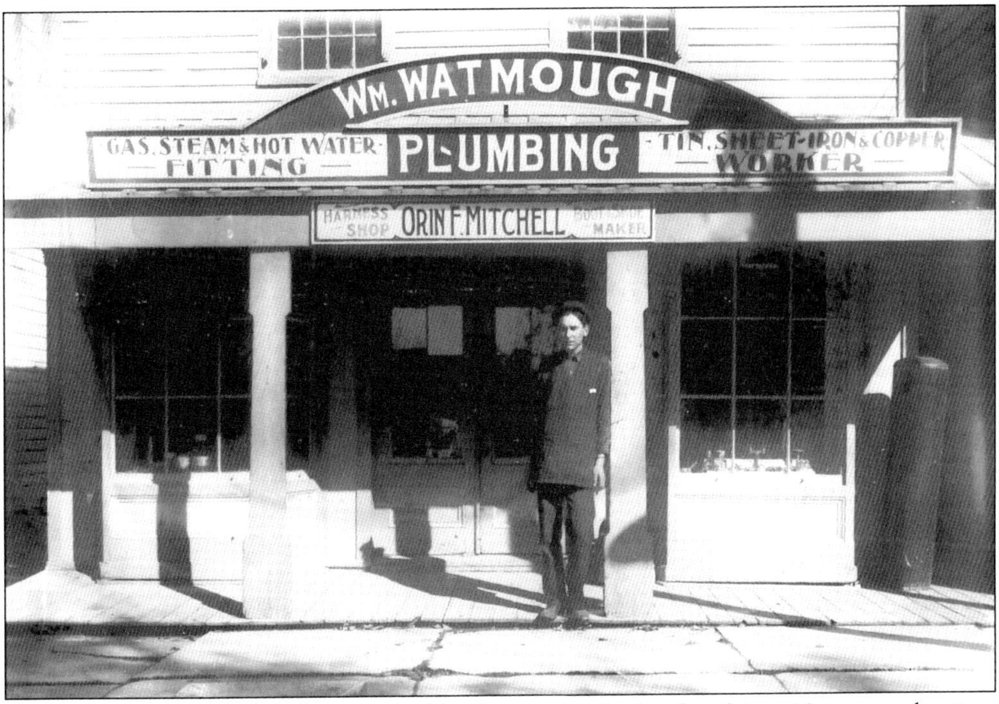

There are many unlabeled photographs like this one in the local archives. Names on the signs and the structure of the building usually assist in identification. This is believed to be the location of Leo Santerre's liquor store in the 1960s. (Courtesy CVA.)

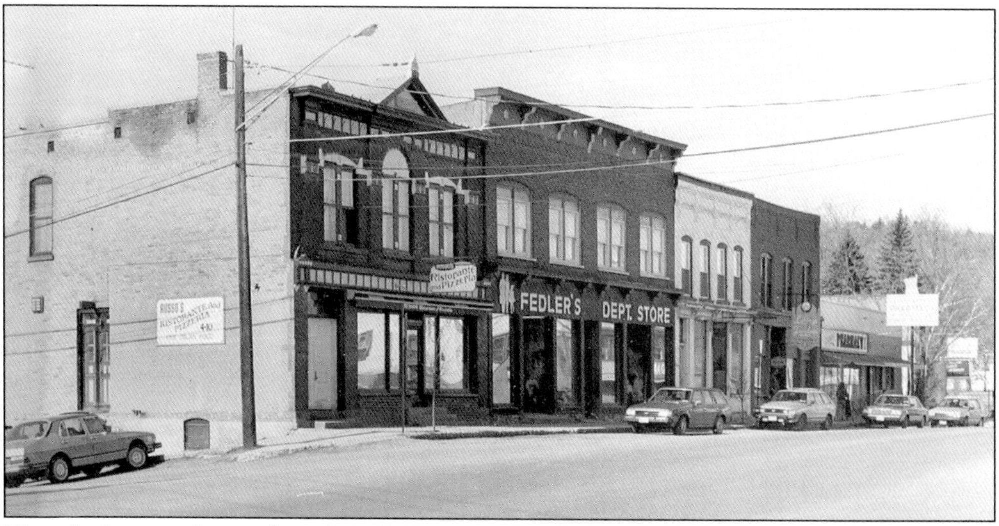

The telephone and power lines have been an eyesore for over 100 years. On August 25, 1891, the village board awarded a contract to Cambridge Light and Power Company. They installed 100 incandescent lamps, each with a brightness of 25 candlepower. They burned on the moonlight schedule, not to exceed 20 nights per month. Each light cost $8 per year to operate and were extinguished by 1:00 a.m.

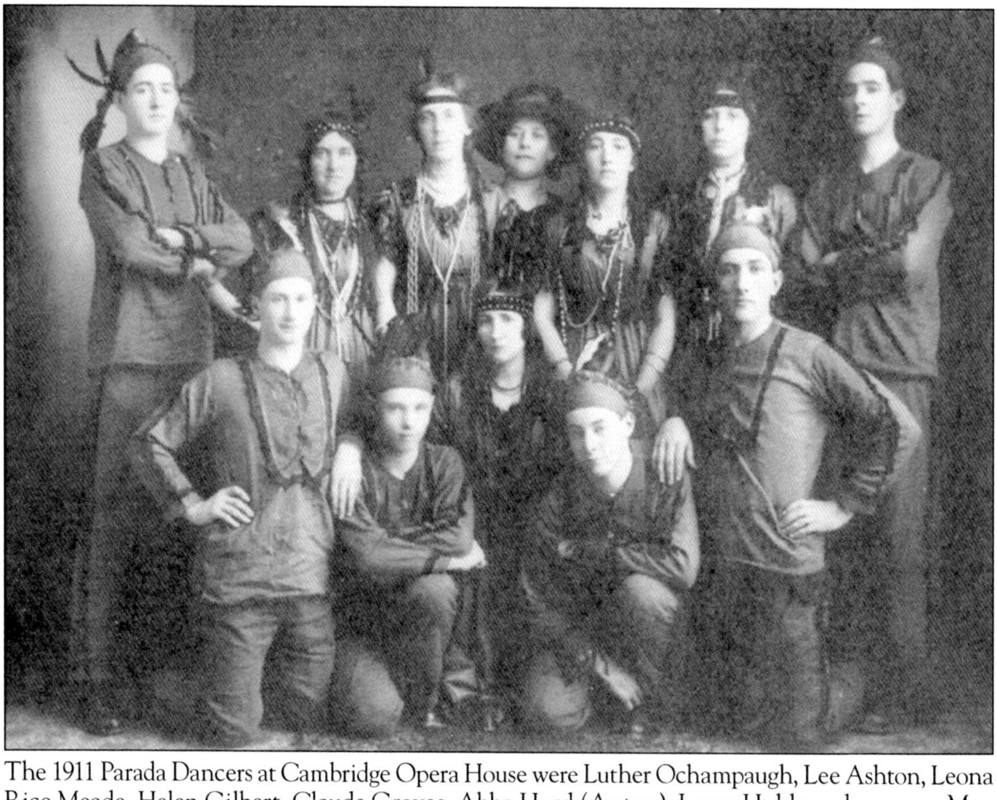

The 1911 Parada Dancers at Cambridge Opera House were Luther Ochampaugh, Lee Ashton, Leona Rice Meade, Helen Gilbert, Claude Graves, Abba Hurd (Anton), Leroy Holden, chaperone Mrs. Harry Hedges, Ethel Kinard, Harry Curtis, James H. Meader, and Elizabeth Meader. James Meader, a multisports star at Cambridge High School, is kneeling at the right end of the front row.

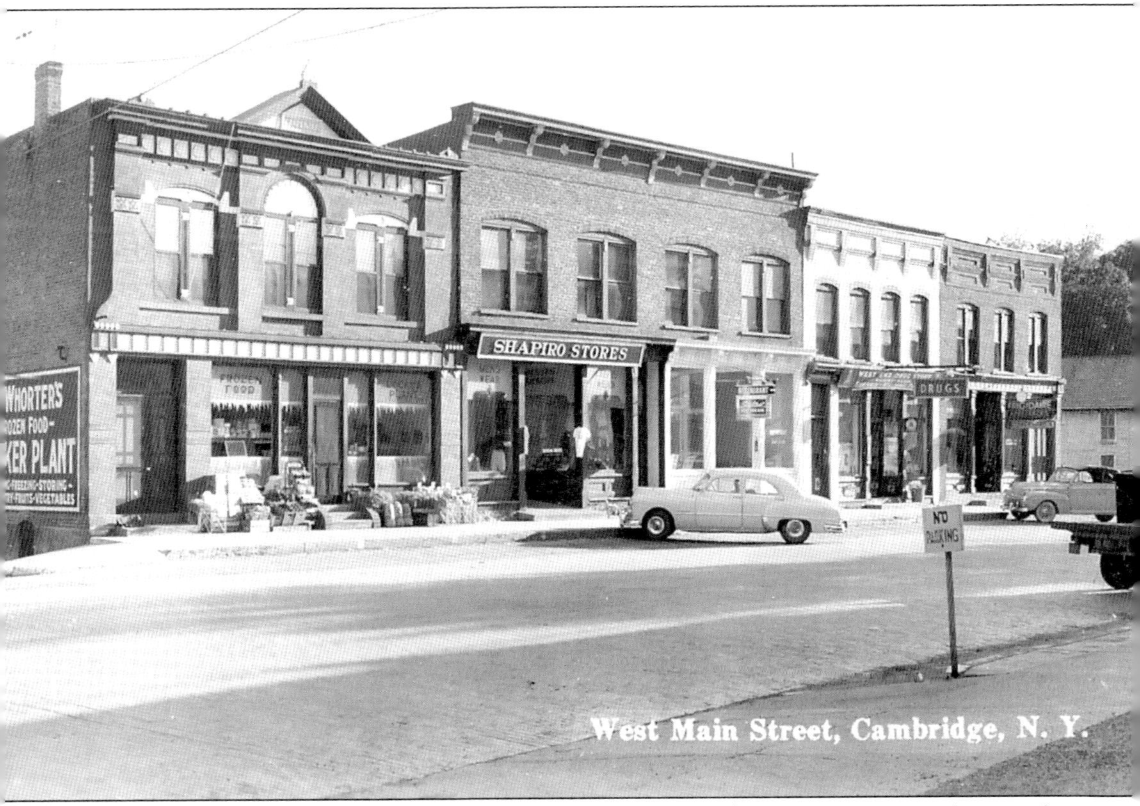

In 1901, the village board voted to pave Main Street at a cost of $10,000. By 1908, with no work started, a second proposal for $20,000 was defeated by the voters, 164-135. In 1911, with still no work started, a third proposal for $30,000 was approved by a vote of 153-96. In 1912, growing anxious for action, the voters approved a fourth proposal for $36,000 by a vote of 225-10. Work finally started in early 1913. Progress was slow. The age-old distrust between the West End and East End led to an unusual construction plan. Work started on the East End at Dorr's Corners (Main and Gilbert Streets). The fill was pushed to the middle of the village to fill in the swamp. After some bricks had been laid, the entire operation was uprooted and moved to the West End near Tannery Pond, where an equal stretch of paving occurred. As the project faltered in early summer, William L. Hitchcock took charge, and the project was completed by year's end. In 1960, the village asked the state to blacktop Main Street.

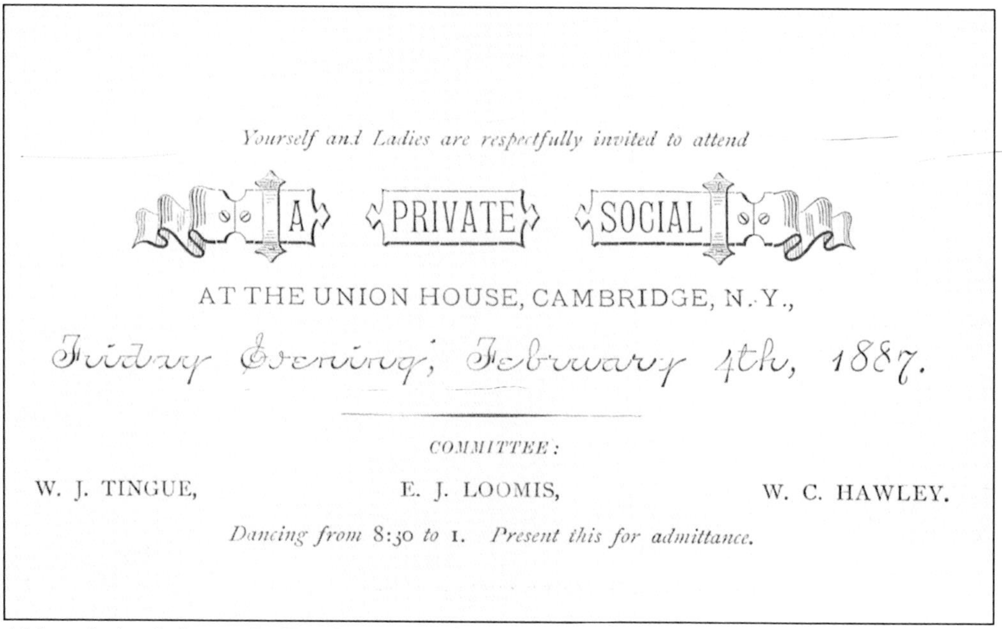

Yourself and Ladies are respectfully invited to attend

A PRIVATE SOCIAL

AT THE UNION HOUSE, CAMBRIDGE, N. Y.,

Friday Evening, February 4th, 1887.

COMMITTEE:

W. J. TINGUE,	E. J. LOOMIS,	W. C. HAWLEY.

Dancing from 8:30 to 1. Present this for admittance.

Although divided into the East District and West District, everyone came together when it was time for a party. These prominent committee members were from distinguished families. Charles Tingue was president of Cambridge on two occasions (1898–1901 and again 1908–1913). Charles Hawley followed in the footsteps of his father by becoming stationmaster. He was active in the formation of the Cambridge Water Works in 1885.

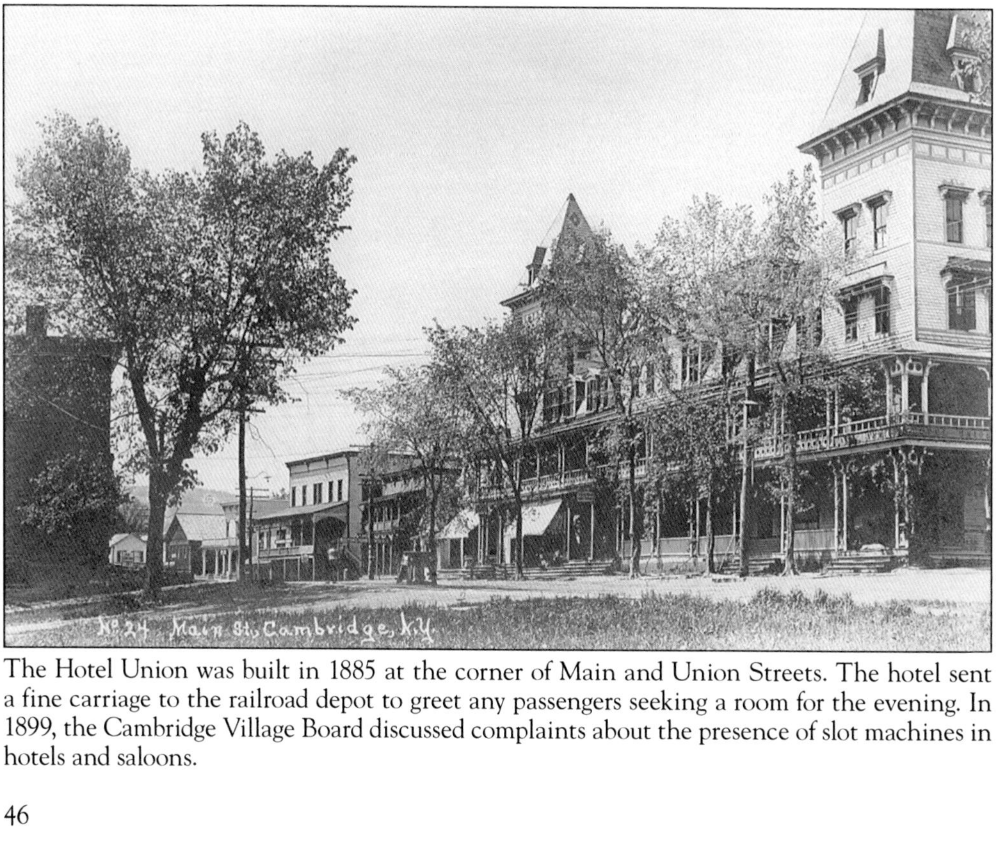

The Hotel Union was built in 1885 at the corner of Main and Union Streets. The hotel sent a fine carriage to the railroad depot to greet any passengers seeking a room for the evening. In 1899, the Cambridge Village Board discussed complaints about the presence of slot machines in hotels and saloons.

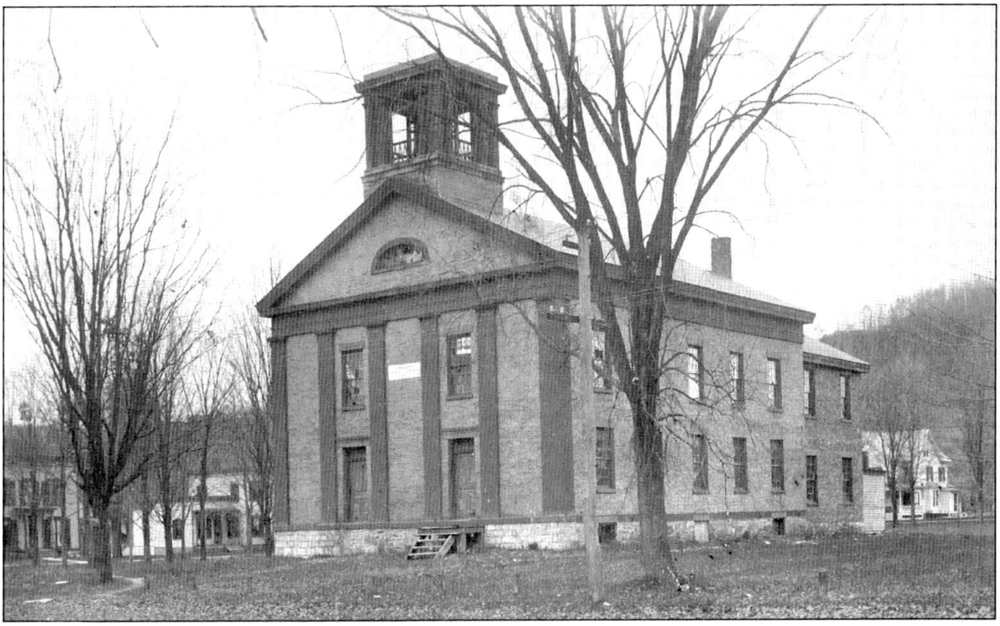

An academy was located on the northwest corner of Academy and Pleasant Streets for over 100 years. The original smaller wooden structure was built around 1800. The New York State Regents granted its petition in 1815 to become Cambridge Washington Academy. The front 40-foot-by-60-foot building was constructed. The 24-foot-by-48-foot rear addition was opened in 1844. As the depression of 1873 approached, the academy closed its doors.

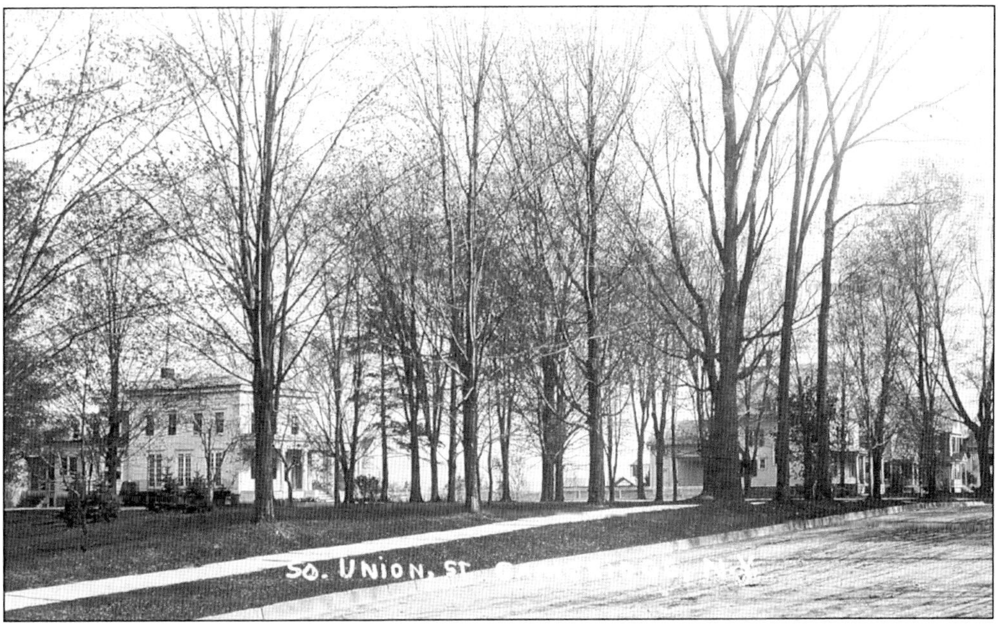

Hiram House owned the stately home on the left in 1859, followed by J. J. Gray. The next owner was Edwin McClellan, who had his brother-in-law, William Mynderse, renovate the house. McClellan called the estate Meikleknox, meaning little hill. McClellan spent much of his time in London, England, but upon his death was returned to Cambridge and laid to rest in Woodlands Cemetery.

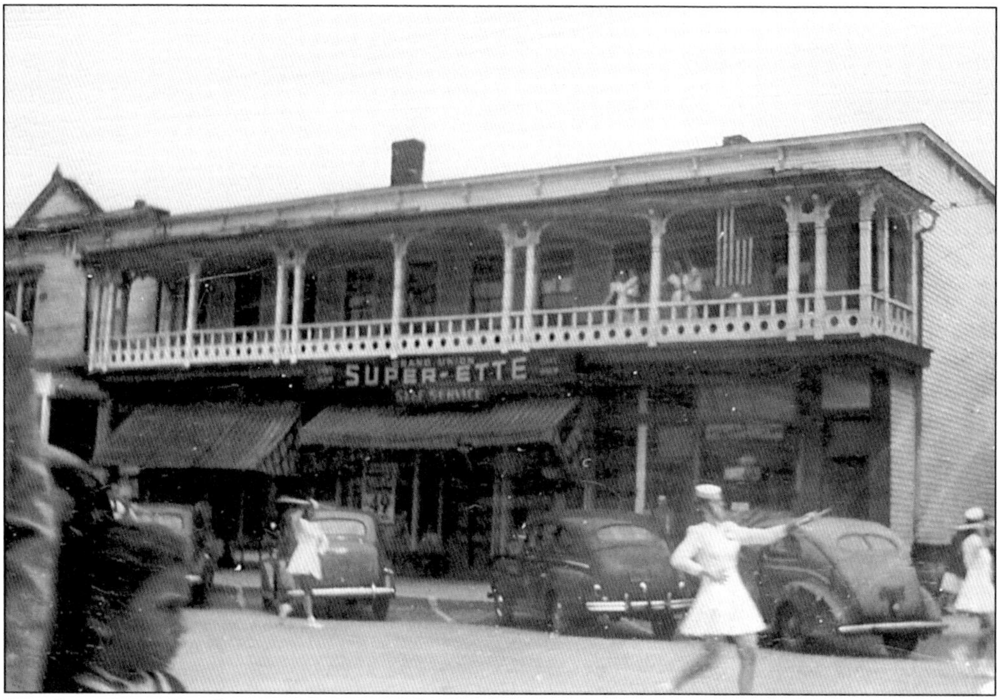

Parades start at Academy Street, proceeding eastward on Main Street and turning south on Park Street. Today a ceremony is held when the parade reaches the school grounds. For years, the ceremony was held in Fuller's Grove on the west side of South Park Street. Here the parade is just underway, passing what was the Union House. At the time of this photograph, the building housed the Grand Union Super-ette.

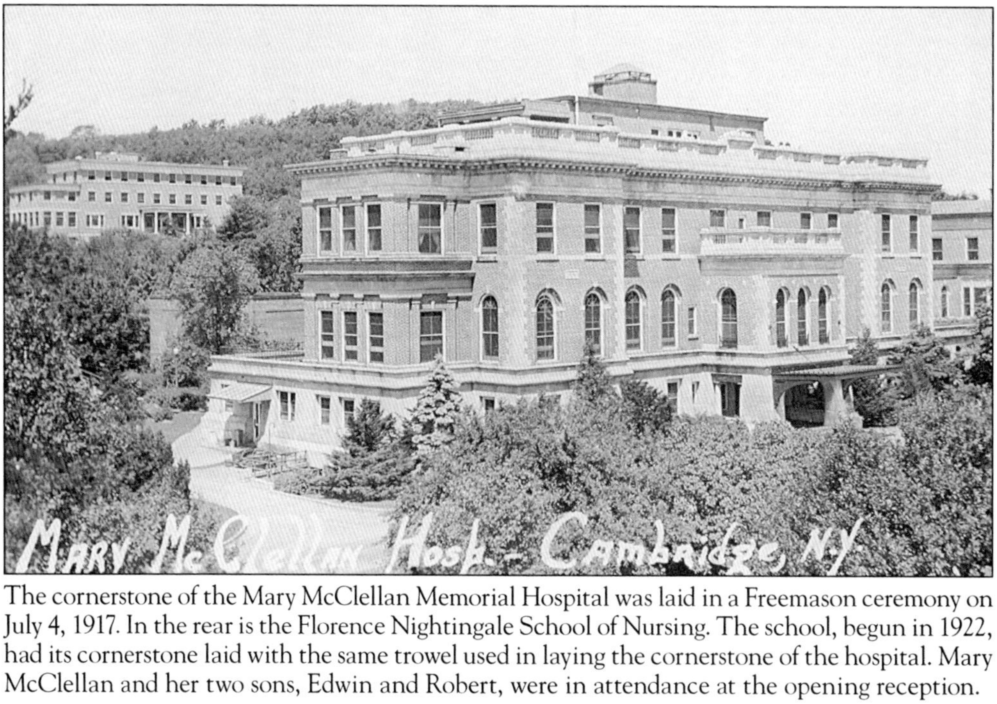

The cornerstone of the Mary McClellan Memorial Hospital was laid in a Freemason ceremony on July 4, 1917. In the rear is the Florence Nightingale School of Nursing. The school, begun in 1922, had its cornerstone laid with the same trowel used in laying the cornerstone of the hospital. Mary McClellan and her two sons, Edwin and Robert, were in attendance at the opening reception.

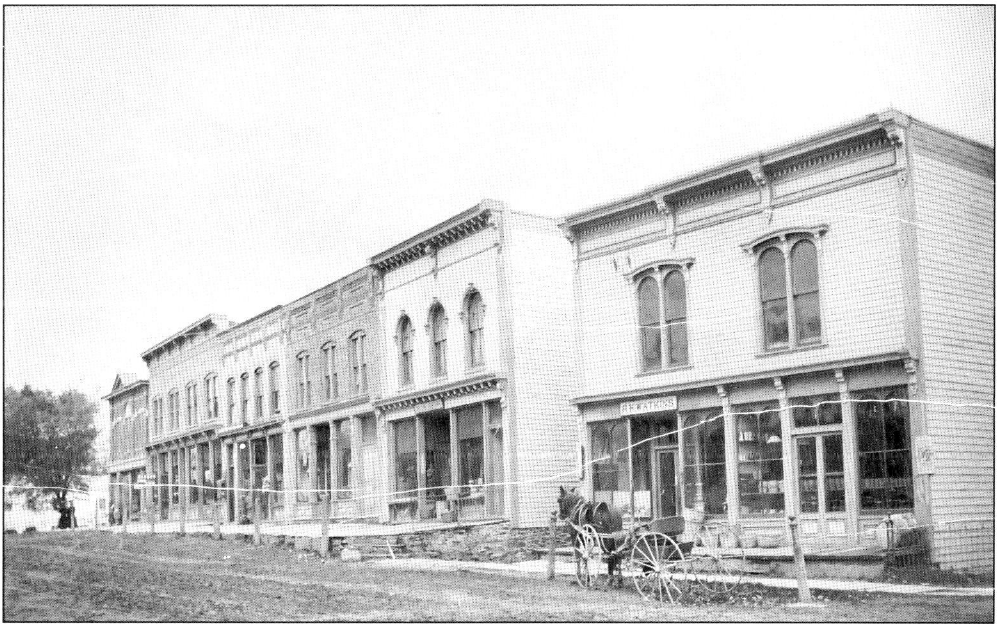

The south side of West Main Street has suffered many fires but always seems to be rebuilt in a similar style. The four buildings to the left still stand today, although the one to the left of H. A. Qua's store is in need of much repair. The R. H. Watkin store, today the location of O'Hearn's pharmacy, sits just east of the Cambridge Creek. (Courtesy CVA.)

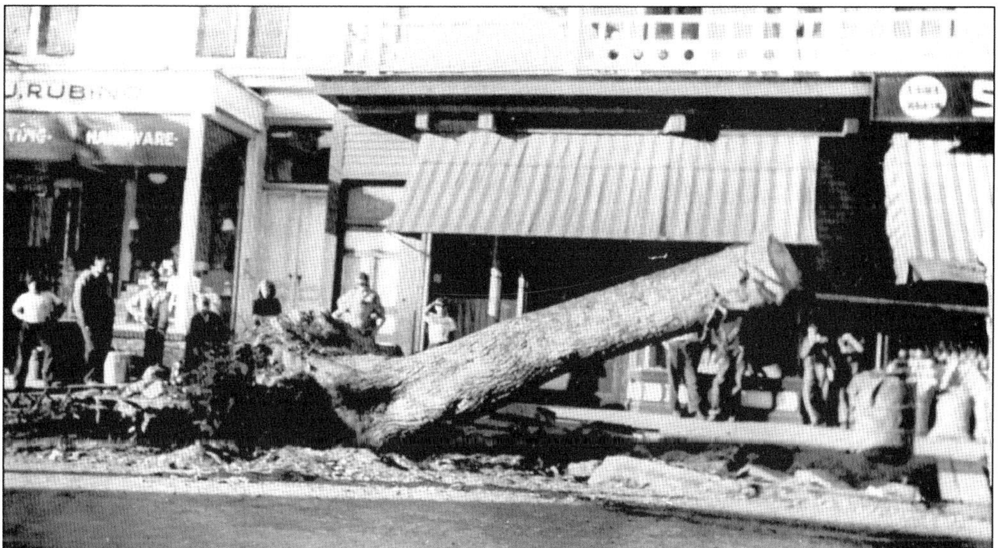

A severe storm in 1947 destroyed the last great elm tree on the north side of West Main Street. James Rubino's hardware and plumbing store is on the left, and the Grand Union Super-ette on the right. (Courtesy CVA.)

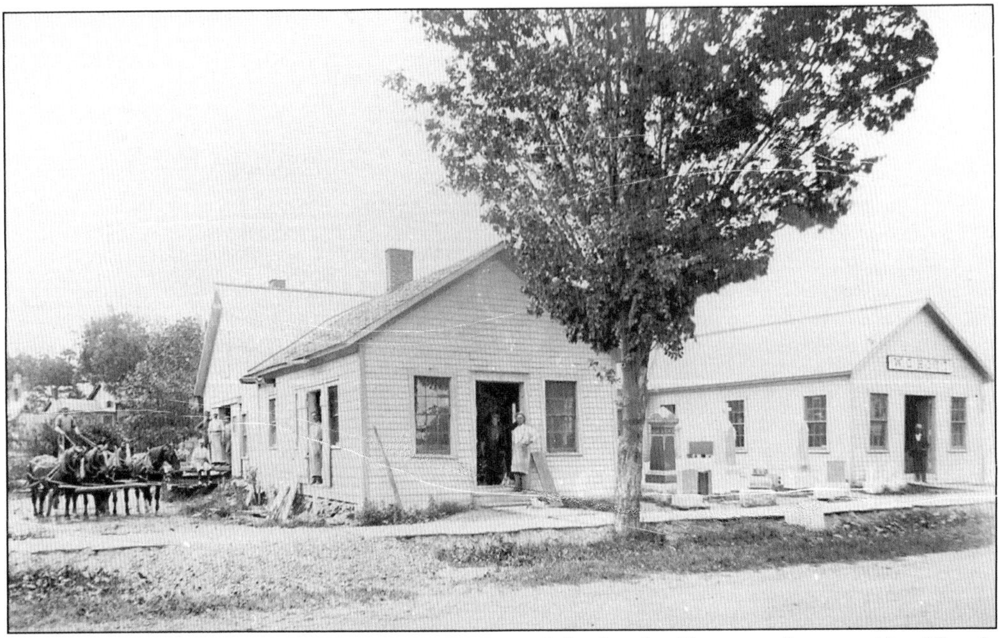

In the early 1900s, W. D. Hoyt Stonecutting occupied the first buildings on the west side of South Union Street. By 1925, these buildings were gone, replaced by the Robert Reis and Company factory, a manufacturer of underwear. Today the building is a church.

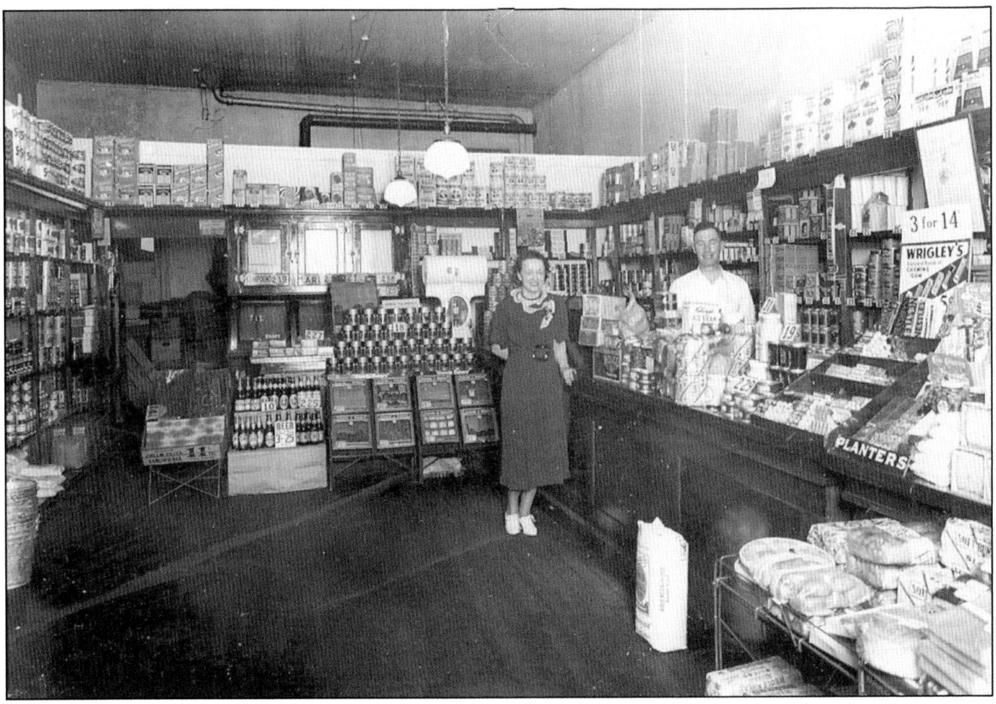

It is unclear who the people in the photograph are, as well as the location of the grocery store. It may be the McWhorter store.

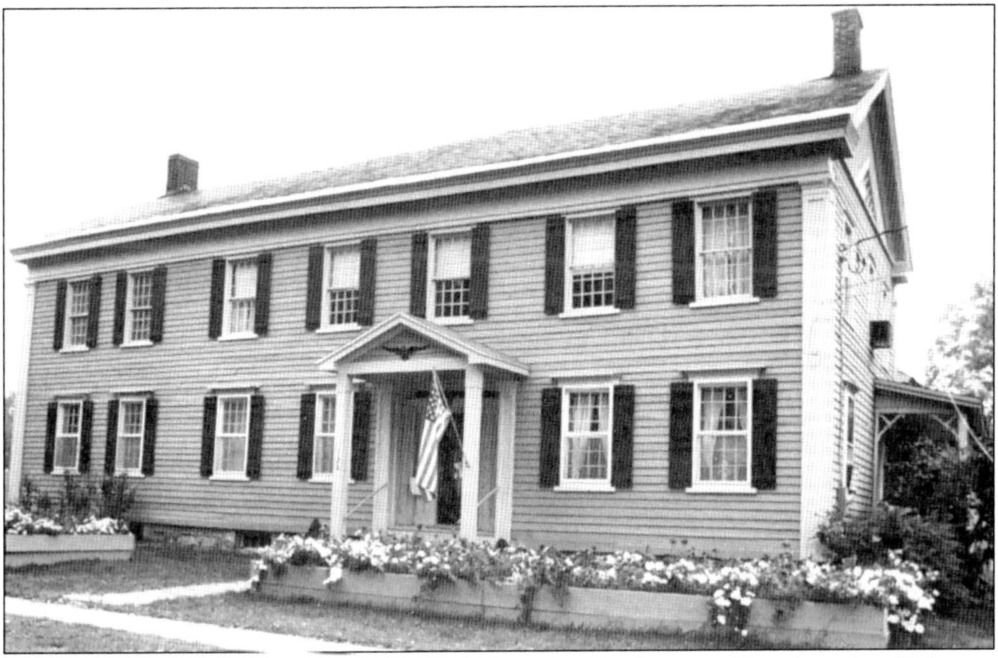

A minority congregation split from the Coila Associate Presbyterian Church in the 1830s over the reconciliation of the Anti-Burghers and Burghers in the Church of Scotland. Longtime pastor, Rev. Alexander Bullions, was suspended in 1838 for his role in the dispute. They worshipped in the Cambridge Washington Academy for six years. In 1844, they built this Old Boarding House on West Main Street. The congregation reunited in 1854.

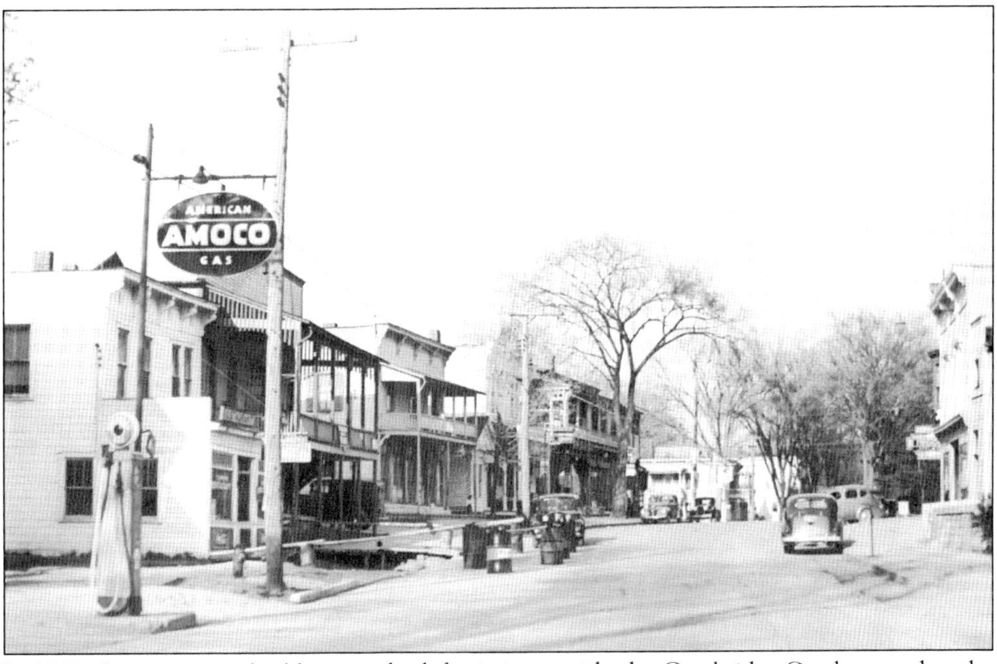

In 1910, the restaurant building on the left, sitting astride the Cambridge Creek, served as the firehouse for the John Larmon Hose Company No. 2. In this photograph, a large portion of the bridge spanning the creek has collapsed.

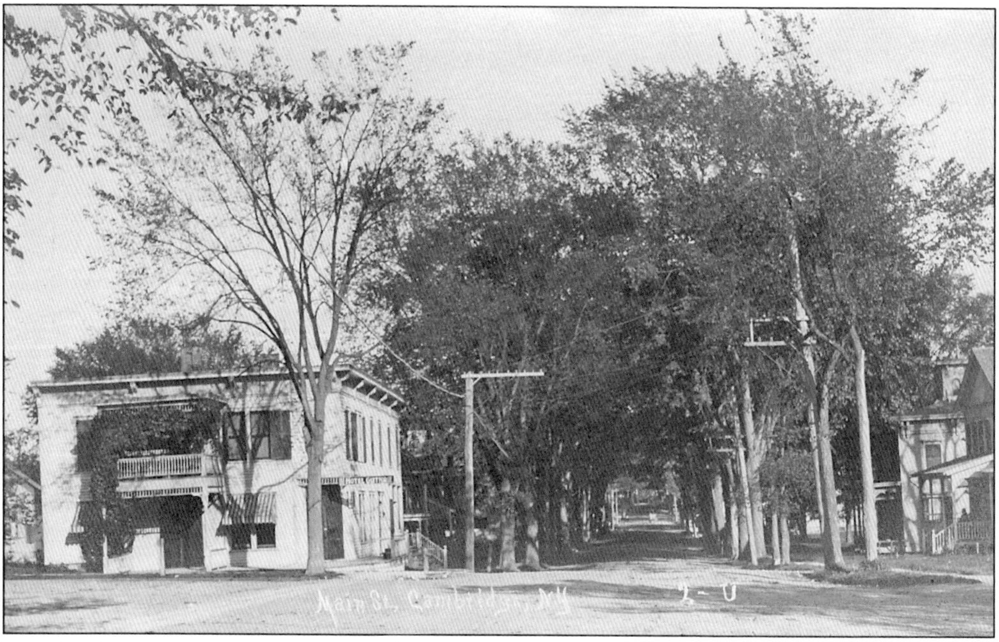

The Guthrie Hotel was located on the northeast corner of Main and Union Streets. One of the first Cambridge post offices was located on this site around 1830. In the mid-1900s, the Odd Fellows (IOOF) used the second floor as their meeting hall. Today this is the home of Ed Levin Jewelry.

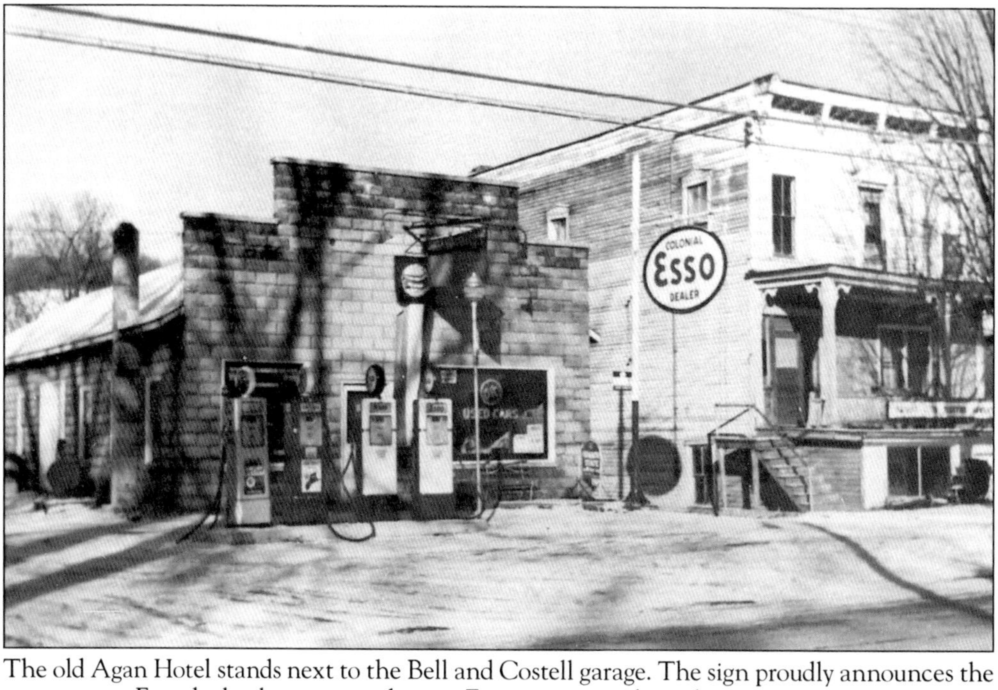

The old Agan Hotel stands next to the Bell and Costell garage. The sign proudly announces the garage as an Esso dealer, but next to the two Esso pumps on the right are Texaco Fire Chief and Sky Chief pumps.

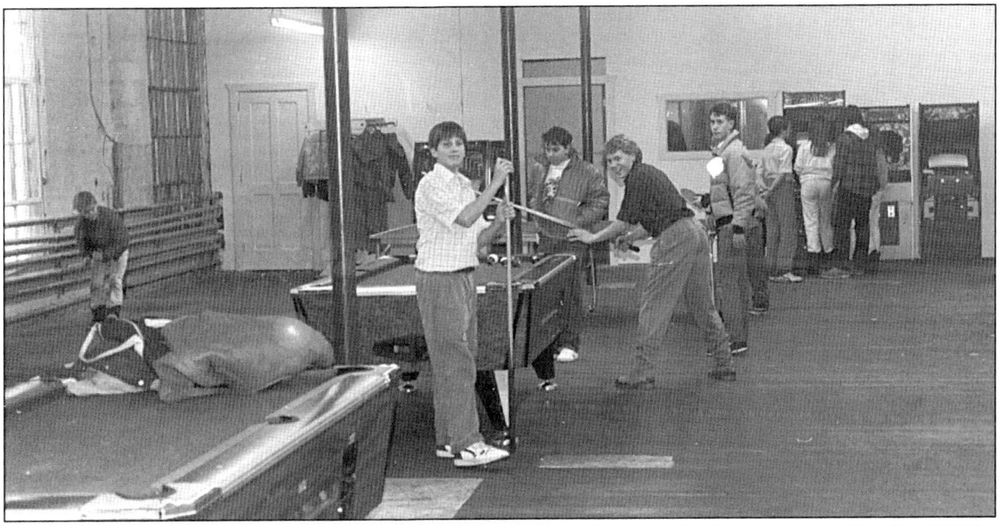

In 1958, the village board appointed the first Cambridge Youth Commission. In the 1980s, the commission opened a youth center on South Union in the old Reis Mill building. (Courtesy CVA.)

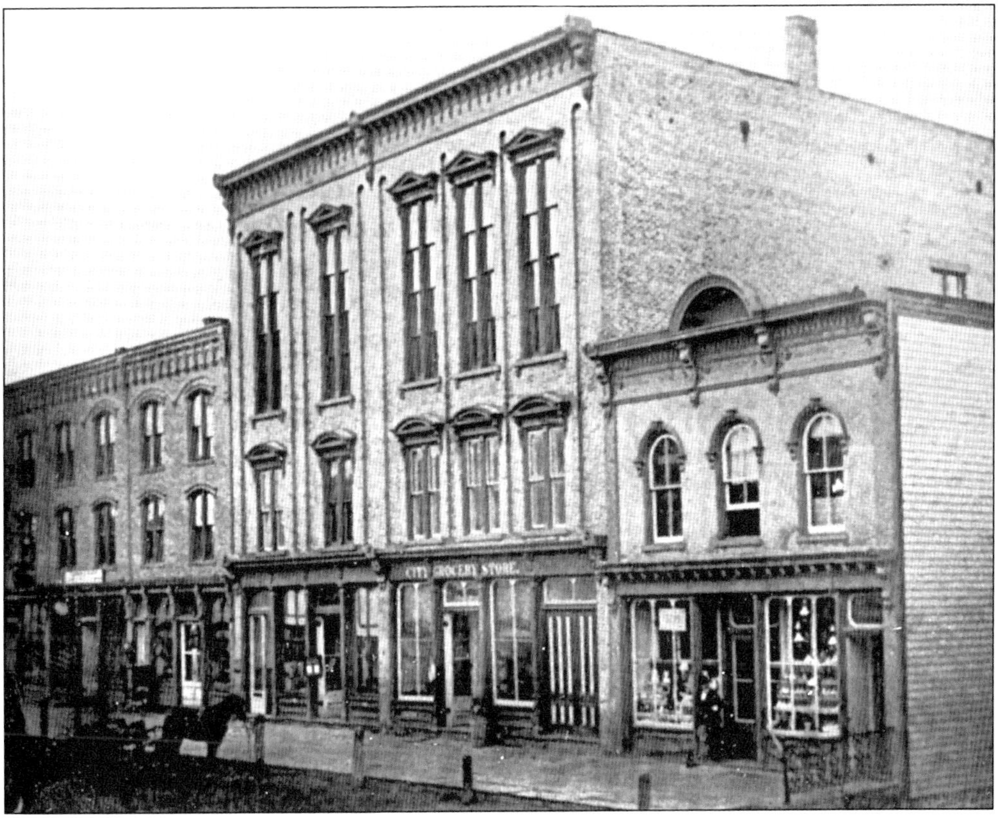

Samuel Clemens, better known as Mark Twain, performed at Ackley Hall on Thursday, January 13, 1870, at the age of 34. The next day, the *Washington County Post* published an unflattering report of the performer. Local folklore tells that Twain responded with an unflattering, albeit witty, report of the audience. (Courtesy CVA.)

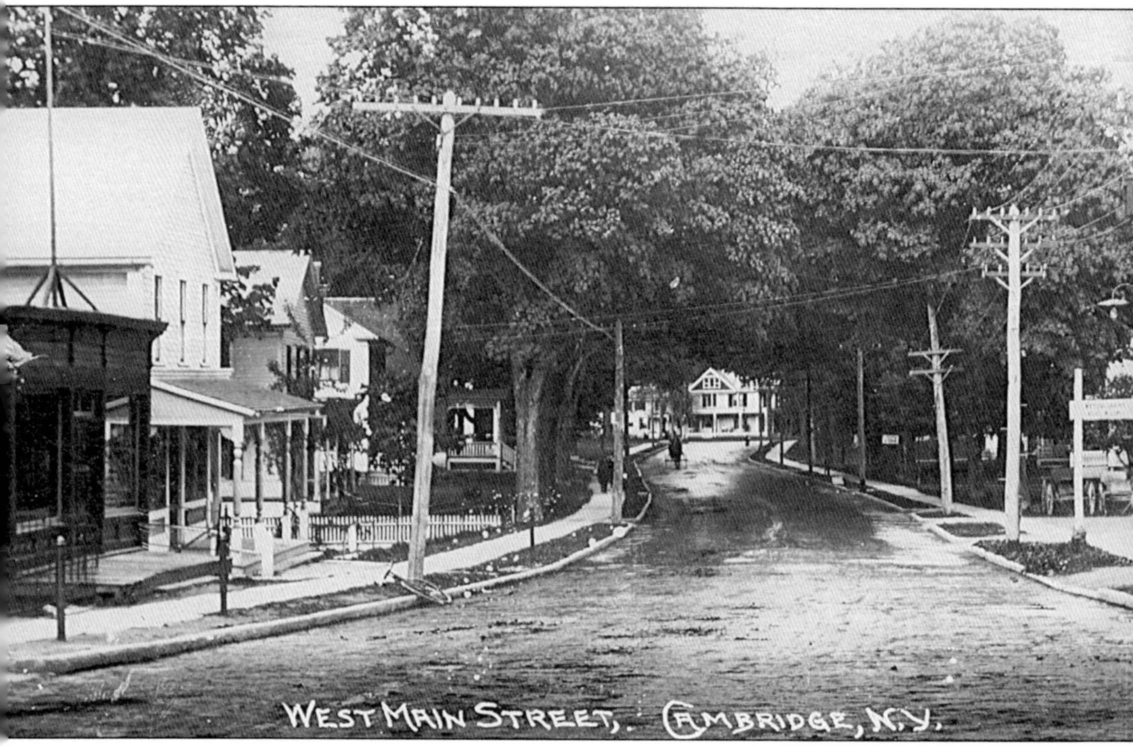

The first speed limit approved by the village board was 15 miles per hour in 1914. In 1923, it was raised to 20 miles per hour, then 25 miles per hour in 1939, and finally to 30 miles per hour in 1964. In 1915, a village ordinance required that all vehicles keep to the right of the center of the road and park only on the right side. Prior to the paving of Main Street with yellow bricks in 1913, many cars drove in the middle of the road to avoid the mud. Cars parked wherever there was a dry spot, regardless of which side of the street it was on. In 1927, the village board voted to remove all stepping-stones (mounting blocks) near the curb since by now the automobile had replaced horse-drawn vehicles. In 1902, the Bennington and Hoosick Valley Railroad Company obtained the franchise to construct a trolley line on Main Street. No work was ever done.

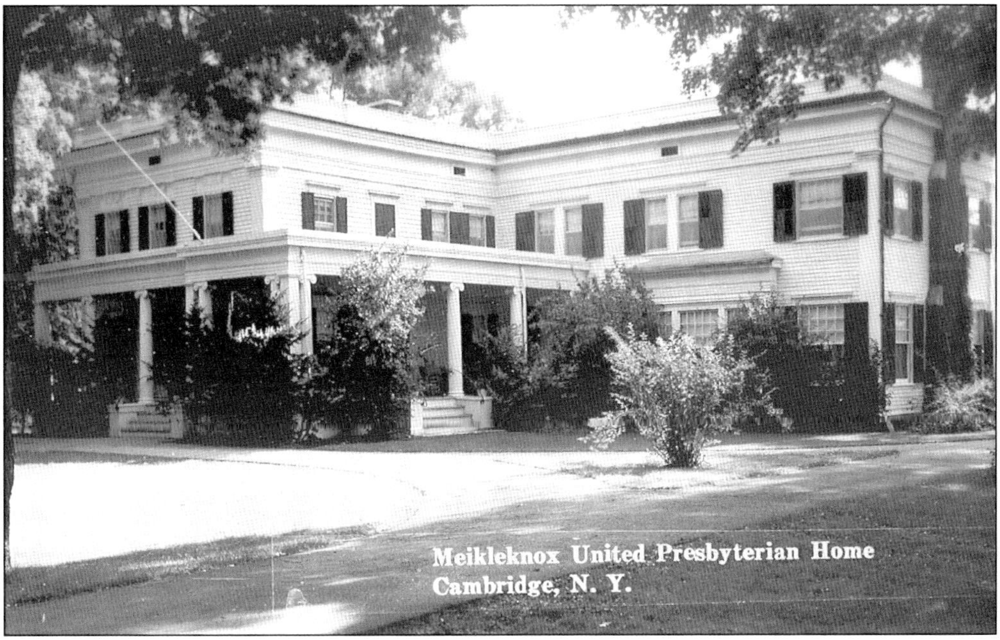

Edwin McClellan (1861–1924), a great humanitarian and philanthropist, started his education in District School No. 9 on Lake Lauderdale, later graduating from Yale College in 1884. In 1898, he joined the Foster-Milburn Company of Buffalo, amassing a fortune in Doan's pills. McClellan's widow, Helen Livingston McClellan, bequeathed their house, Meikleknox, to the Washington County Historical Society, which sold it to the United Presbyterians as a retirement home.

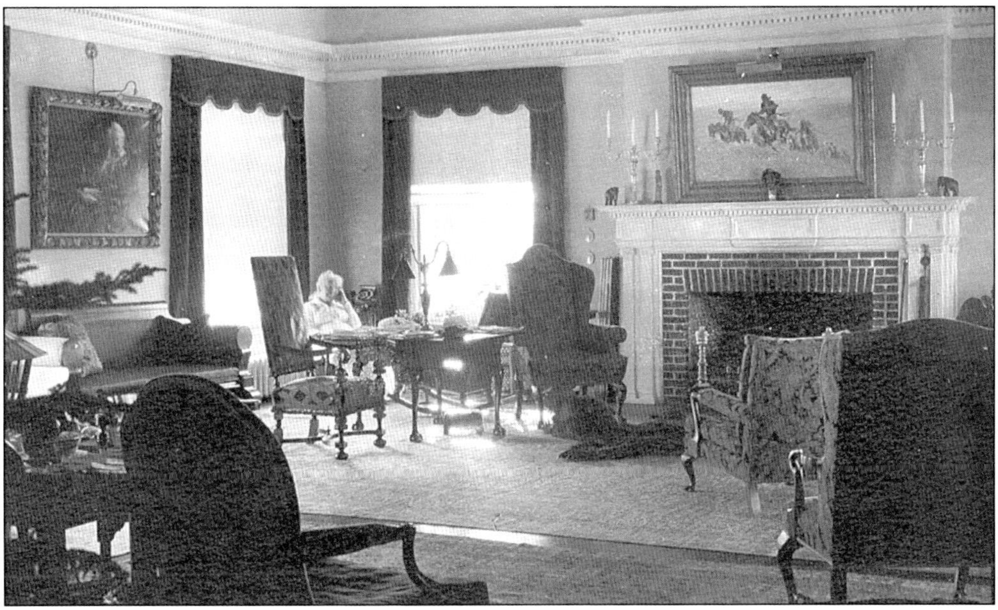

Mary McClellan sits in the corner of Meikleknox, the estate of her son, Edwin. A donation to Yale University in memory of her husband by Edwin's widow, Helen Livingston McClellan, created the Edwin McClellan dormitory. The two McClellan boys predeceased their mother—Edwin in January 1924 and Robert in December 1924.

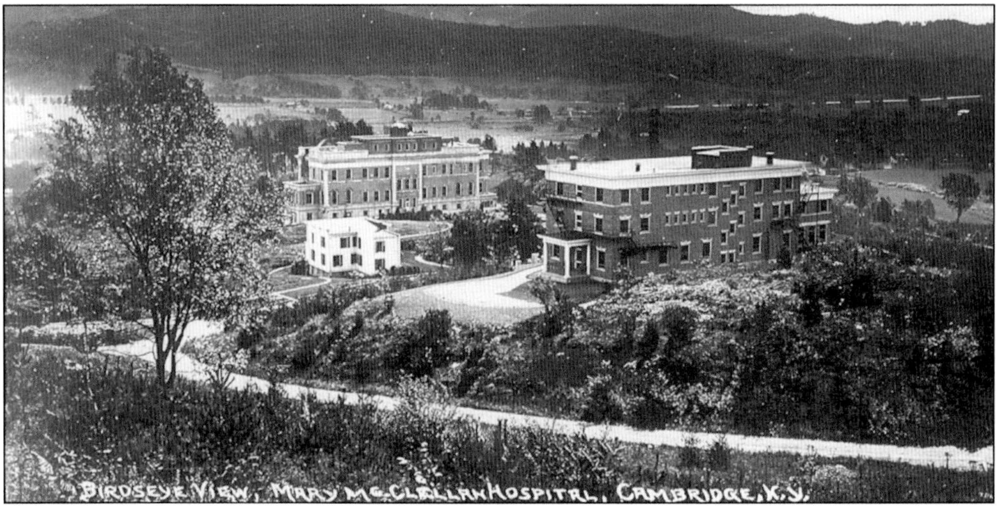

The Florence Nightingale School of Nursing (right) was erected by Robert McClellan and his wife, Irene Ward McClellan. The nurses' home and training school was affiliated with Skidmore College at Saratoga Springs and the Yale School of Nursing at New Haven, Connecticut.

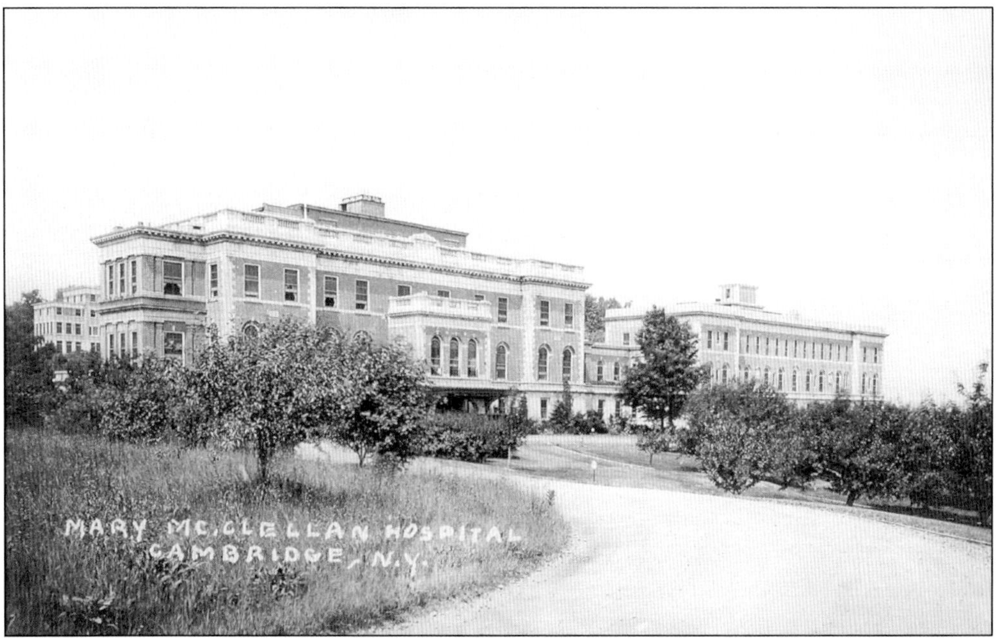

The first and only patient on opening day, January 5, 1919, was Mrs. J. Smith. She was admitted to room A. The first baby was Ella Mary Shannon, born on February 26, 1919. Beds in the public ward cost $3 per day, while a private room cost $7. Visiting hours were from 3:00 p.m. to 4:00 p.m. and from 7:00 p.m. to 8:00 p.m. Patients were fed vegetables from a nearby garden.

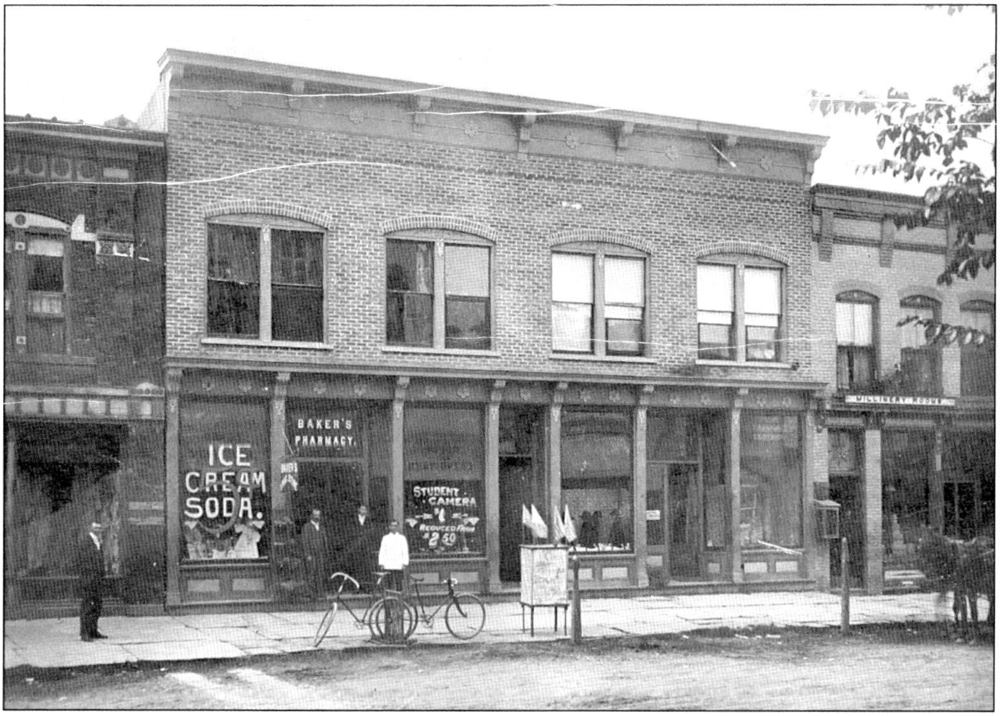

In 1866, a fire starting in the Jennings Brothers Meat Market on the north side by West Main Street near the Cambridge Creek spread across the street. The bucket brigade shifted to the creek on South Union Street. Capt. Henry Gray rushed into Newman's basement saloon (just right of this photograph) with two kegs of black power. The explosion created a fire break and saved the remainder of the block. However, Newman sued Gray for destroying his saloon.

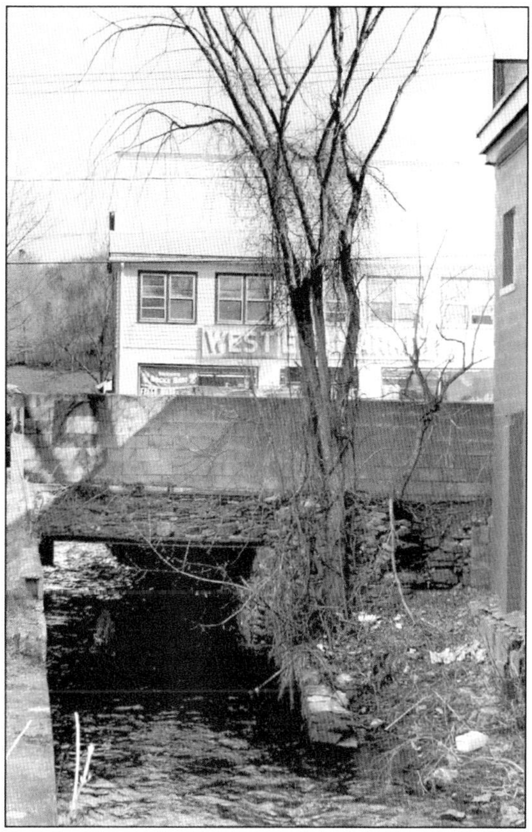

This street-level view looking northward across West Main Street shows the Cambridge Creek as it flows toward the Cambridge swamp. In 1910, the Modern Woodmen of America met in the third-story hall above the West End Market. (Courtesy CVA.)

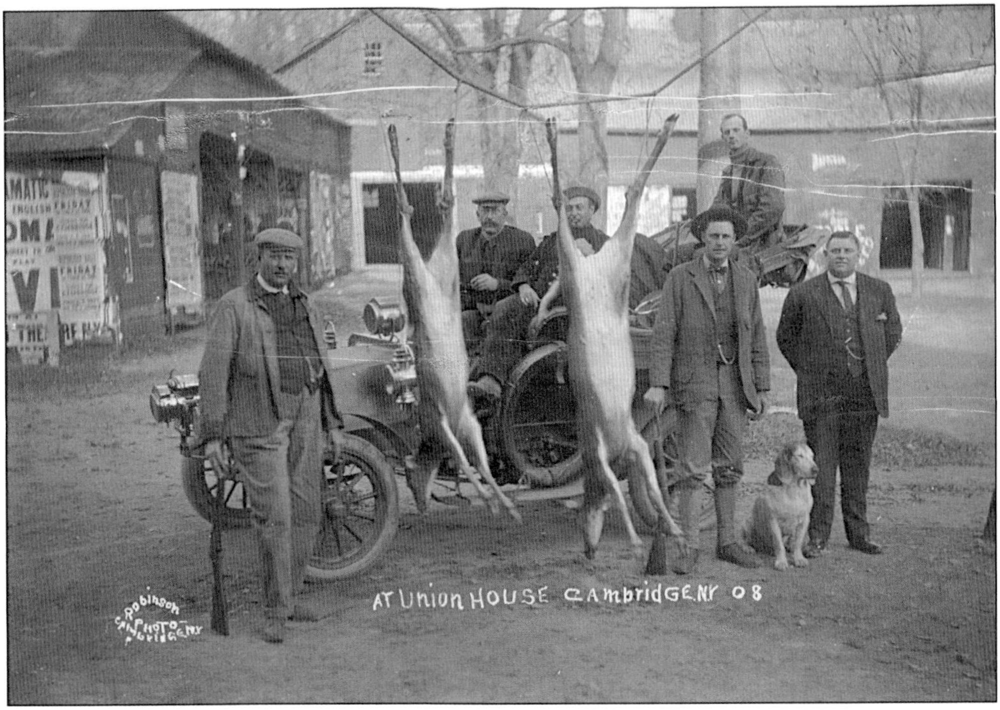

The deer hanging out back (above) and over the bar (below) give an indication that the bar at the Union House was probably not the place for dainty young ladies in the early 1900s.

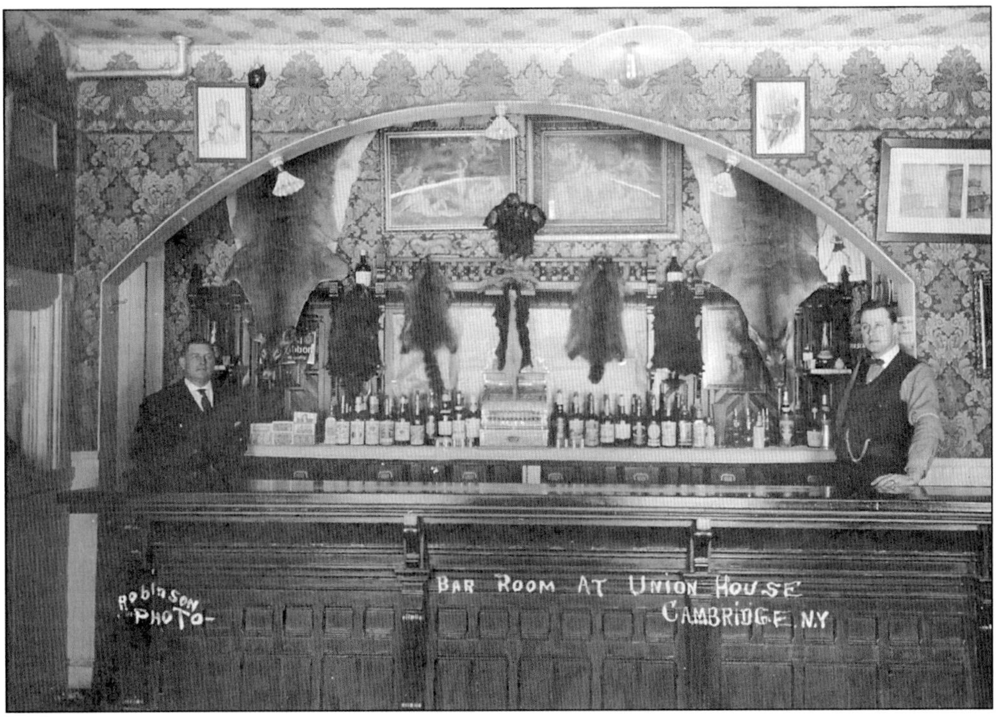

Three

MIDDLE

The Cambridge area was long known as The Corners. From the east to the west, there were four communities along Main Street, each situated at a major intersection. Between the two middle corners (Cambridge Corners and North White Creek) was a swampy area along Blair's Brook.

The Cambridge swamp significantly impacted the development of the village. During and after heavy rains, Main Street was very muddy. The middle of the community was so impassable that the East and West Ends may as well have been 50 miles apart rather than only half a mile.

In the 1850s, B. P. Crocker was one of the first to support the development of the middle of the village. Another early proponent was James Smart. Crocker built the brick structure next to the railroad tracks, and Smart constructed the *Washington County Post* office.

However, it was not until Jerome B. Rice that the issue of the dividing swamp was addressed. Rice had over 3,000 loads of fill dumped in the middle of the village, raising the ground level sufficiently to build his Rice Seed campus. The 4-foot drop from the Rice footbridge to the underlying Owl Kill illustrates how much Rice changed the middle of the village.

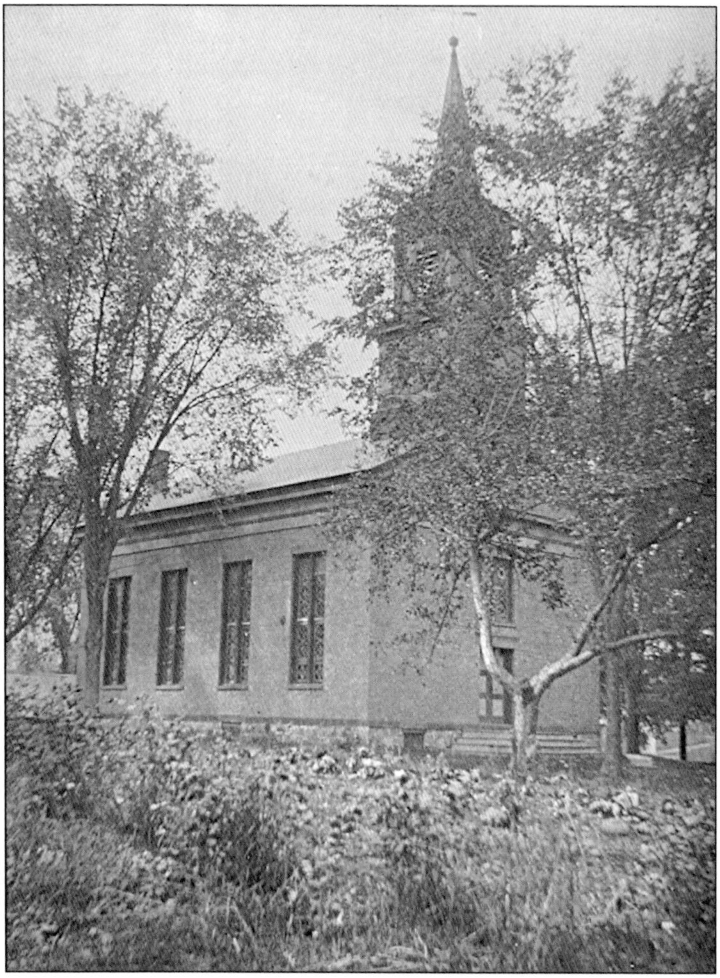

The Protestant Presbyterian congregation was organized in 1769. A house of worship was started in 1775 at the southern edge of Cambridge Corners but not completed until after the war. In 1785, the congregation split, and the new group worshipped at the yellow meetinghouse in Coila, later forming the Associate Presbyterian congregation. In 1792, a second group split from the original congregation, building the white meetinghouse in North White Creek on the northeast corner of Main and Park Streets. In 1844, the original congregation, now known as the United Presbyterians, sold their dilapidated old church for $80 and built this brick church on West Main Street for $1,400.

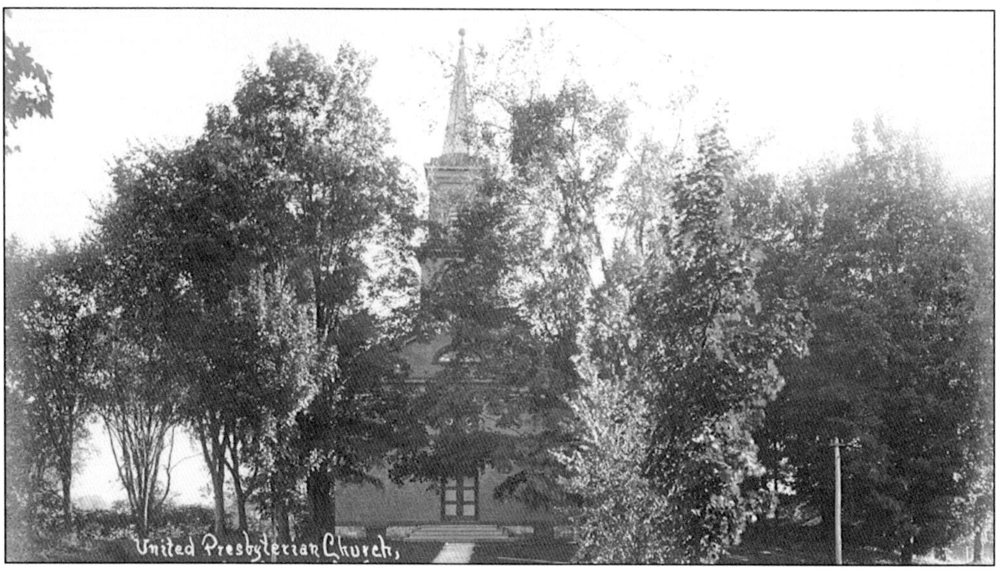

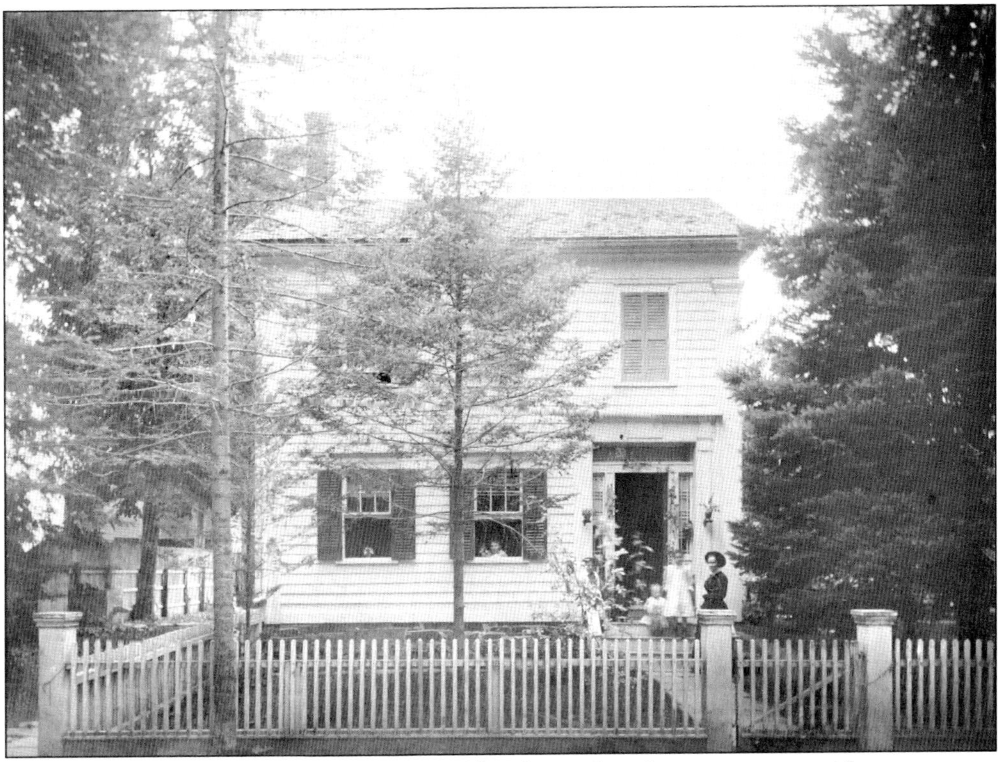

The parsonage for the United Presbyterian Church stands today as a private residence.

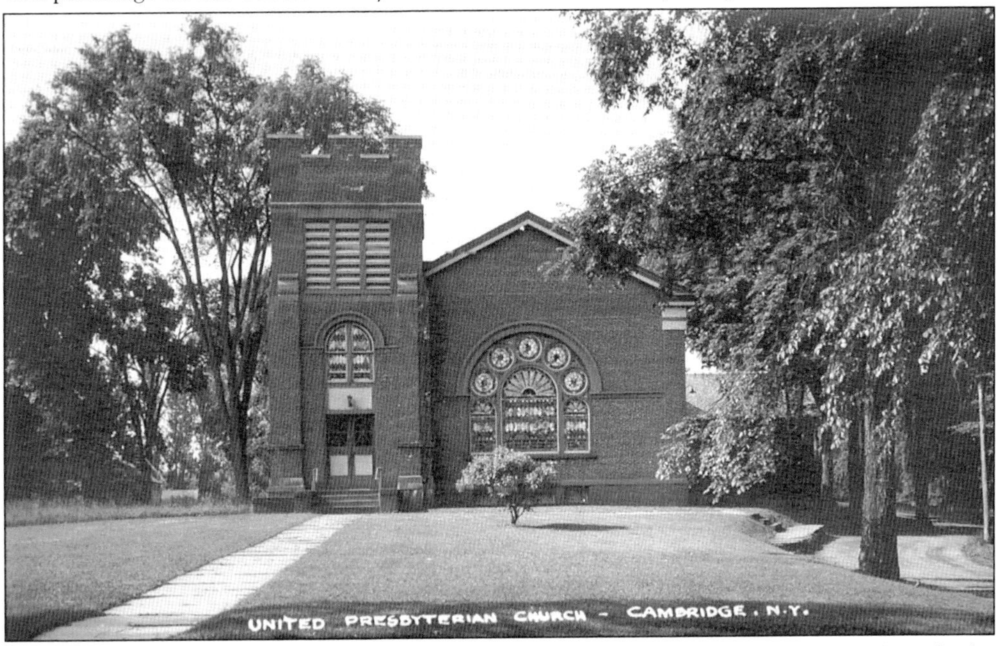

In 1909, the original brick United Presbyterian Church was remodeled and greatly enlarged. The 1844 steeple was removed and replaced with a brick tower and a new stained-glass window. A meeting room and a foyer were added along with a bell chamber. Also included in the change were a kitchen and dining room, new pews, and carpeting.

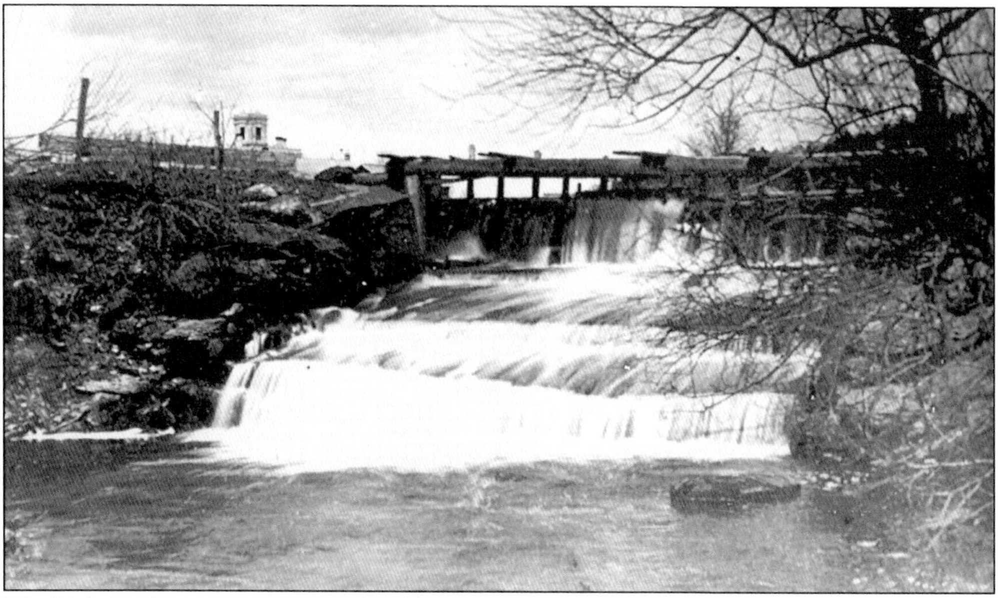

The Blakeley dam was located south of the old school, where Cambridge Creek and Blair's Brook (Owl Kill) unite. Carcasses and animal parts were dumped in the creek at the Coila tannery pond near Center Cambridge Road. They flowed down the creek, becoming lodged at the dam, creating a foul odor throughout the village. In 1864, the newspaper declared the streets a public barnyard. (Courtesy CVA.)

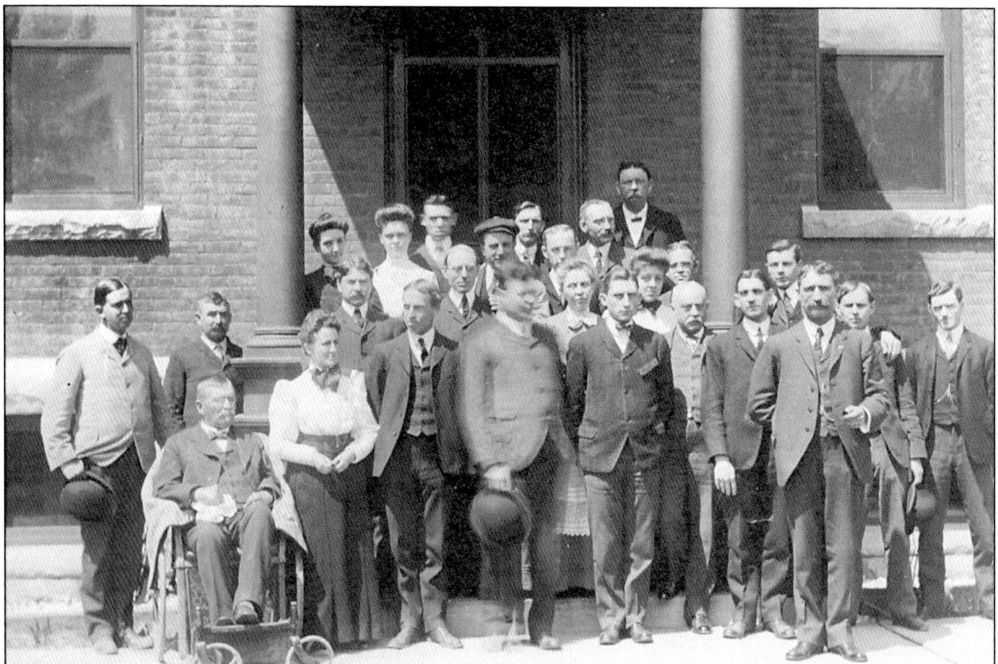

The employees of the Rice Seed Company stand in front of the administration building constructed in 1895. Jerome B. Rice is on the left in the wheelchair. Note that there are five women among the 21 men. In 1917, the "seed house girls" shipped smokes and sweets to soldiers serving in World War I.

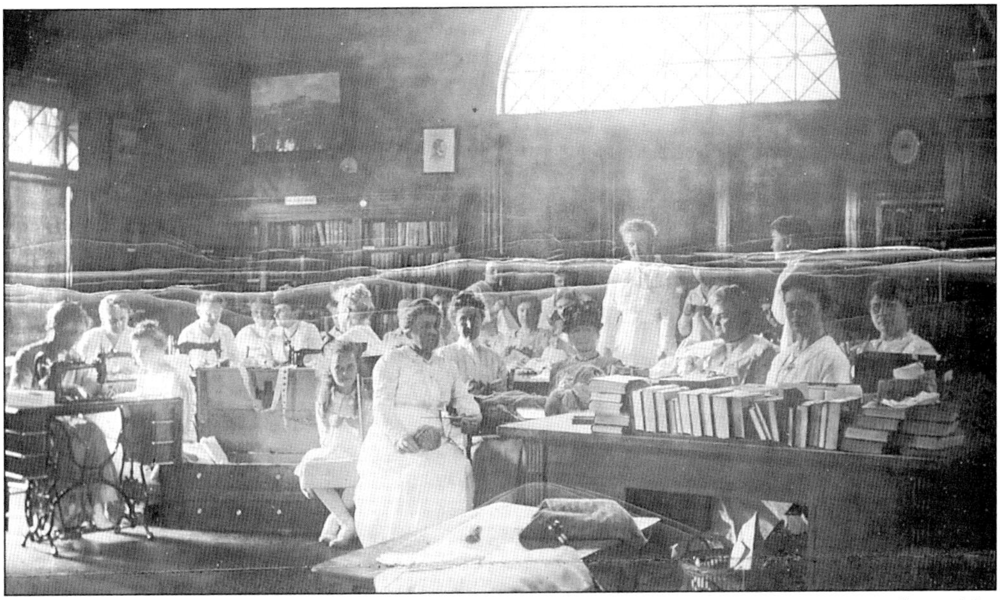

In May 1917, the American Red Cross established their West End sewing center at the public library. The sewing hours were Monday, Wednesday, and Thursday from 1:00 p.m. to 5:00 p.m. Mrs. Tingue was in charge of knitting, while Mrs. Hedges was in charge of inspecting and packing. (Courtesy CPL.)

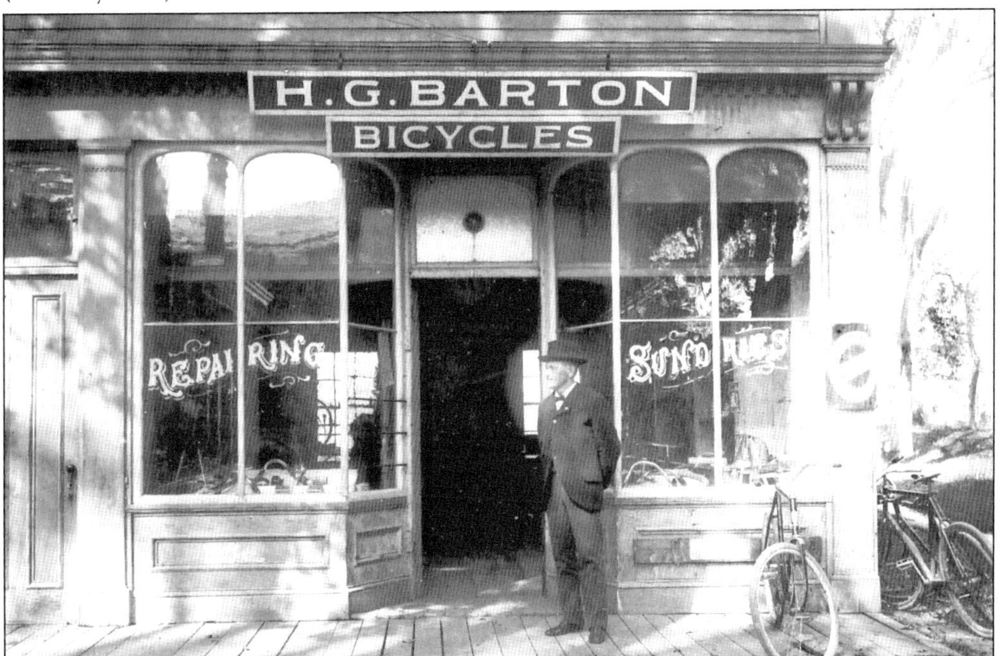

The Barton bicycle repair shop was between the Barton furniture building and the Cambridge Bakery across from the present-day bank. A wooden sidewalk was necessary with the unpaved Main Street. A bicycle rider had a difficult climb up the hill to the West End (left). As the middle of the village was filled in over the years, the slope became less, but bicyclists today still are aware of the incline.

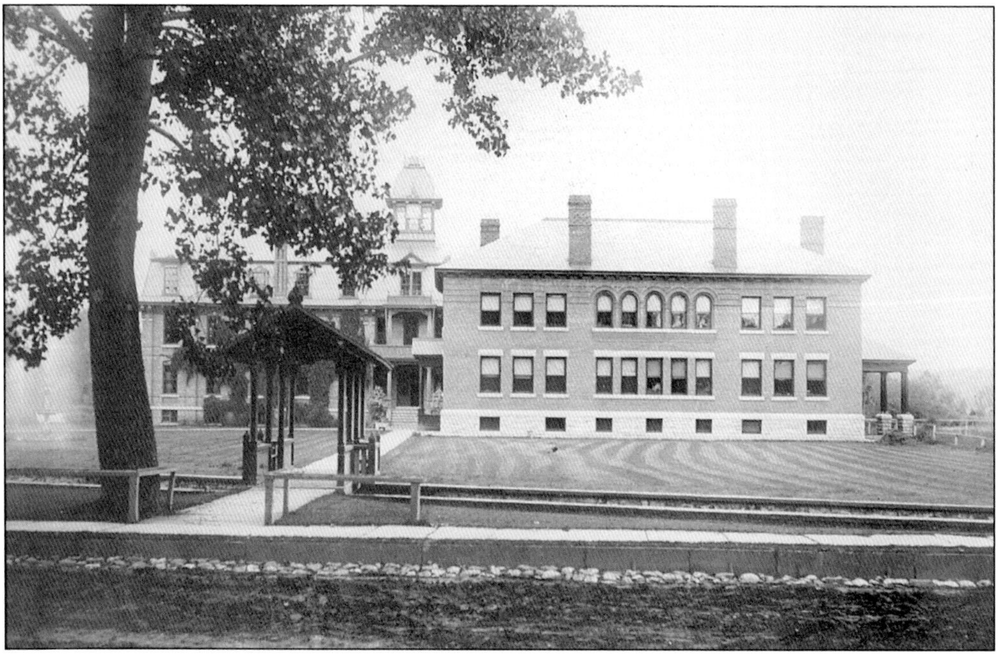

The footbridge over Blair's Brook (now Owl Kill) in front of the Rice Seed Company was designed by Florans Hoxie. In 1883, the Rice Seed Company paid for the stone and had the Owl Kill lined and topped with pavers. The level of the brook, about 4 feet below grade, indicates the amount of dirt required to fill in the Cambridge swamp.

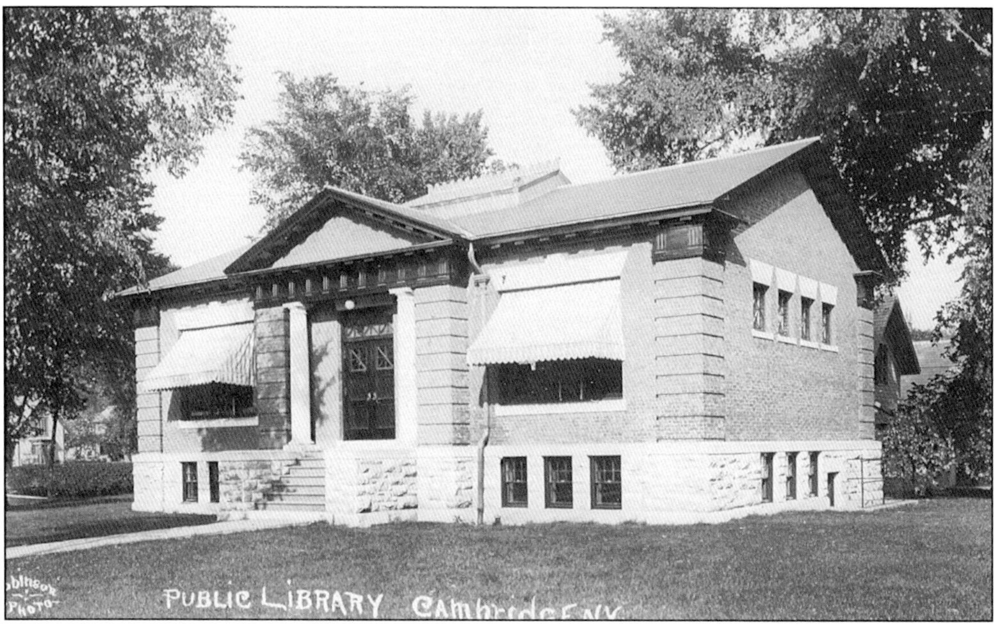

In 1799, a small, private school was built on William Hay's property on Academy Street. In 1801, the Philo Club was formed to provide a collection of reference books for what would become the Cambridge Washington Academy. In 1891, the Cambridge Union School was built, and 13 years later, this library was constructed on its front lawn, thanks to a generous donation from Sallie Law Williams.

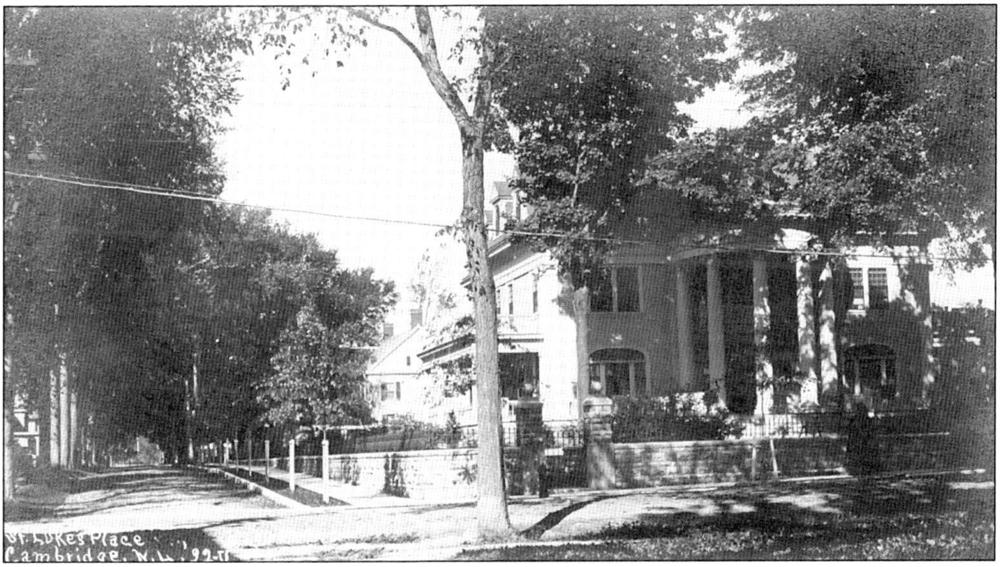

In the late 1880s, St. Lukes Street was called Pearl Street. By 1904, J. B. Rice had filled in the Cambridge swamp and created the current Pearl Street, which ran south (bottom) from this intersection. This gave rise to North Pearl and South Pearl Streets. A 1925 map refers to the street shown here as St. Lukes with North Pearl in parentheses, indicating the name change may have been recent.

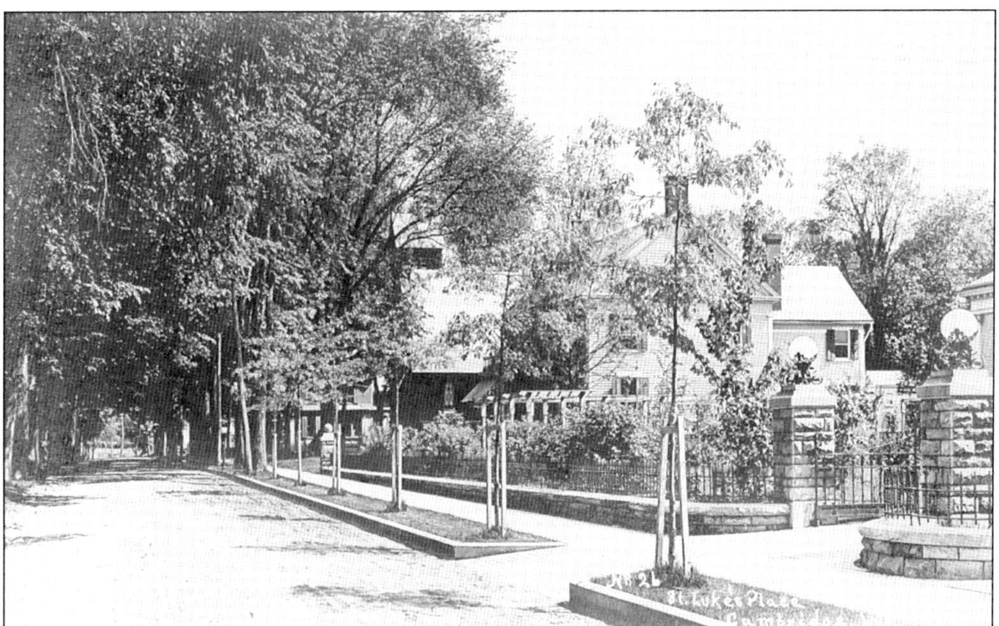

Evensong, sung by the city choir, was widely attended at the St. Luke's Episcopal Church on Sundays at 5:00 p.m. Afterward, many in the crowd had to hustle one block east (right) to catch the 6:18 p.m. train. If the church service ran long, the train waited.

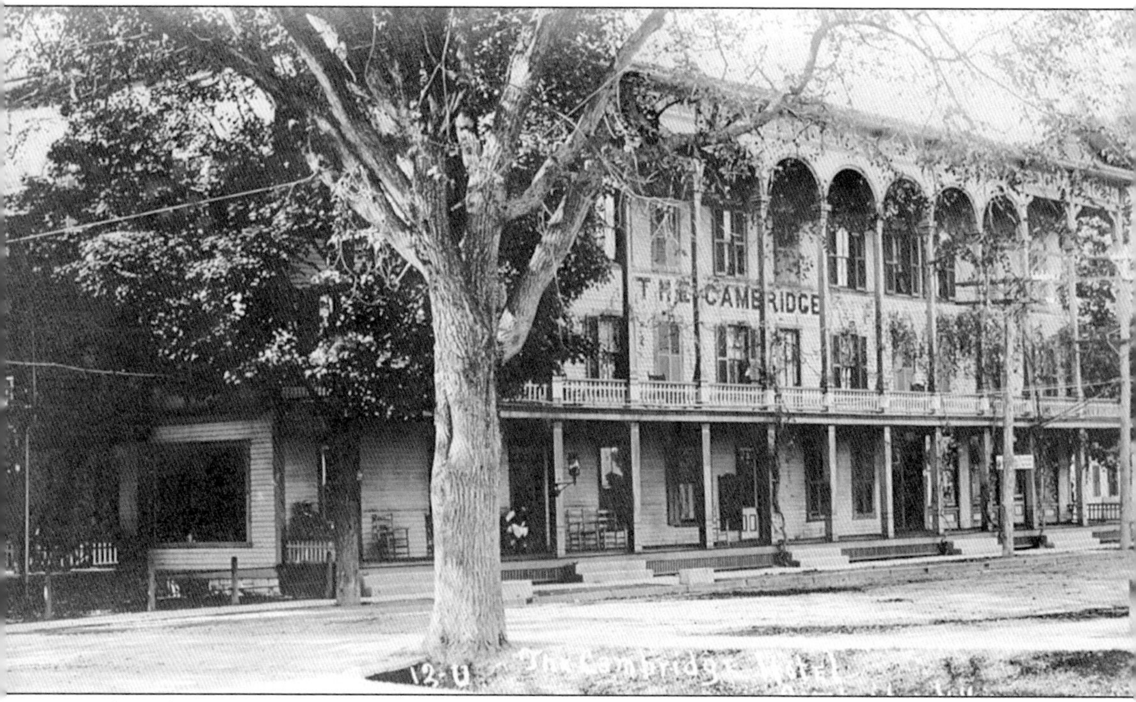

When the railroad was built in 1852, little development had yet occurred in the middle of the village. In fact, when Woodlands Cemetery was dedicated on June 2, 1858, its treasurer, B. P. Crocker, could see the cemetery hill from the window of his brick building just west of the new railroad tracks. In 1885, Crocker sold land across the street, at the northwest corner of Main and Broad Streets, with the stipulation the new owners must erect a hotel. About the same time, the West End started building a new Union Hotel, triggering the "Great Hotel Race of 1885." The Cambridge Hotel, having the advantage of being situated close to the supplies delivered by railroad, opened a few weeks before its West End rival with 40 elegant guest rooms. The economy in Cambridge must have been booming in 1885 since, in addition to the two hotels, the water works company started that year.

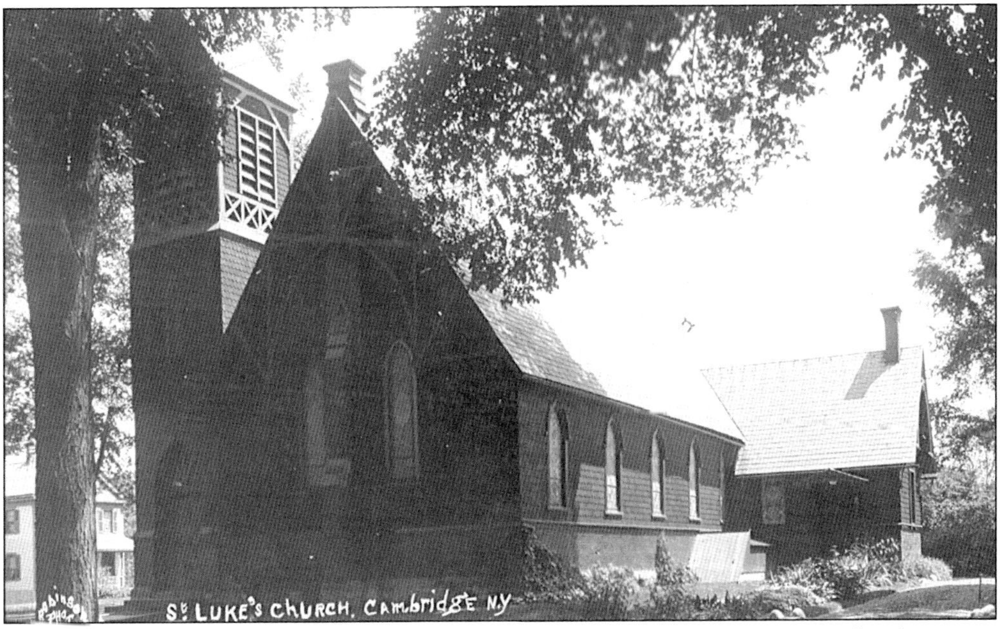

The Episcopal church was organized in August 1866 at Woodworth's Union Hall. The vestry, elected on September 23, 1866, included Edward Hawley, Perry Wager, Ransom Hawley, and Charles Hawley. The cornerstone was laid on July 9, 1867, with the first service on November 24, 1867. The church was consecrated on September 15, 1870, only after all debts had been paid.

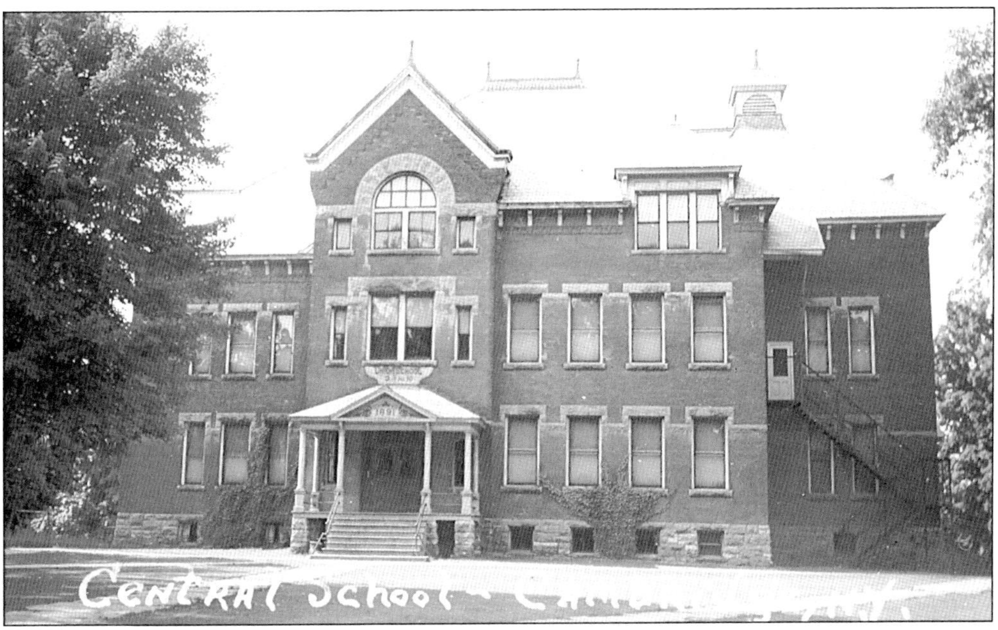

For almost 100 years, the East and West Ends maintained separate schools. In the late 1800s, Jerome B. Rice filled in the Cambridge swamp separating the districts and in 1888 convinced the village to unite to build one school. The Cambridge Union School District No. 10, named for the school on the East End, opened in 1891.

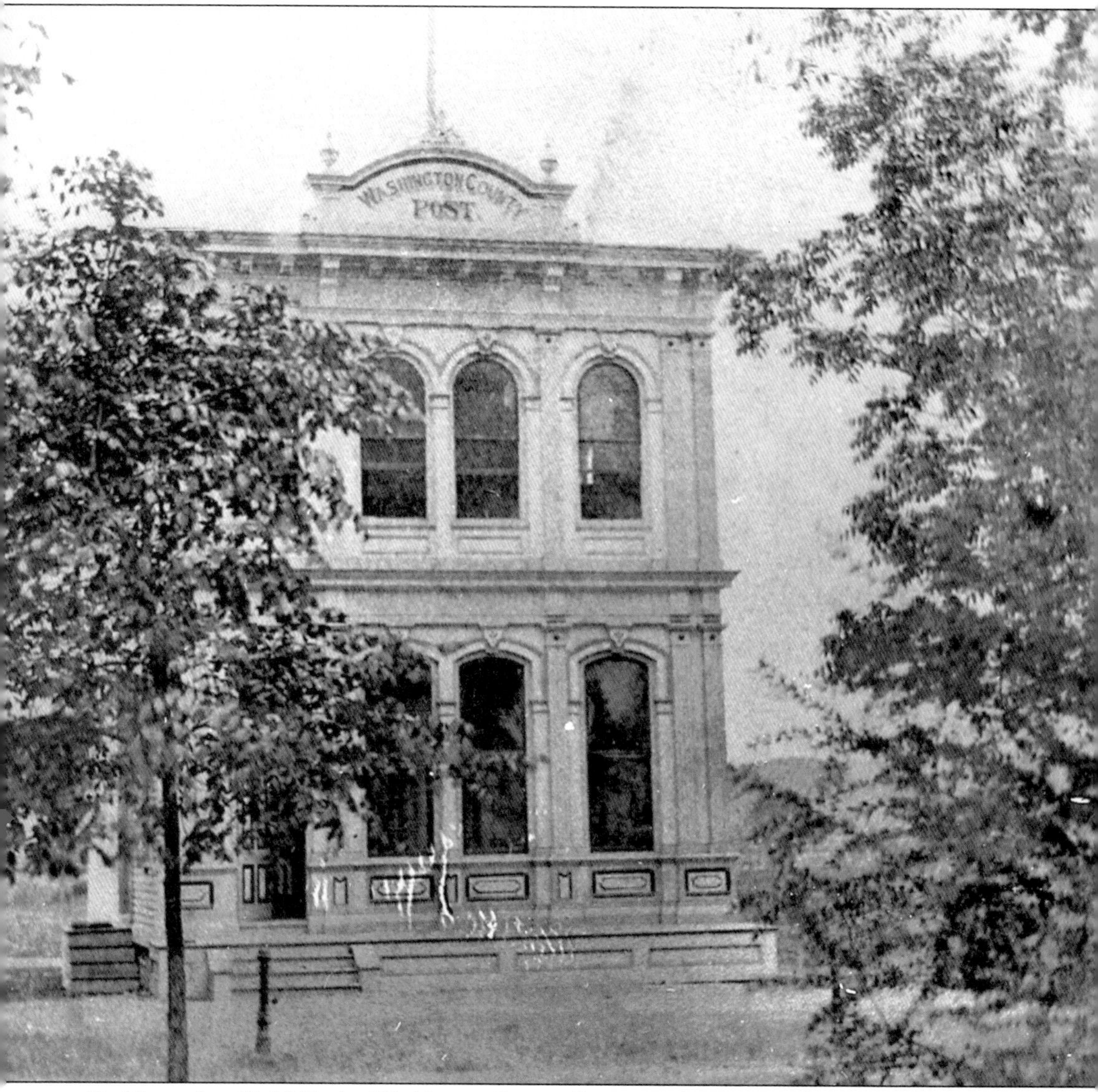

On November 17, 1865, the *Washington County Post* moved to its new home on the southwest corner of Main and Pearl Streets. This building, still in existence today, was erected on the Blair lot by then publishers James Smart and Henry Noble. The newspaper started in Salem on January 1, 1798, first as the *Northern Centennial*, then the *Northern Post*, and finally as the *Washington County Post*. When the paper's owner ran into financial difficulties in 1848, Robert Young purchased it and moved it to the Aaron Crosby store in North White Creek. Young issued the first number on March 15, 1849, with North White Creek, not Cambridge, listed on the masthead. In 1852, when R. K. Crocker was the editor, the paper moved to the second story of B. P. Crocker's new brick building just west of the railroad tracks. The *Washington County Post* name is still visible today in the faded bricks on that building.

This Civil War recruiting poster encouraged all patriotic young men to enlist at the recruiting tent opposite the Cambridge Valley House. This hotel may have been the brick hotel. However, it may have been located near the corner of Broad and First Streets, later known as the Central House. Though most people born in the Cambridge Valley never ventured far from home, approximately 350 men served in the war. (Courtesy CVA.)

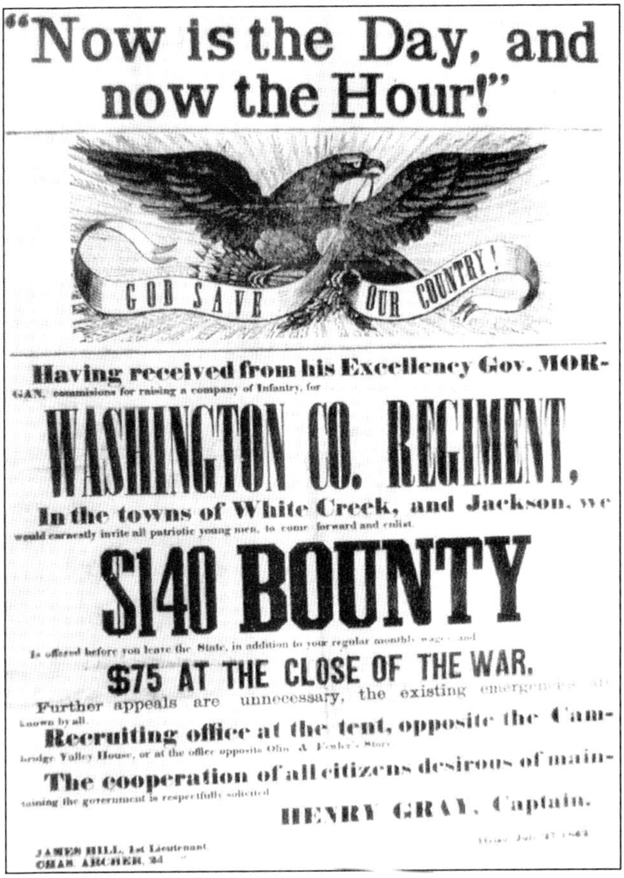

The Laverty house at 25 West Main Street was torn down in 1961 to make room for the new home of the Cambridge Valley National Bank, now the Glens Falls National Bank. Cambridge lost several of its landmarks in the early 1960s as progress tried to modernize the village. Since then, the emphasis has shifted to preservation and restoration.

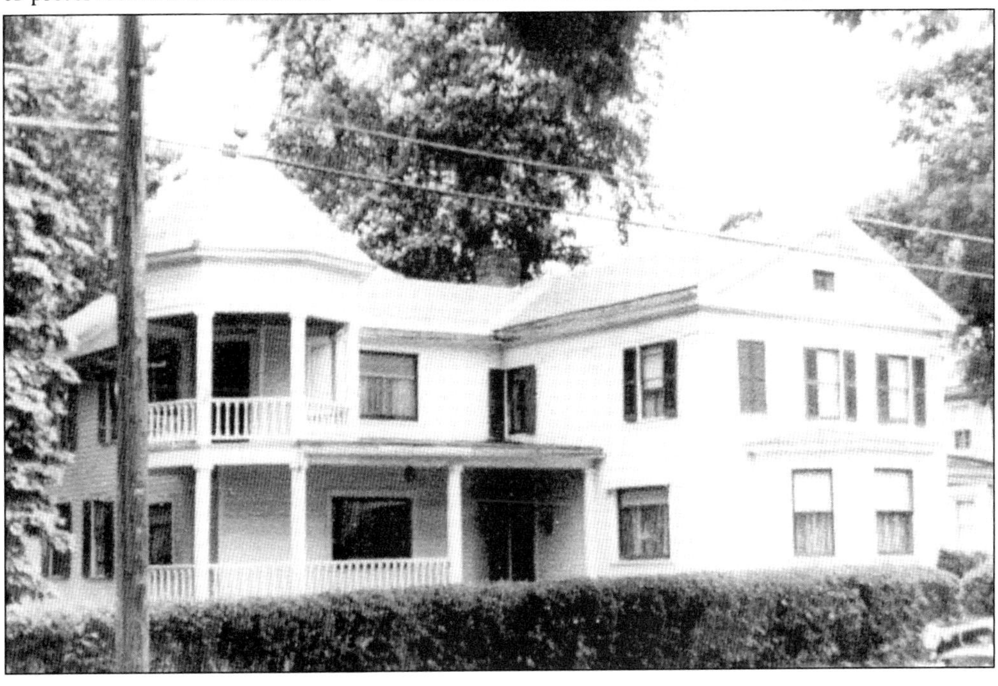

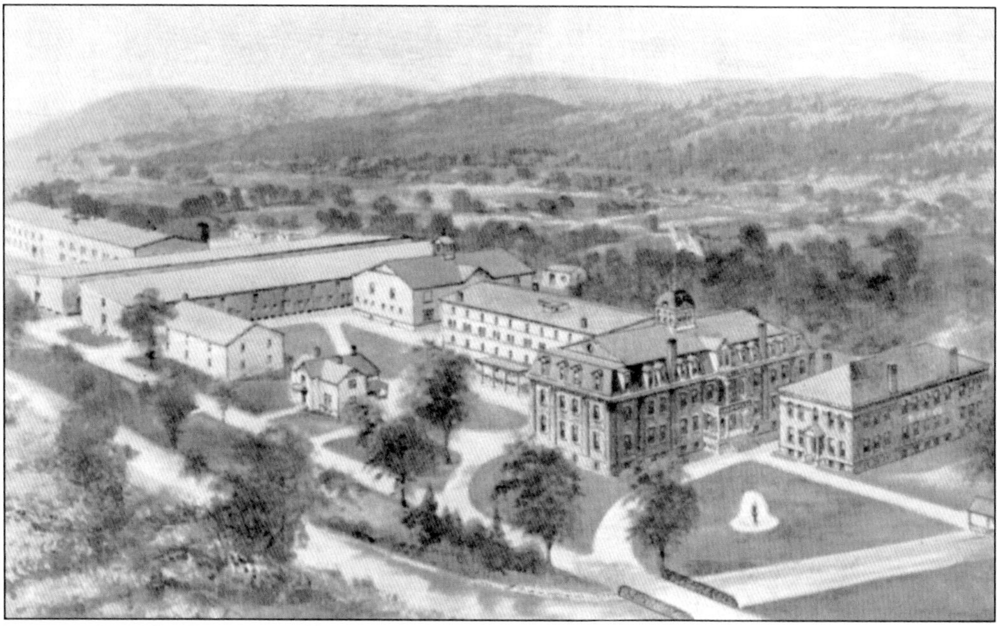

In 1844, R. Niles Rice moved his seed operation to the building known today as the West End Market, along the Cambridge Creek. Around 1880, his son, Jerome B. Rice, helped unite the East and West Districts by filling in the intervening swamp. Over 3,000 loads of fill served as foundation for the Rice Seed campus. In 1888, Rice sold westward adjoining land for the Cambridge Union School.

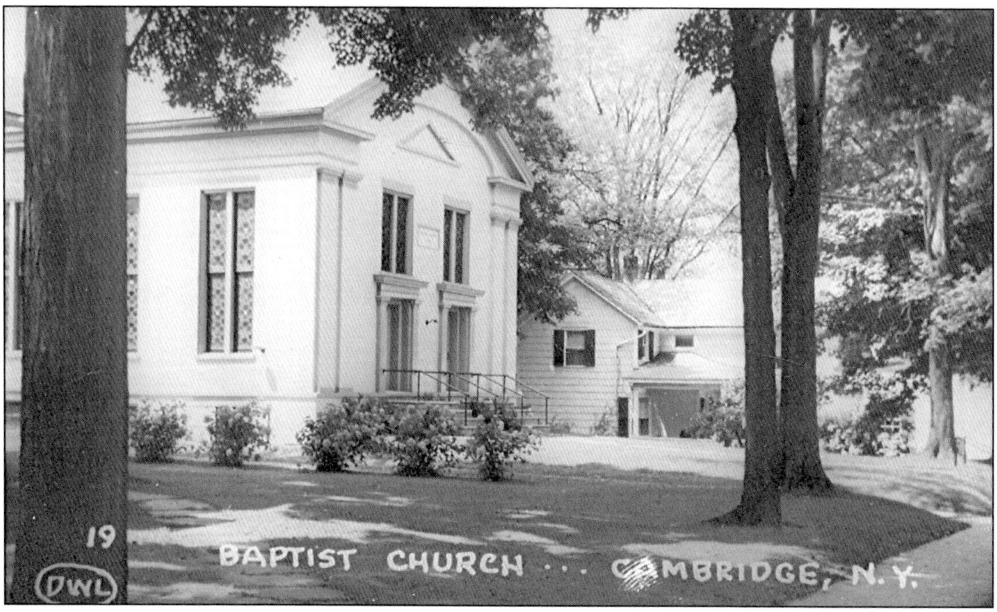

In 1903, the First Baptist Church closed for over two years. Rev. Thomas Cull revived the church in 1905, and membership was at 90 in 1916. The early church suffered from large turnover, having 19 pastors during its first 72 years. By comparison, in the 90 years from 1807 to 1897, the Coila Presbyterian Church had only two pastors: Rev. Alex Bullions (1807–1857) and Rev. Henry Gordon (1857–1897).

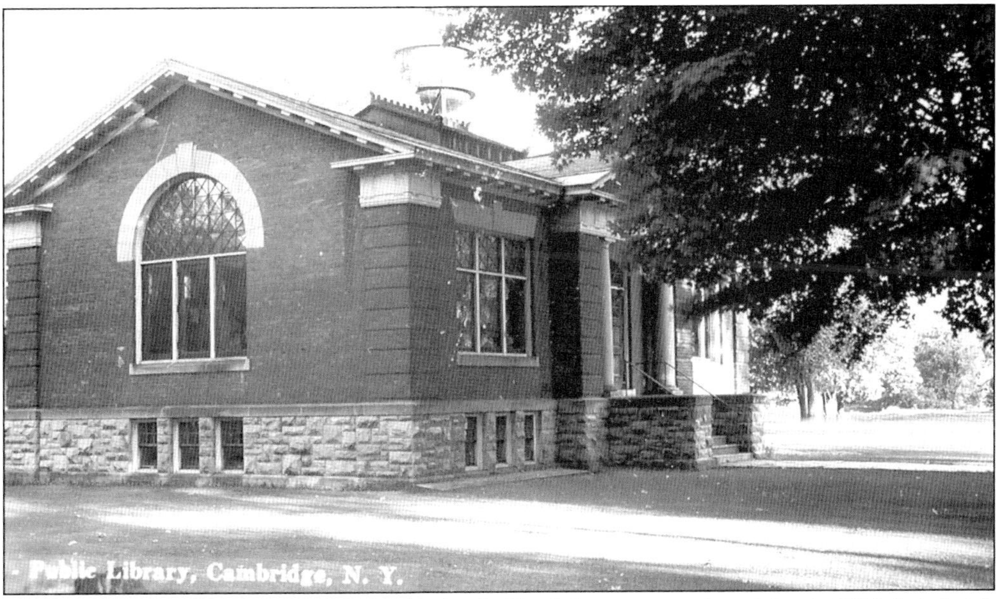

The 30-foot-by-50-foot, one-story Cambridge Public Library opened on May 1, 1904. It is brick with a rough stone foundation and stone columns on either side of the entrance. The steps are blue slate, and the original shelves and woodwork are North Carolina pine. The first librarian was Ethel Law, niece of benefactor Sallie Law Williams. Law was succeeded by May Carpenter, a Cambridge legend for generations.

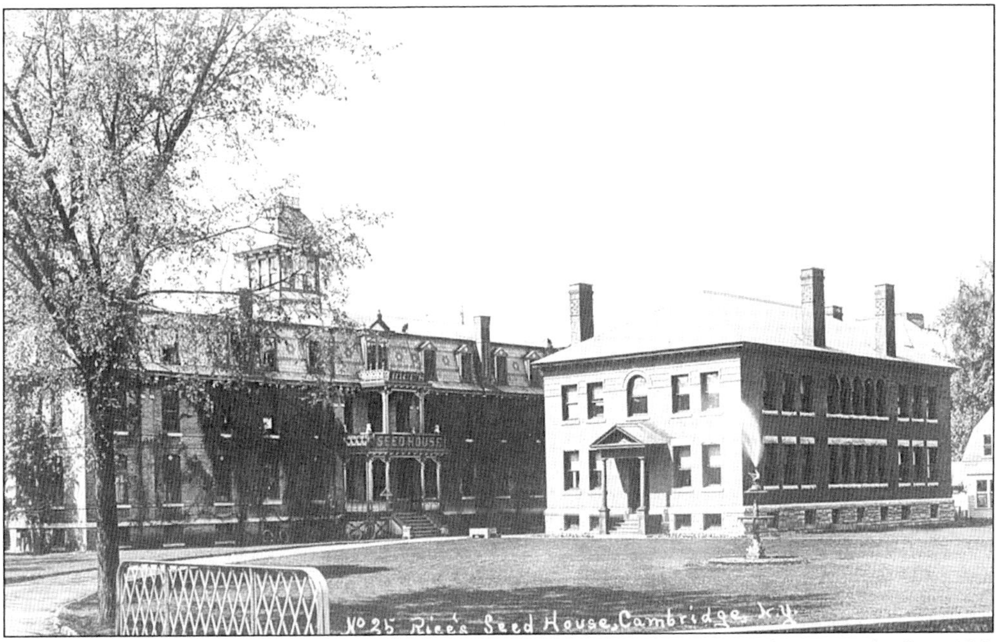

The seed business in the Cambridge Valley was started by Simon Crosby in Coila. By 1836, S. W. Crosby was running the business from the Tracey building and his home at Dorr's Corners. R. Niles Rice united the seed businesses, developing into the second largest in the nation. In 1895, when the brick office building (right) was added, Rice Seed employed over 200 people, including about 30 travelling salesmen.

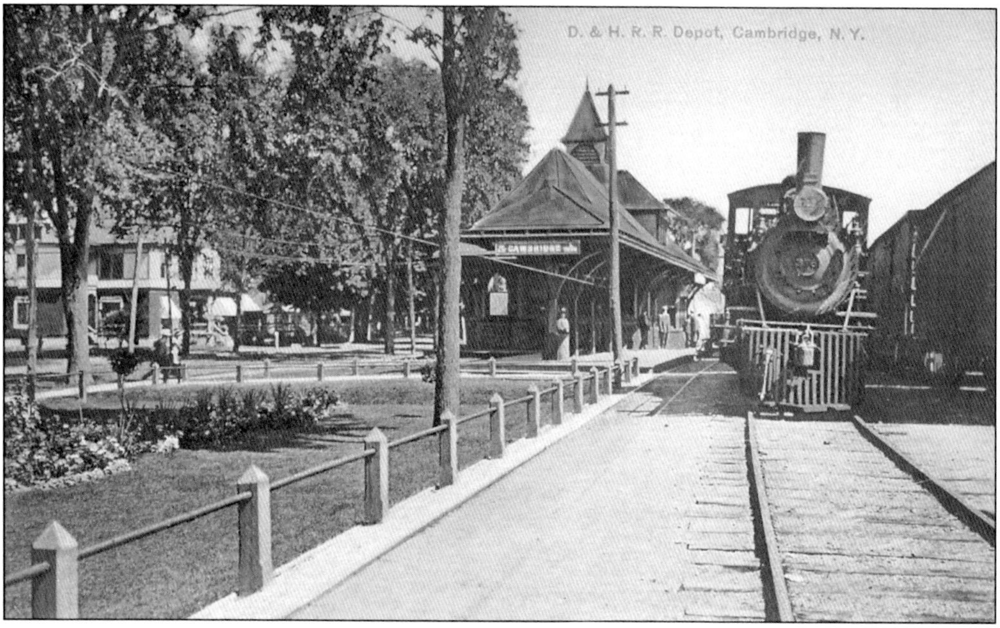

The Troy and Rutland (later Washington and Rutland) Railroad was built halfway between Cambridge Corners and North White Creek in 1852. Later this north-south line connected with an east-west Boston and Maine line in Eagle Bridge. The Rensselaer and Saratoga line acquired the Washington and Rutland in 1865. The Rensselaer and Saratoga line was acquired by the Delaware and Hudson in 1871.

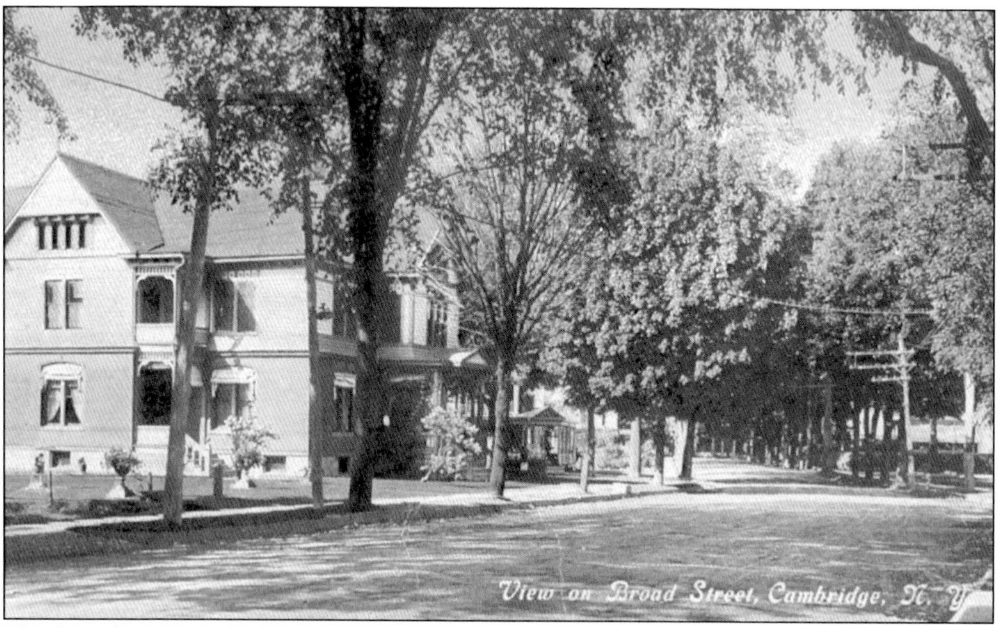

The large house on the left, on the southwest corner of Broad and First Streets, belonged to Ransom Hawley and later his son, Charles. They worked at the train depot across the street, so the house is still referred to as the stationmaster's house. In 1862, Hawley started a telegraph to Salem. By 1863, when other lines were completed, this became the first telegraph connecting Montreal and New York City.

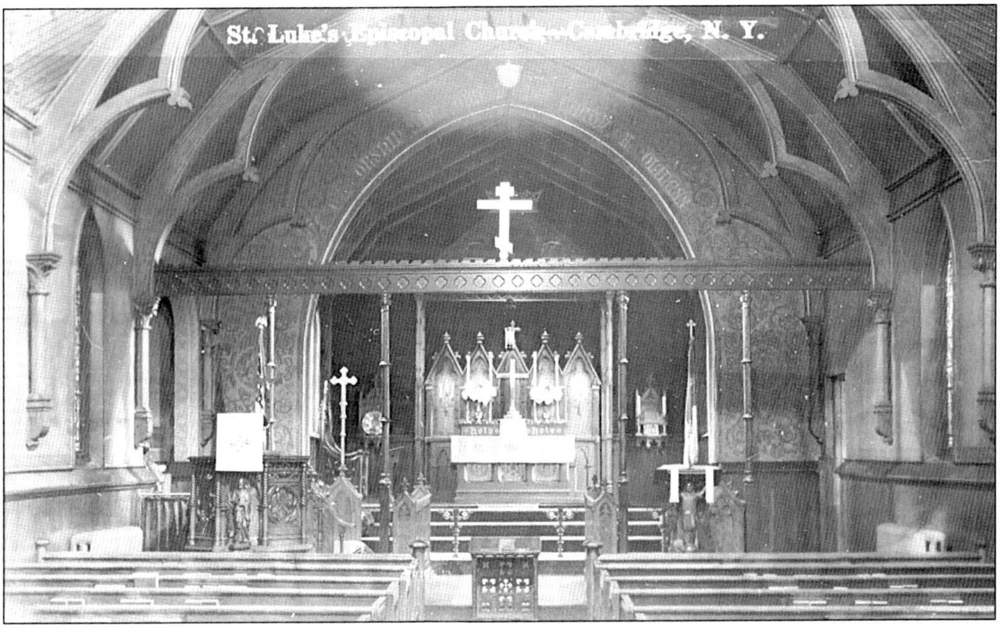

A fire severely damaged the St. Luke's Episcopal Church in the late 1800s. A restoration service was held on June 29, 1892. In June 1906, Tiffany windows were installed in the church through a generous donation from the Law sisters: Mrs. Granville Wright (Anna Frances Law) and Mrs. Laurence Williams (Sallie Law).

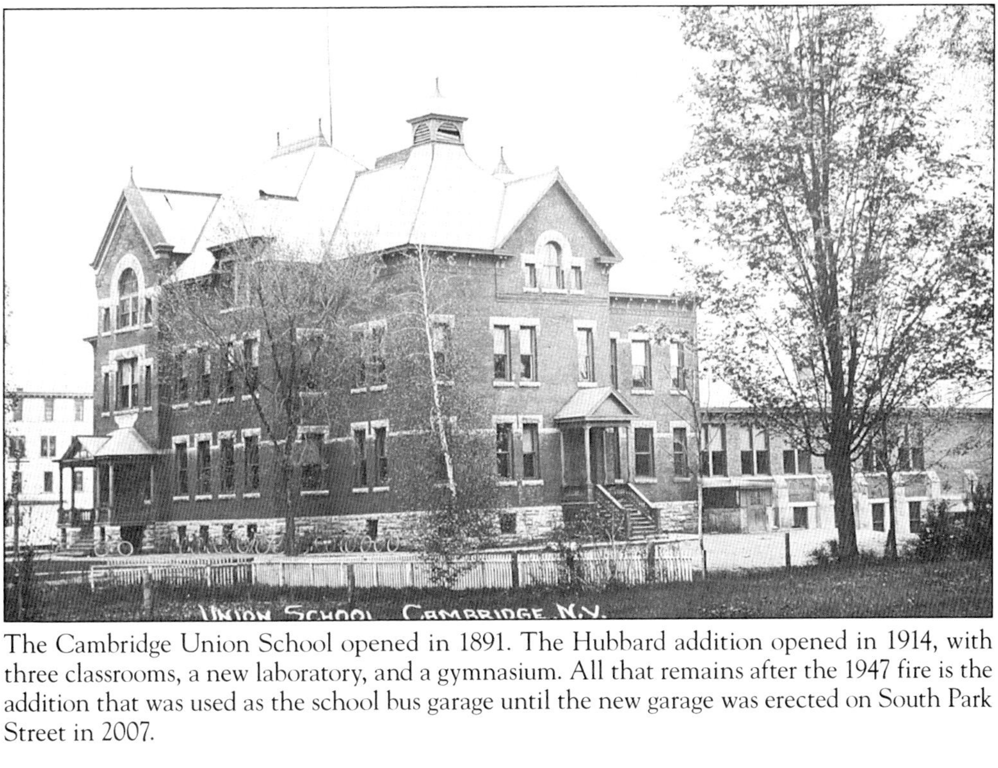

The Cambridge Union School opened in 1891. The Hubbard addition opened in 1914, with three classrooms, a new laboratory, and a gymnasium. All that remains after the 1947 fire is the addition that was used as the school bus garage until the new garage was erected on South Park Street in 2007.

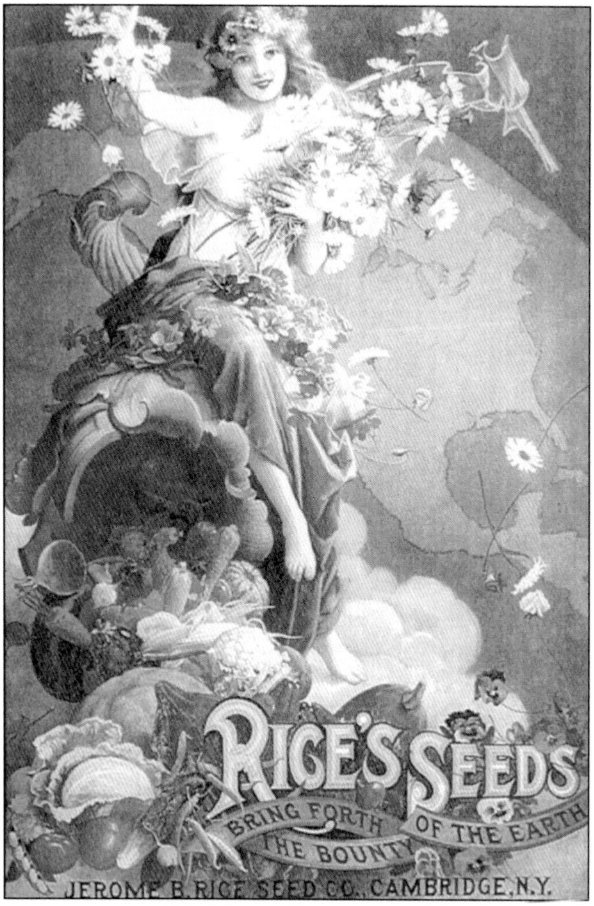

Rice memorabilia is cherished in Cambridge, as evidenced by this 2008 poster created by the local historical society. Some wooden crates used for shipping in the early 1900s ended up as siding when building houses during the Depression. During a recent renovation on Academy Street, original siding was exposed that still showed the Rice Seed logo.

St. Luke's Episcopal Church got its first full-time priest in April 1868. The church had eight different priests before 1880, possibly since there was no place for the priest to live. In 1896, the rectory, visible just beyond the church, was built at a cost of $5,500. This was a sizable amount, considering the church cost $6,700 to build.

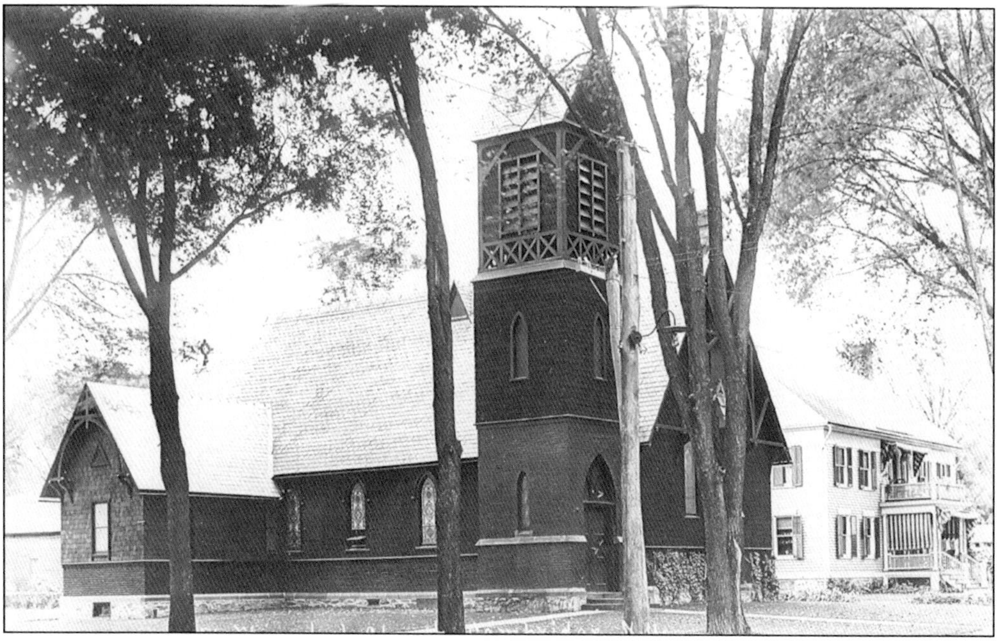

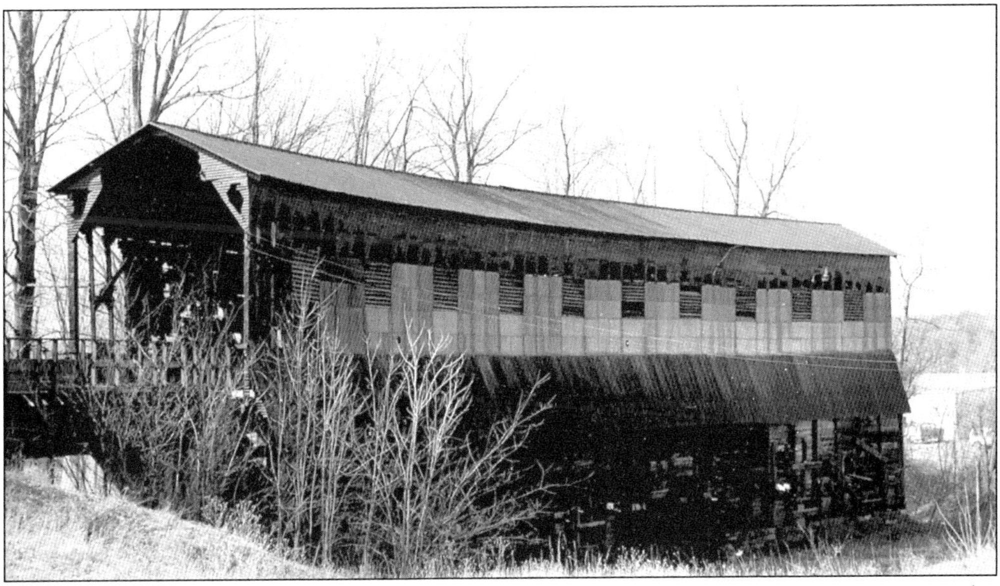

The coal trestle faced east on a railroad spur just south of the lumberyard. Florans Hoxie, who designed the Hawley House and Rice footbridge, designed this trestle at about the same time.

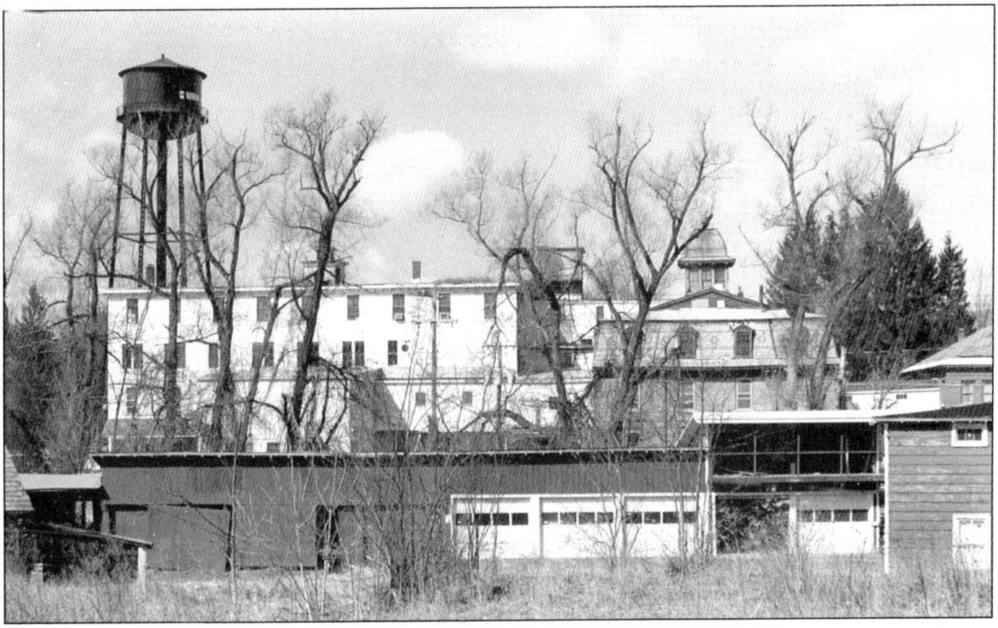

VARAK Park stands to the west of the old Cambridge Lumber Company. VARAK Park was the brainchild of five local businessmen who hated to see the Asgrow property (Rice Seed) go unutilized. They were Francis Vitro, Bo Anderson, John Rich, Everett Ashworth, and Jim King, hence the name VARAK. (Courtesy CVA.)

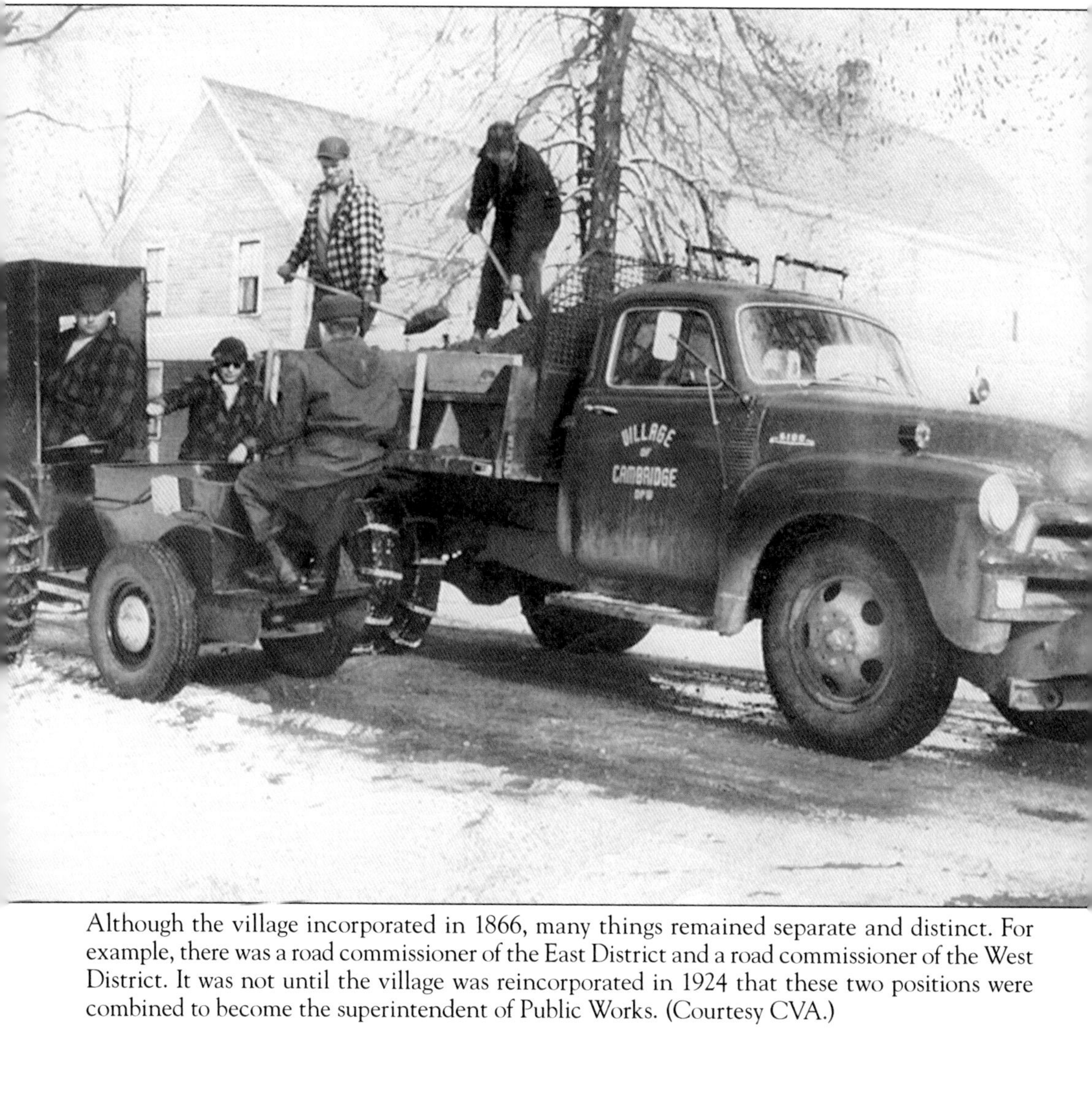

Although the village incorporated in 1866, many things remained separate and distinct. For example, there was a road commissioner of the East District and a road commissioner of the West District. It was not until the village was reincorporated in 1924 that these two positions were combined to become the superintendent of Public Works. (Courtesy CVA.)

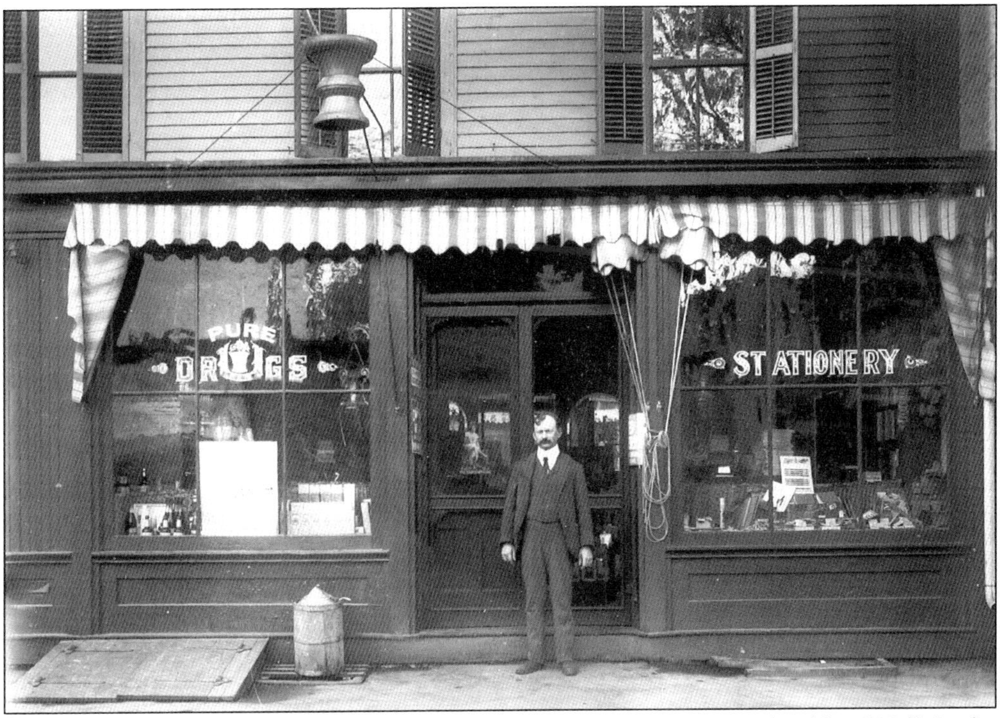

The Robertson Drug Store was in the Hubbard block one building west of Hubbard Hall. In the mid-1900s, Arno Wilson ran a Philco television repair shop in the building. In 1966, the village board voted for the police department to open an office in the rear of the building.

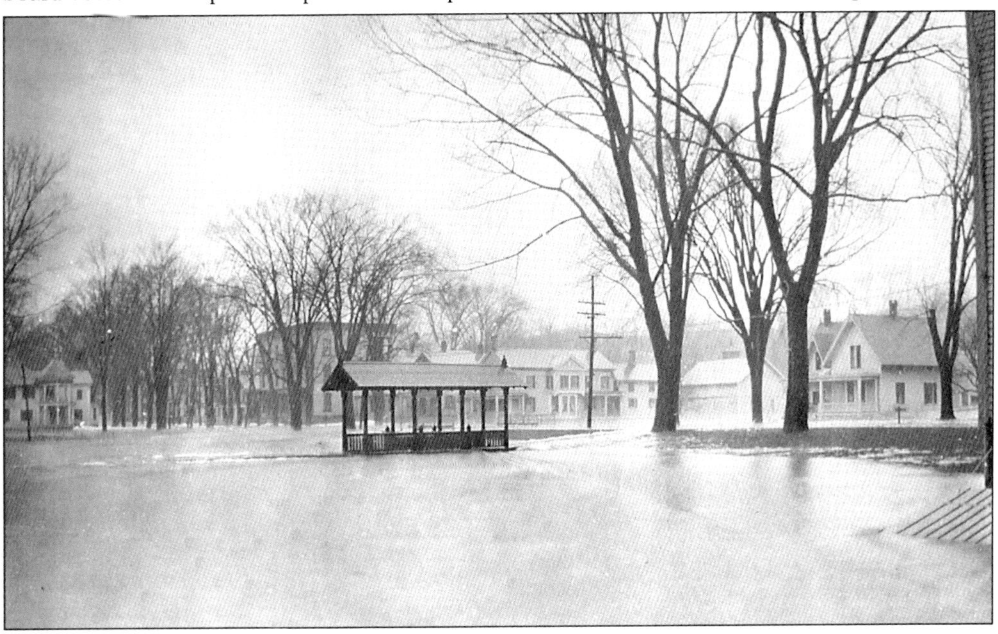

As late as this 1930s photograph, Blair's Brook (Owl Kill) overflowed and flooded West Main Street and the lawn of the Rice Seed Company. The Oatman furniture and undertaker building is visible beyond the footbridge. To the left is the Laverty house that was torn down in the early 1960s to make room for the new office of the Glens Falls National Bank. (Courtesy CVA.)

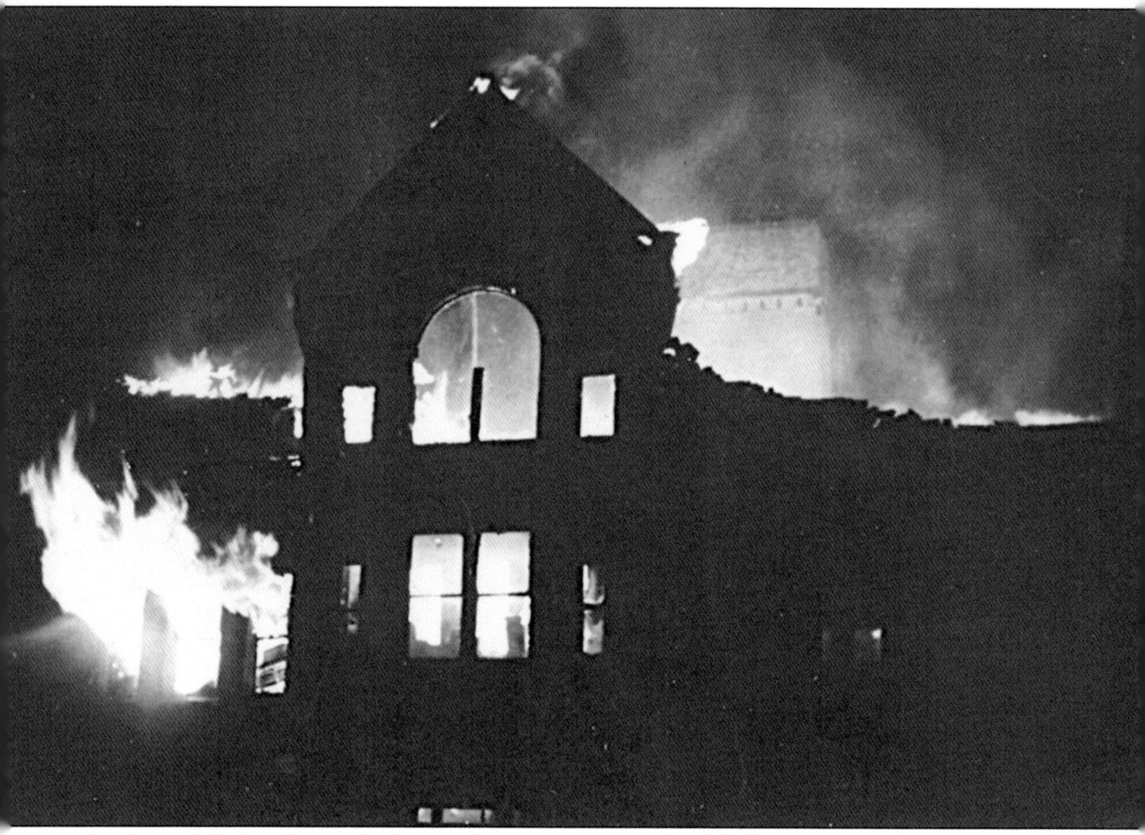

In the mid-1940s, Cambridge began discussing a new school. Following a close vote in 1946, the Hitchcock farm at the south end of Park Street was selected as the location. Through the summer of 1947, heated debates and votes ensued, with the East End and West End unable to agree on the design and cost of the new school. Suddenly (some still say mysteriously) early on Monday August 18, 1947, the Cambridge School caught fire. By sunrise, the fire was under control but continued to smolder for days. The building was ruined. The blaze was so hot that Charlie Ackley spent the wee hours of the morning with a water hose atop the roof of his furniture store across the street. Over the next four years, students attended classes in churches and businesses around the village. With the old school gone, progress on the new one should have been fast. However, when the cornerstone of the new school was laid in September 1950, the community had not agreed yet on the final design or cost. (Courtesy of Kirk Spurr.)

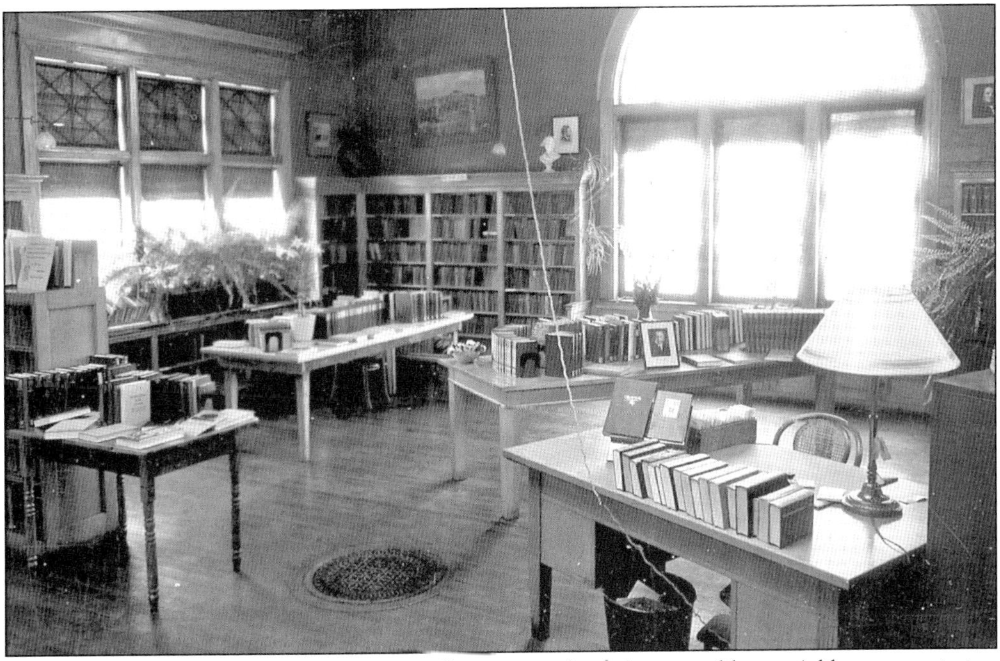

In the 1860s, James Smart spearheaded an effort to raise funds for a new library. A library association was formed and met in the YMCA room over the Hubbard block. Later a reading room opened in the Crocker brick building by the railroad tracks. Lecture series were held. In 1875, a spelling bee was held in Ackley Hall to raise money, with many local dignitaries participating.

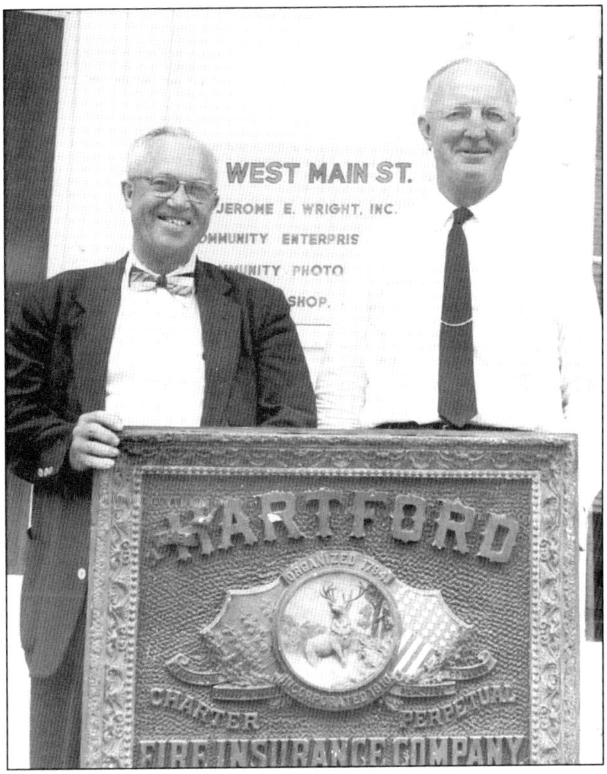

For over 100 years, the Hitchcock family ran an insurance business started by John Eddy in North White Creek in July 1856. Affiliated insurance companies included Aetna Fire Insurance, Glens Falls Insurance, Hanover Insurance, Phoenix of London, Niagara Fire Insurance, Continental Insurance, Northern of London, Royal Insurance, Aetna Casualty and Surety, and Boston Insurance. Here Bob Wright, of Jerome Wright Insurance, accepts an award from Hartford Fire Insurance. (Courtesy CVA.)

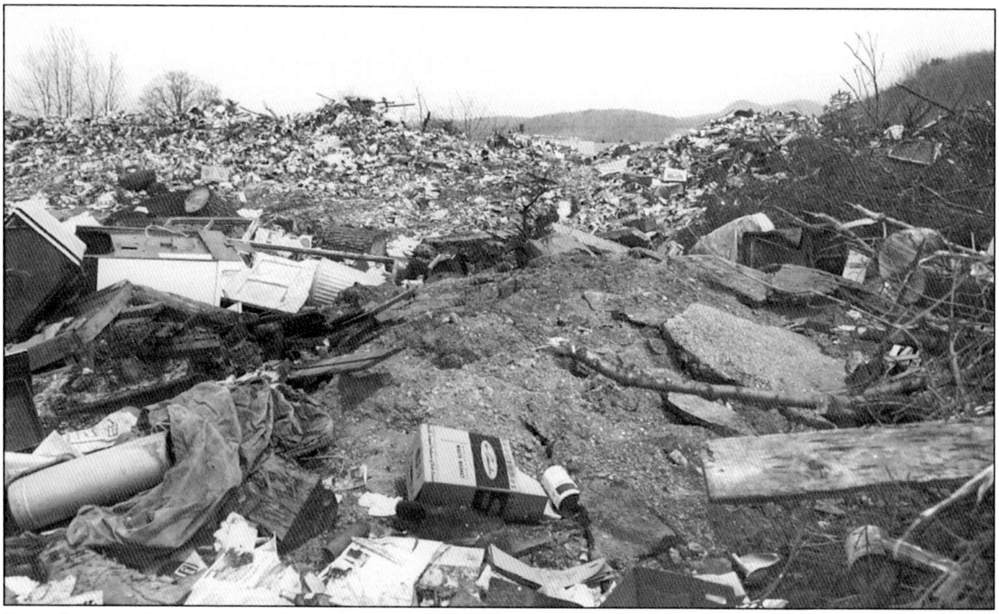

First discussed in 1912, a village dump was finally created on the Newcomb land on Pearl Street in 1949. In 1957, the Town of White Creek started using the village dump. In 1964, the landfill projects of the Village of Cambridge and Town of White Creek were combined, later adding the Town of Jackson. A new landfill on Plains Road was overseen by Morris Bentley, superintendent of landfill. (Courtesy CVA.)

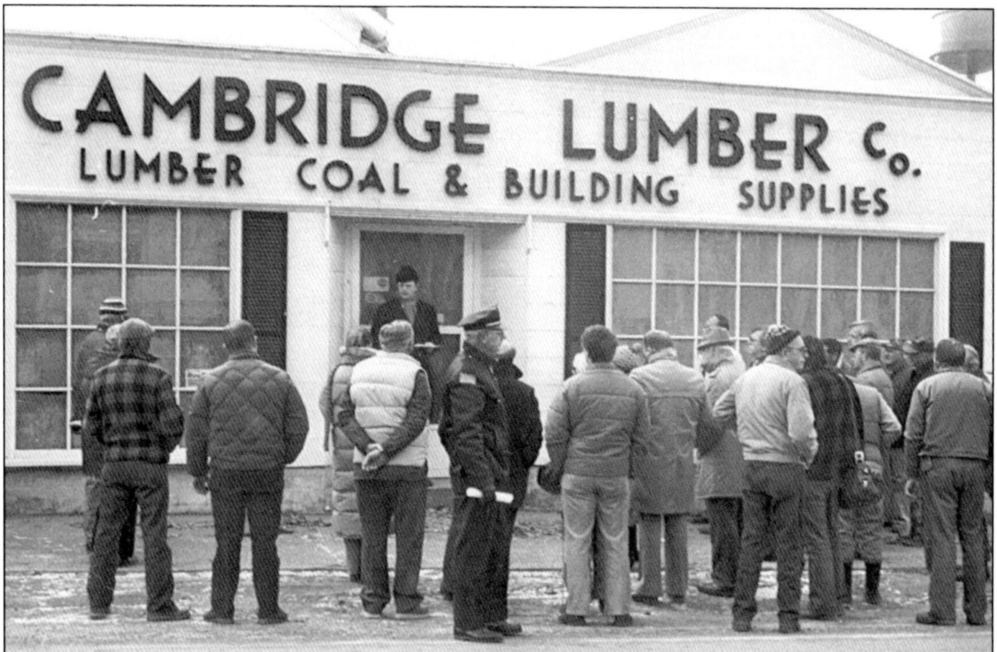

In the early 1900s, the lumberyard next to the firehouse was operated by T. McConnell. By 1925, Charles McGhee had taken over, followed in the 1950s by Graeme (Tink) Parrish. In the 1980s, the building was sold at this on-site auction to VARAK Park. Recently the building has been restored through village grants. (Courtesy CVA.)

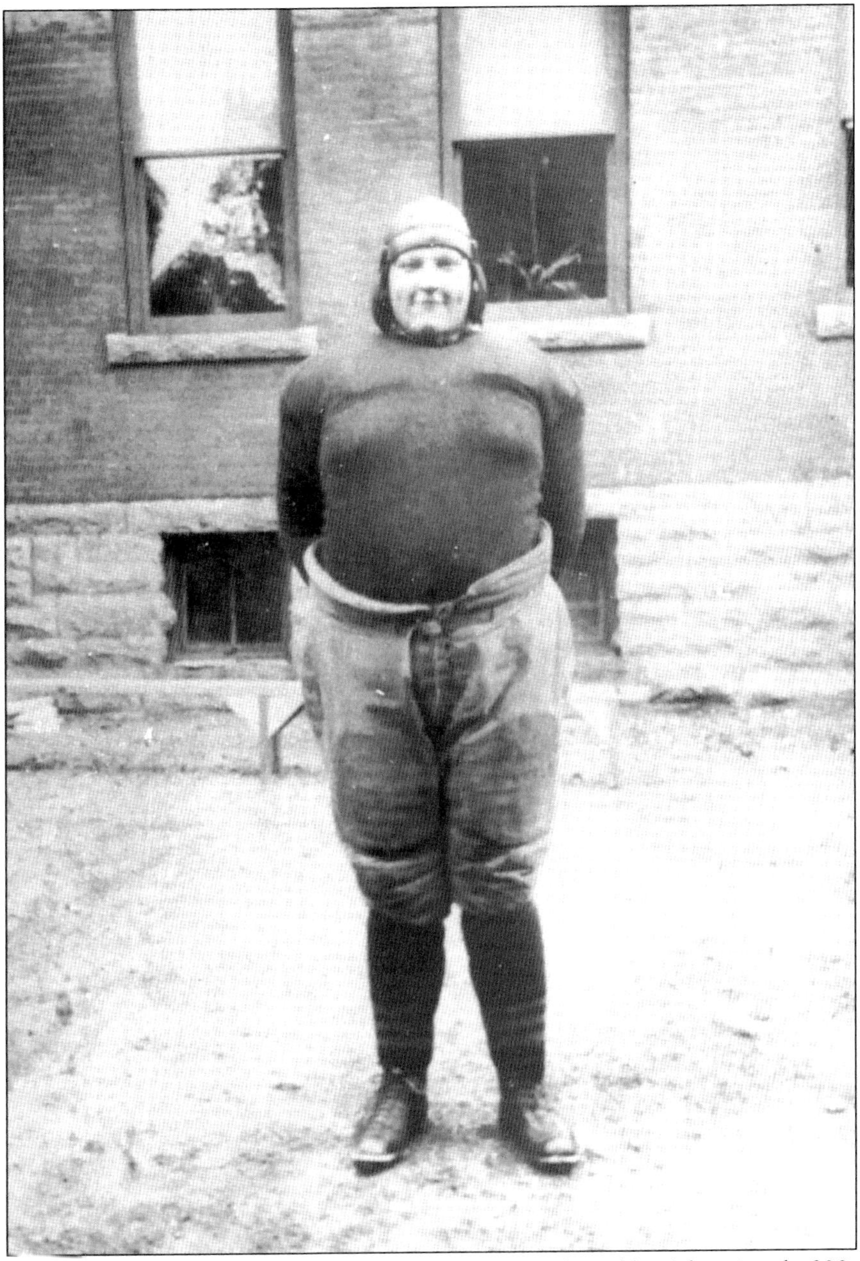

The front line of the 1925 Cambridge football team was anchored by 6-foot 4-inch, 300-pound Martin Church, then only an eighth grader. After leaving school, Church studied tuba under the locally renowned Professor Nichols. He became a professional tuba player, touring with a vaudeville company. During his two-year football career, Church was moved sometimes to fullback in short yardage situations. In 1925, Cambridge completed a perfect 9-0 season by beating Albany High 46-6 on Alexander Field at Union College to claim the championship of the Northeastern New York League. The team attracted such large crowds that new bleachers were installed behind the school. Also on the 1925 team was John Galloway, who later starred as the "Galloping Ghost" at Colgate University. Several years later, the Ghost returned to coach the Cambridge team. (Courtesy CVA.)

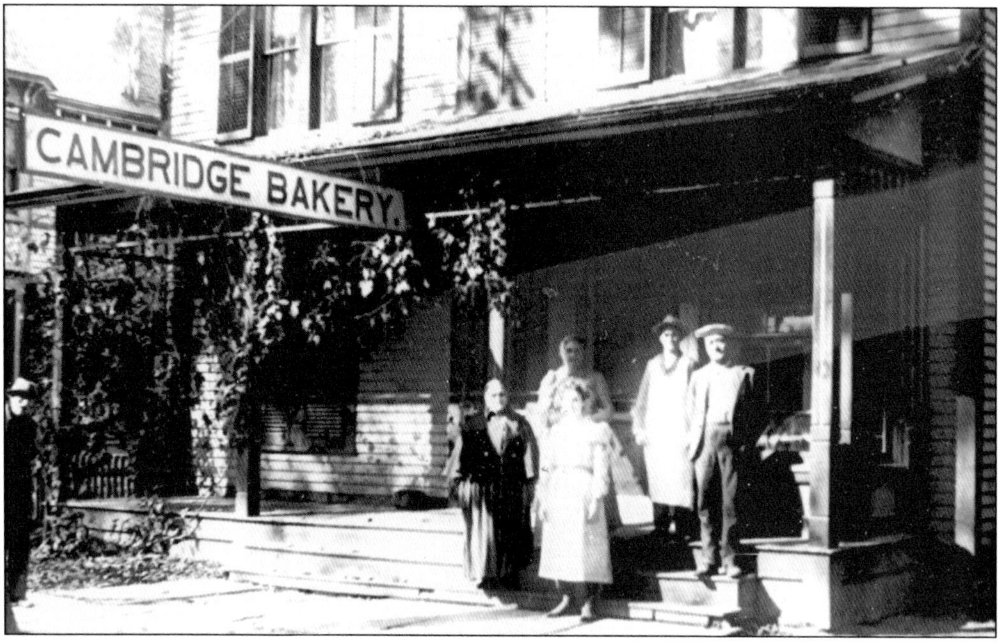

The Cambridge Bakery occupied the right half of this building in the early and mid-1900s. Products were displayed in the large bay window. Baking was done in a large concrete block addition in back. Friday was baked beans day. After Gus Severson stopped to deliver ice in his horse-drawn wagon, he would refresh his horse at the village watering trough at the northwest corner of Main and Union Streets.

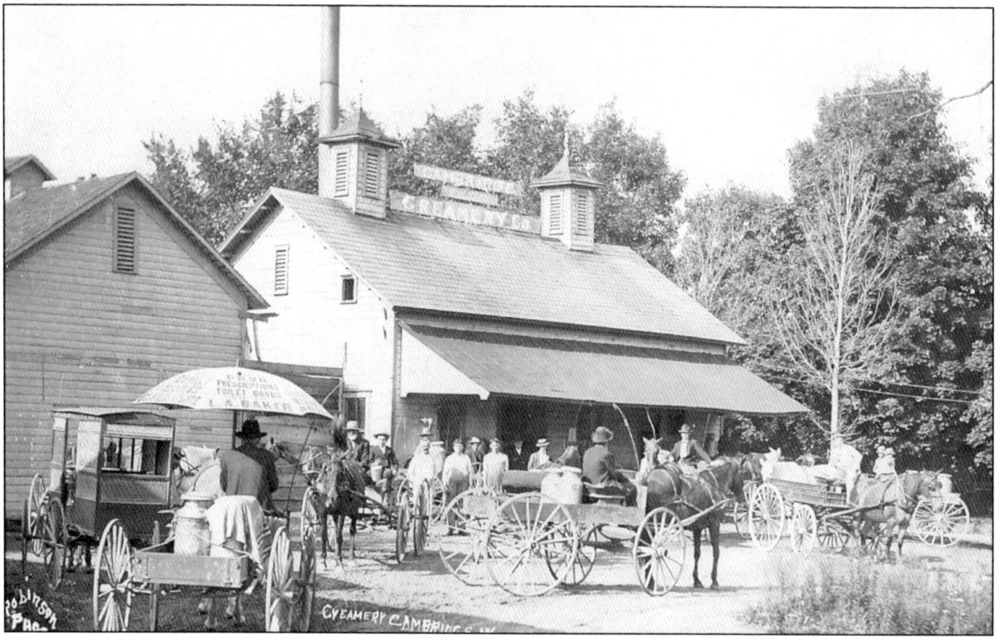

The Cambridge Creamery stood near the railroad tracks between Railroad and Pearl Streets. In 1904, when it was called Cambridge Elgin Creamery Company, Amos Conkey had a flour, feed, and lumber company next door, and C. A. Brownlee had a feed and gristmill across the street. The nearby railroad shipped the valley's milk as far as New York City and Boston.

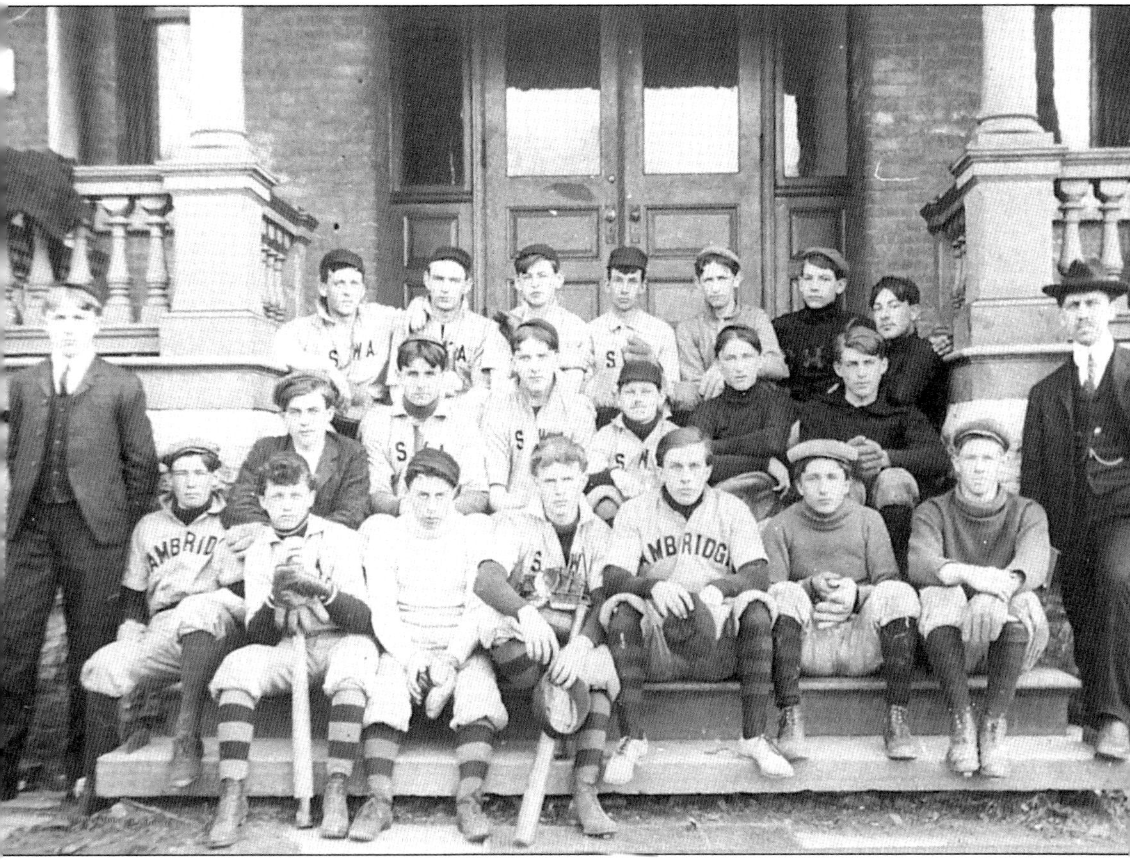

This photograph, taken on the steps of the Cambridge Union School, appears to be an all-league baseball team from the 1930s. Two unidentified Cambridge players appear in the first row. Ten of the players have S.W.A. on their jerseys, which probably stands for Salem Washington Academy. Today young ballplayers hone their skills on the Cambridge Youth Athletic Association fields between Division and North Park Streets. The Star Baseball Club is purported to be the first organized baseball team in Cambridge. Their first game was played on June 29, 1867, against the Arctic Baseball Club of Greenwich. In a game that took less than three hours to complete, Cambridge won 177-43. The snow may have been flying by season's end for the Stars, as their last game was played on November 5.

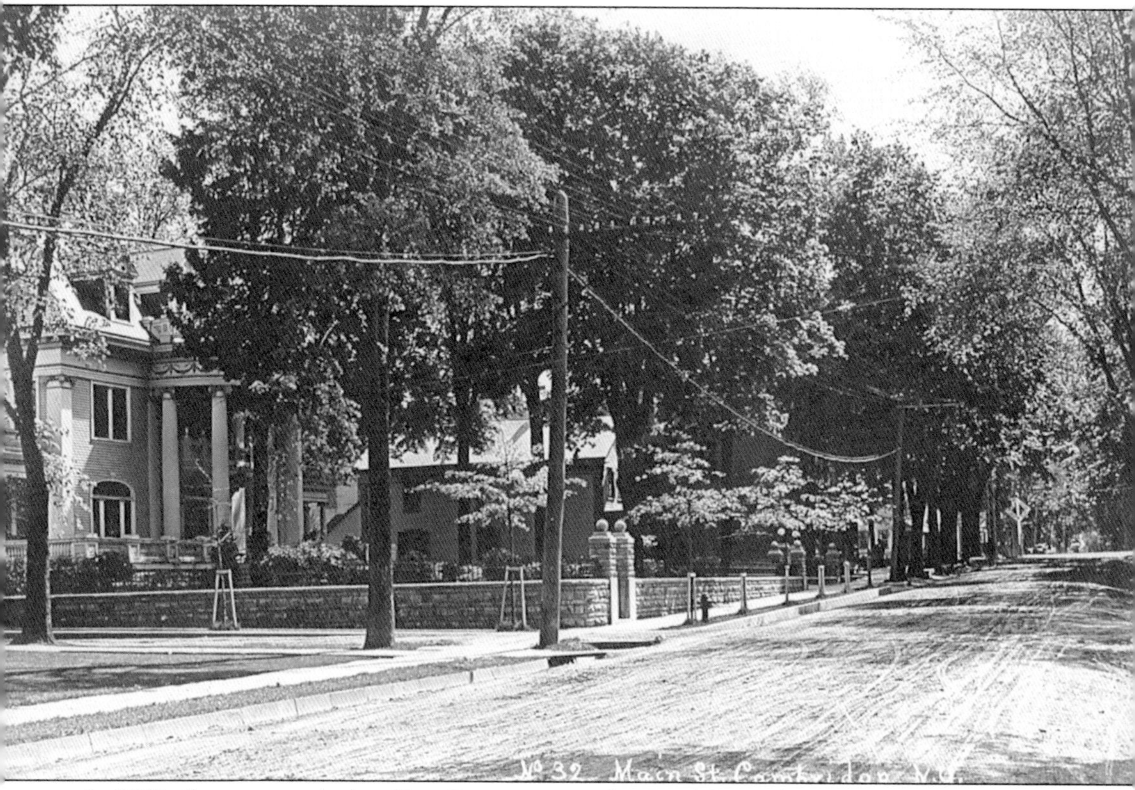

In 1887, tile sewer was laid on First Street westward to Pearl Street (now St. Lukes Street), across Main Street and into Blair Brook at the bridge near the Rice Seed Company. The proponents of this endeavor included George McKie, James Smart, A. B. McNish, C. T. Hawley, Robert Blair, and R. Niles Rice and his son, Jerome B. Rice. It is not surprising that the sewer followed a route that passed by the houses of each proponent. In 1891, the sewer was extended to include East Main Street to the brook and in 1895 extended to parts of Broad, Spring, First, and Pearl (St. Lukes) Streets. In 1949, the village board discussed a village sewer system at a cost of $200,000, but nothing was done. In 1950, the possibility of state aid for a sewer system was investigated, but again no action was taken. Finally in the 1980s, the village voted to have residents install individual septic systems.

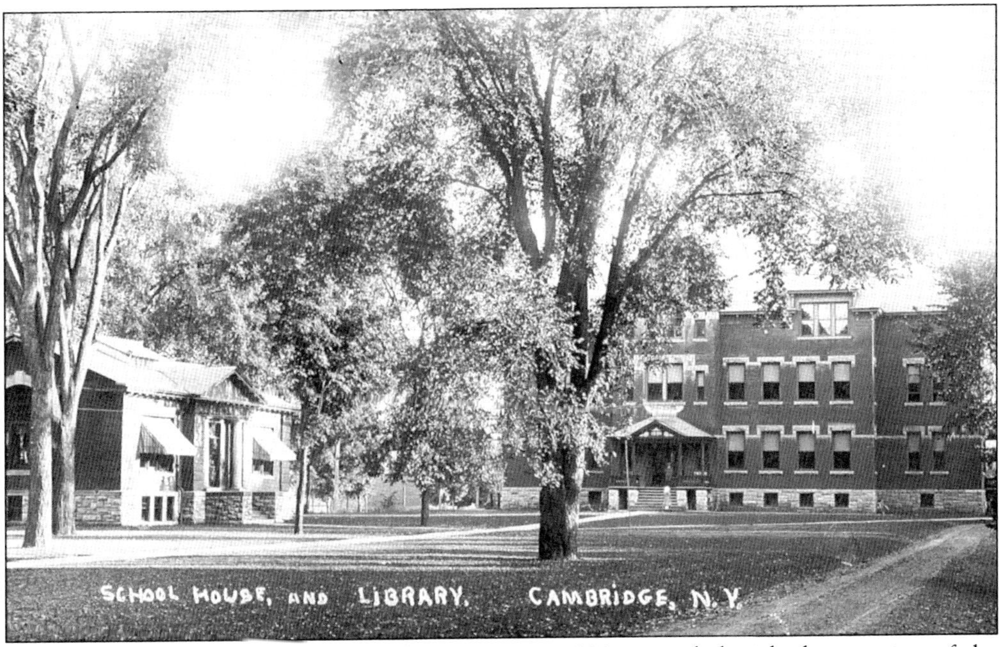

The installation of streetlights on Main Street in 1891 coincided with the opening of the Cambridge Union School. This brought to an end two village positions, that of lamplighter of the East District and lamplighter of the West District. Power failures were frequent, and in 1893, service was taken over by Consolidated Electric Company of Greenwich. The old gas lamps and posts were disposed of in 1895.

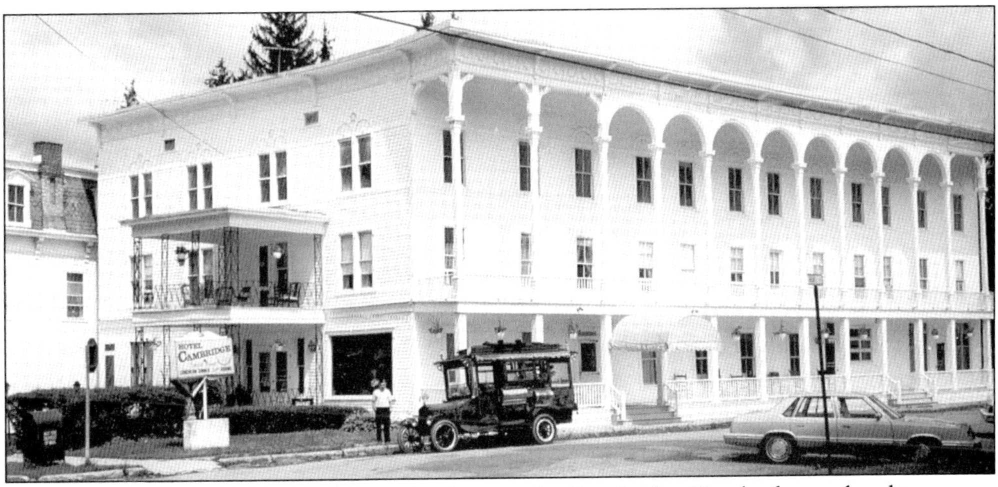

Prof. Charles Watson Townsend, a regular diner at the Cambridge Hotel, often ordered ice cream with his apple pie. Mrs. Berry Hall dubbed this pie à la mode. When a *New York Sun* reporter overheard Townsend ordering pie à la mode at Delmonico Restaurant in New York City, he published a story demanding that New York City provide fare equal to that found in Cambridge.

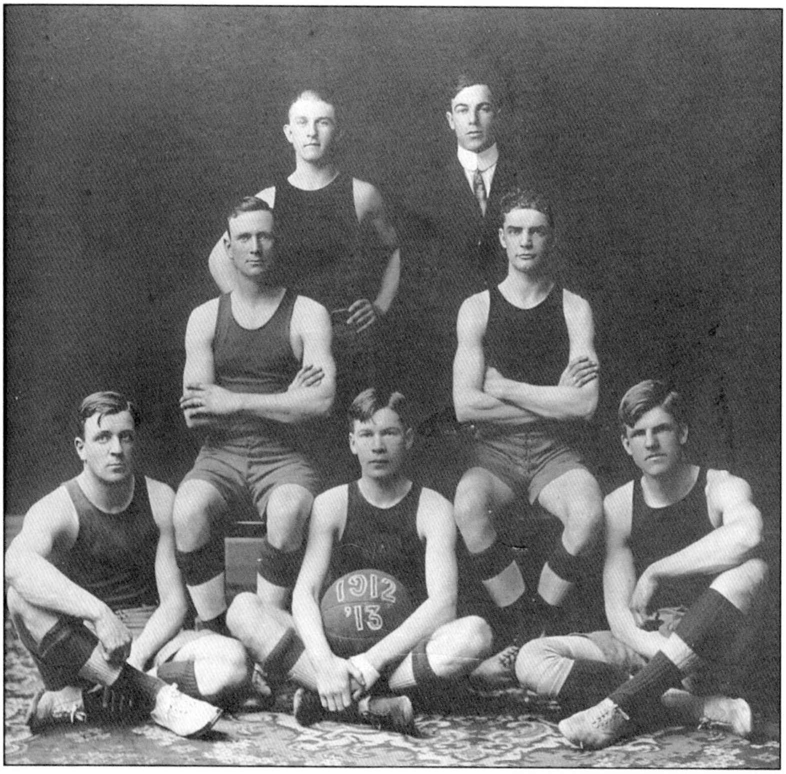

Before the Hubbard addition was built in 1914, the Cambridge High School basketball team played its games on the second floor of the old white church (Grange Hall) at the northeast corner of Main and Park Streets. (Courtesy CVA.)

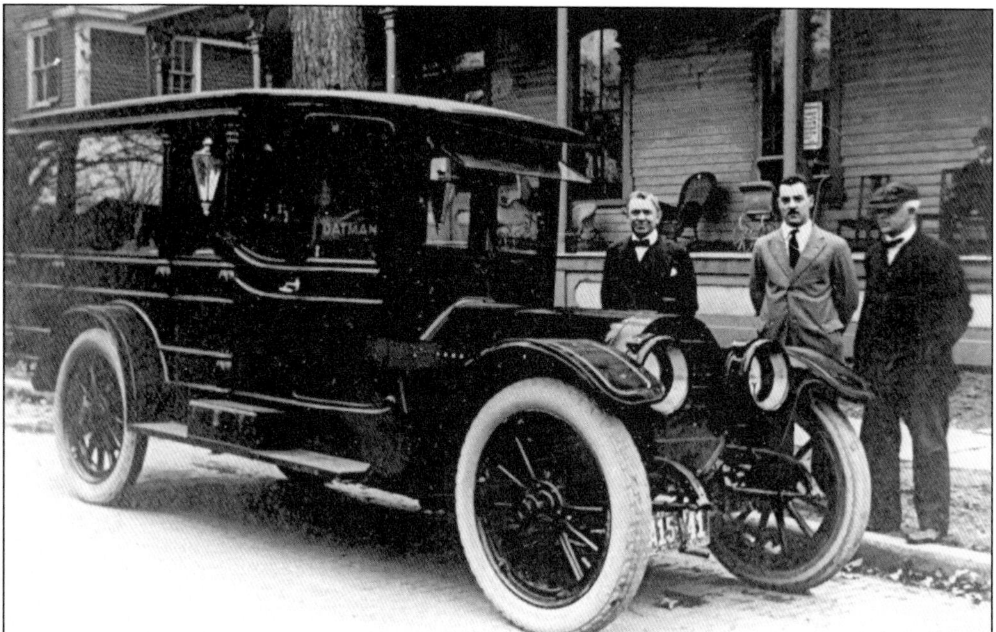

Barton used the upstairs of the West End Market for his furniture business before moving to the large yellow building on West Main Street across from the current bank. After that, the building was operated by Oatman and then Ackley, each of whom ran an undertaker business in addition to the furniture business.

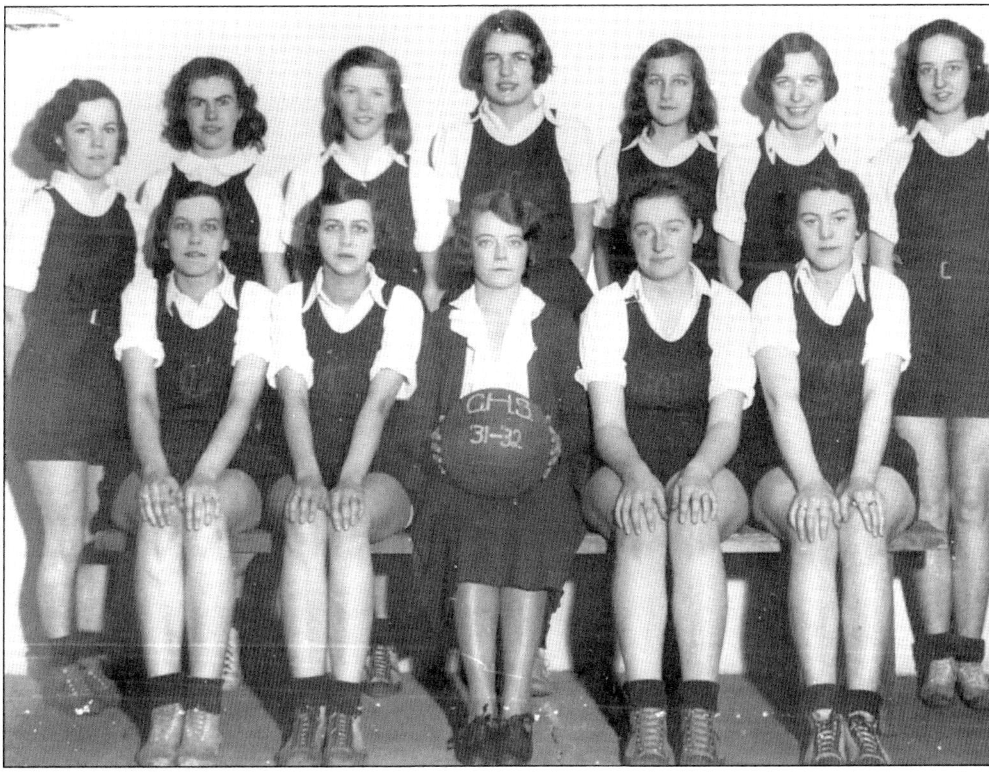

The Cambridge girls' basketball team traveled around New York in the early 1930s, trying to find suitable competition. In the first league game of the 1933 season, they beat Berlin 81-2, while the boys were typically scoring only 15 or 20 points a game. Dot Burch Benson (seated second from left) once scored 72 points in a single game, more points than the boys' team scored that entire season.

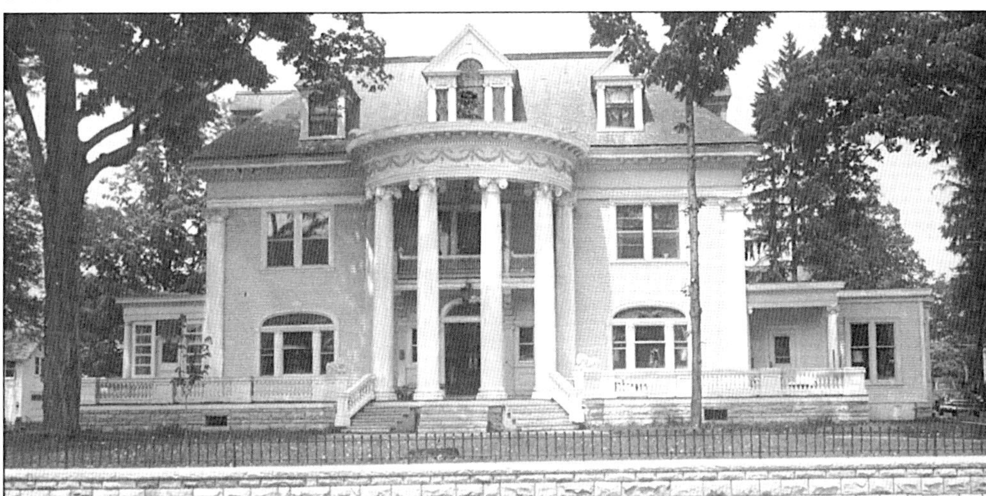

Construction on the Rice mansion began in the summer of 1901. Jerome Bonaparte "J. B." Rice was confined to a wheelchair, so an elevator was installed, requiring large hydraulics in the cellar. The stone wall was built in late 1903, and the family moved in during January 1904. On Wednesday, October 25, 1905, a huge housewarming party was held.

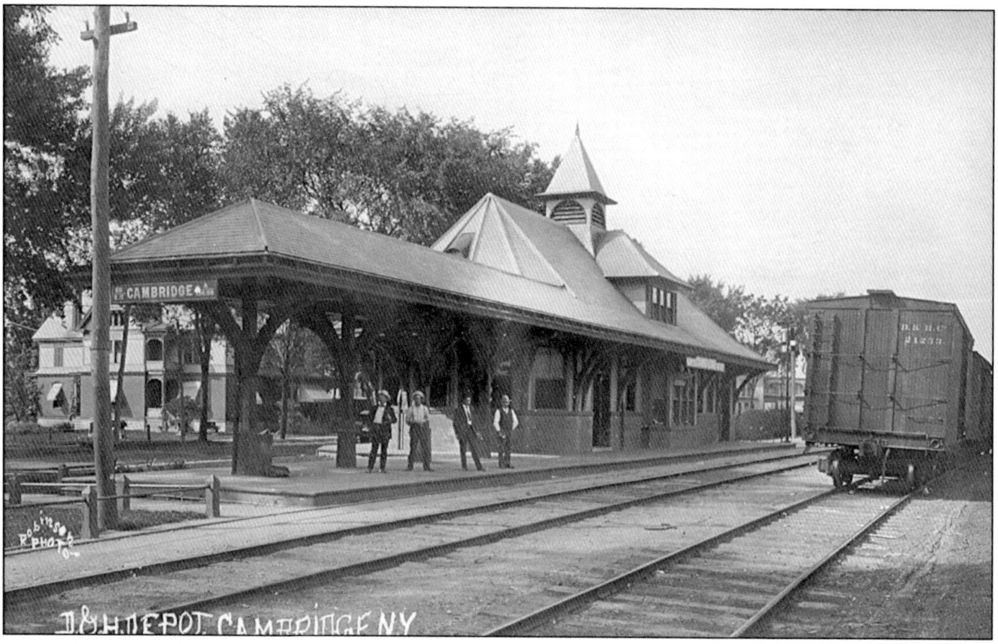

Six Delaware and Hudson trains a day passed through Cambridge in the early 1900s. In the mid-1900s, new automobiles were shipped to Cambridge automobile dealers in enclosed boxcars, not on flatbeds. Skilled local drivers would carefully turn the new automobiles within the railroad car, maneuvering for the ramp.

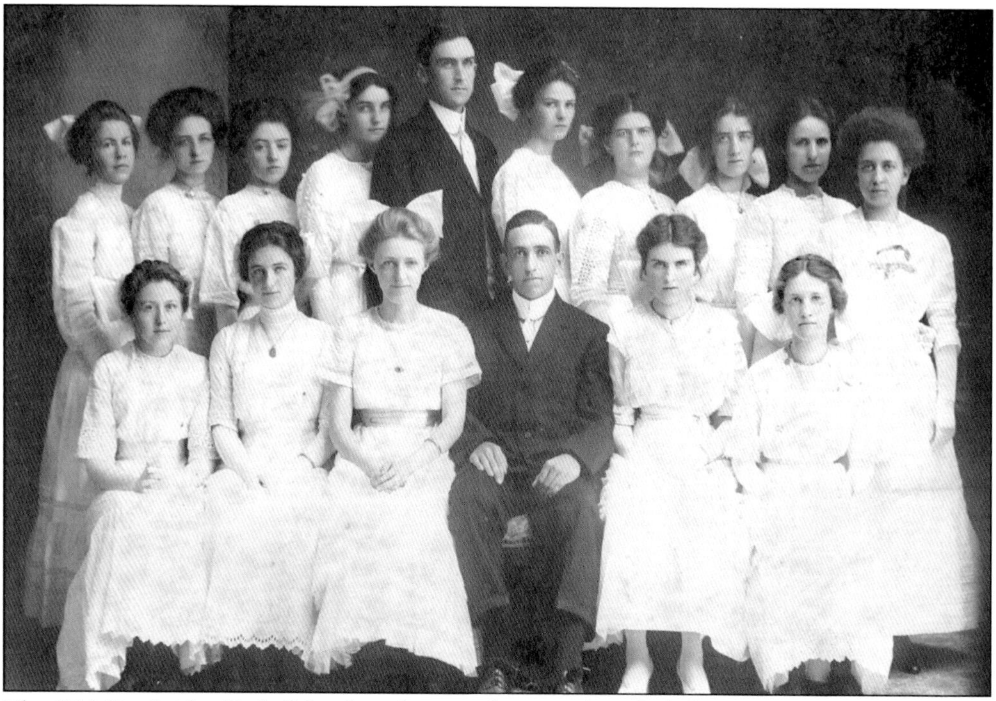

The 1911 Cambridge High School graduation photograph included two men: Professor Kingsley (second row) and Lionel Edie (first row). Six years later, Edwin Cornell's daughter, Elsa (first row, third from left), married Malcolm Parrish.

The First Baptist Church was organized on July 8, 1843. Thomas Stevens served as moderator and Noah Fowler as clerk. There were already five other organized churches within a square mile, but that did not deter the congregation. The church was built in 1844 and dedicated in June 1845. At that time, there were only 26 members, but they grew to over 100 by 1860.

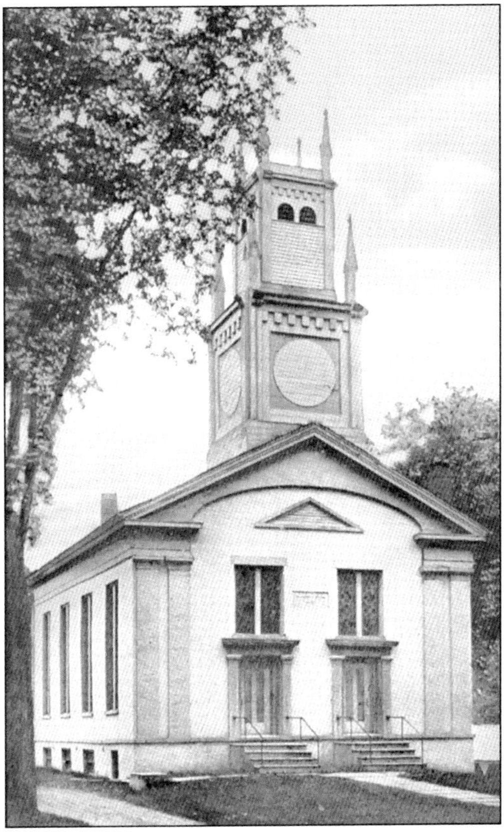

The Cambridge football team played on the field behind the old school. West Main Street is to the northeast beyond the trees. The west side of the Rice Seed campus is visible in the background on the right (east). Cambridge alternated between 6-man and 11-man football over the years. (Courtesy CVA.)

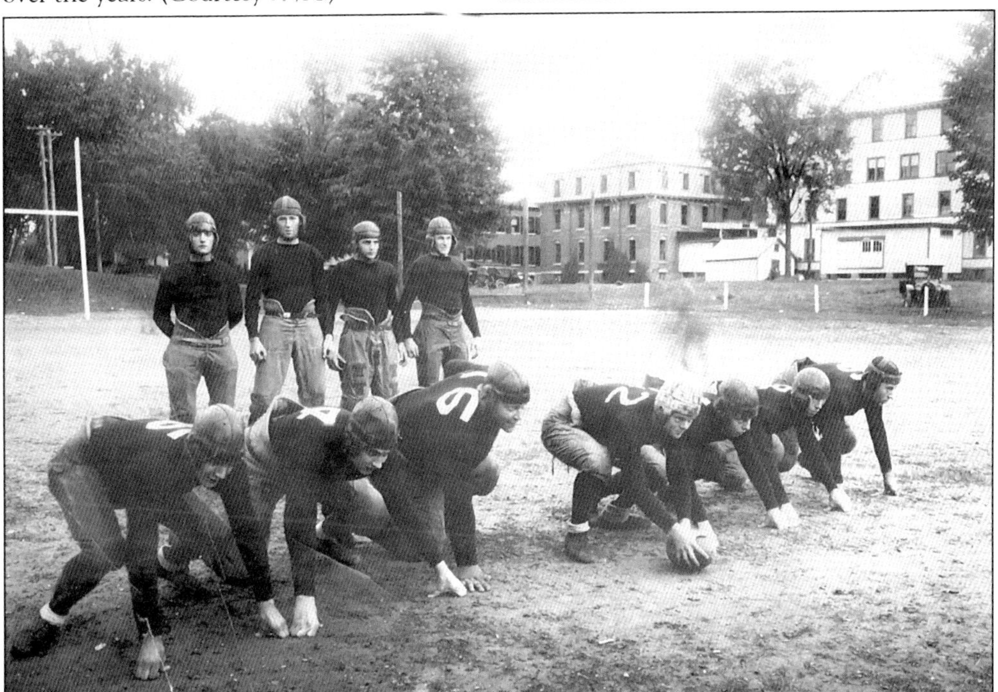

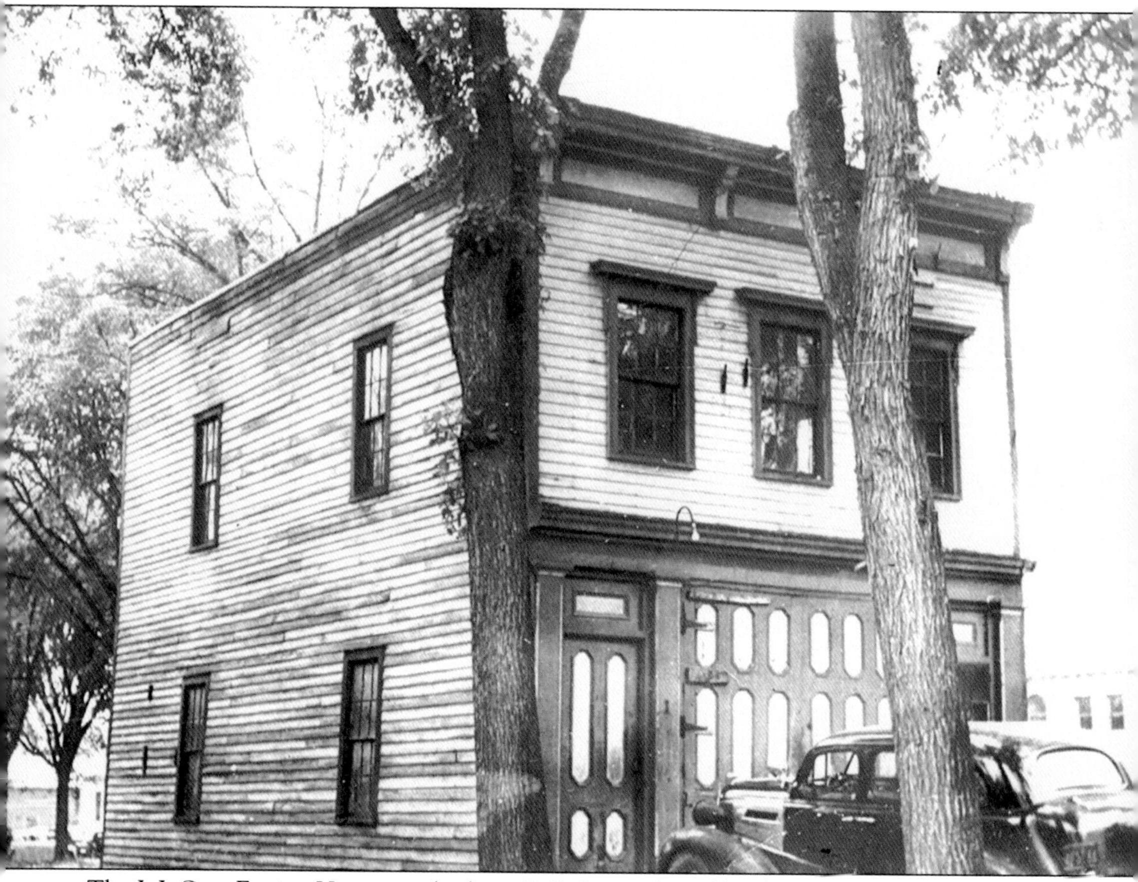

The J. J. Gray Engine House was built in 1868. It was shared by the Russell Hose No. 1 (later J. B. Rice Hose) and the Hook and Ladder company. The Larmon Hose No. 2 used a building on West Main near the creek, and the Hallelujah Hose used a building on North Union. In June 1950, the village board voted to tear down this building and erect a new firehouse. The J. J. Gray Engine House was taken down in August 1950, but one month later the proposed plans for the new building were rejected. The first proposal of $25,000 was later increased to $37,000, with the final cost being $36,553.75. In 1951, a piece of land was purchased from the Charles A. McGhee Company to the left and rear of this building. The new firehouse also served as the municipal building. The first village board meeting was held in the new building on May 1, 1951. In 1954, plans were made to put a kitchen in the firehouse.

Four

Surrounding

The village of Cambridge spans the towns of Cambridge, White Creek, and Jackson. As the boundary lines on the maps have changed over the years, it usually takes a generation or two before the residents acknowledge the change.

In 1864, Jackson was the largest grain-producing township in Washington County, accounting for over 30 percent of all grain in the county. Jackson also produced more pounds of wool than any other town in the county, with all three towns producing more than 25 percent of all wool in the county. Jackson was the largest producer of pounds of pork, almost twice as much as the next largest town. All three towns ranked at or near the bottom in dairy production.

In 1865, Cambridge Corners was fifth largest community in the county, and North White Creek was the sixth, behind Whitehall, Fort Edward, Union Village (Greenwich), and Sandy Hill. After the communities merged the following year, their combined population of 1,590 still ranked them fifth in the county. The population of the towns, over 97 percent white, has not changed by more than four percent in the last 150 years.

In the late 1800s, the towns each created mutual fire insurance companies. In case of a loss, an assessment was made on each insured person to reimburse the one suffering the loss. In 1870, Jackson only suffered one loss, costing $1,100, about $50,000 in today's money. The White Creek Company required keeping a surplus. In 1941, this amounted to $639,380 divided among 186 policies.

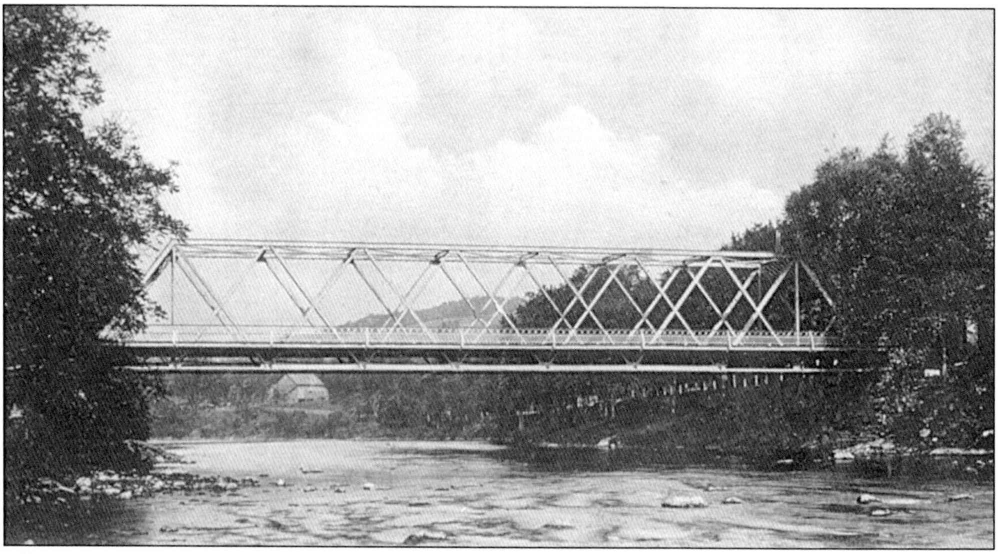

The Hoosick River forms the boundary between Rensselaer County (left) and the town of White Creek in Washington County (right). A covered bridge, built in 1827, allowed Northern Turnpike traffic to bypass Buskirk's Bridge and the ensuing steep Oak Hill. Travelers now crossed the Eagle Bridge, entering Cambridge via the flat Turnpike Road. In 1875, the covered bridge was rebuilt, and it was replaced in 1898.

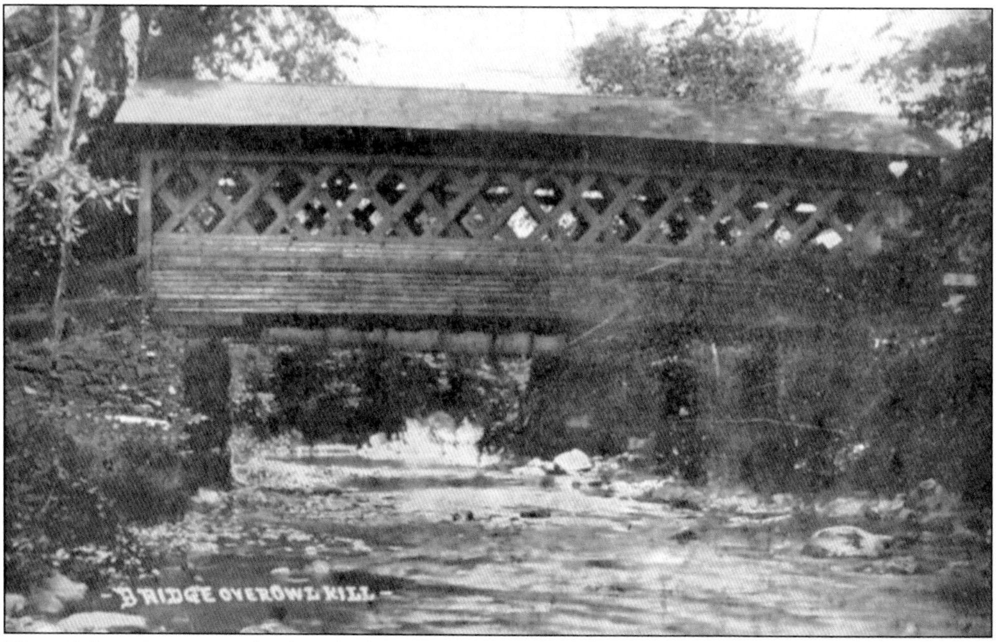

The 46-foot Carpenter bridge, built in the late 1800s, crossed the Owl Kill just north of the intersection with the Hoosick River. In 1932, it was bypassed by a steel deck bridge on New York Route 67. When the bridge was dismantled in 1947, Gerald Moses used the beams to build his house, which sits just to the east (left) of this photograph.

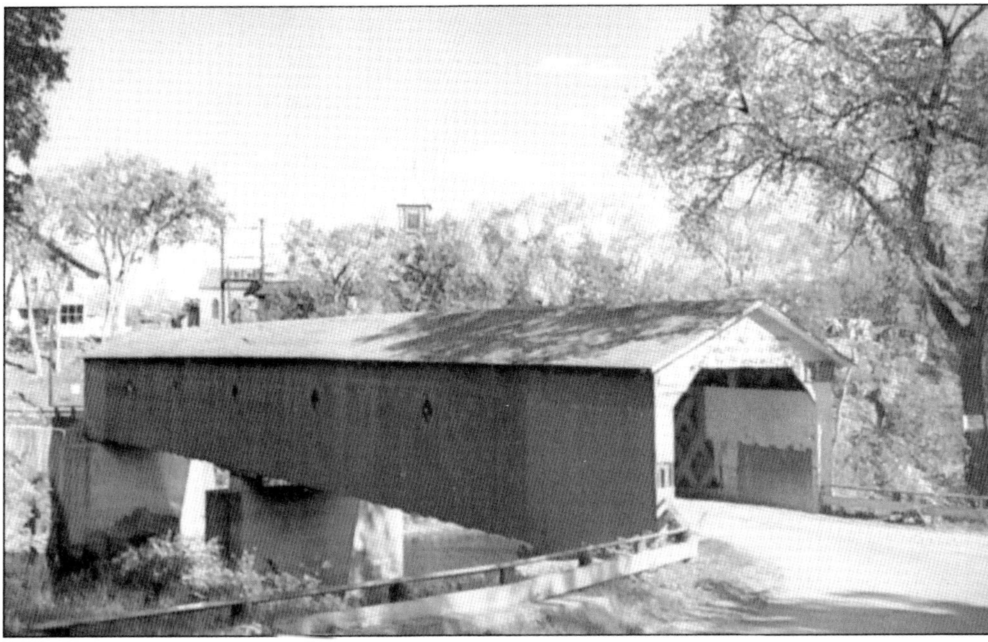

The Shushan Covered Bridge is a two-span, 160-foot bridge across the Battenkill. It was built in 1858 by Milton and James Stevens. Today it is a museum, having been replaced by a steel deck bridge.

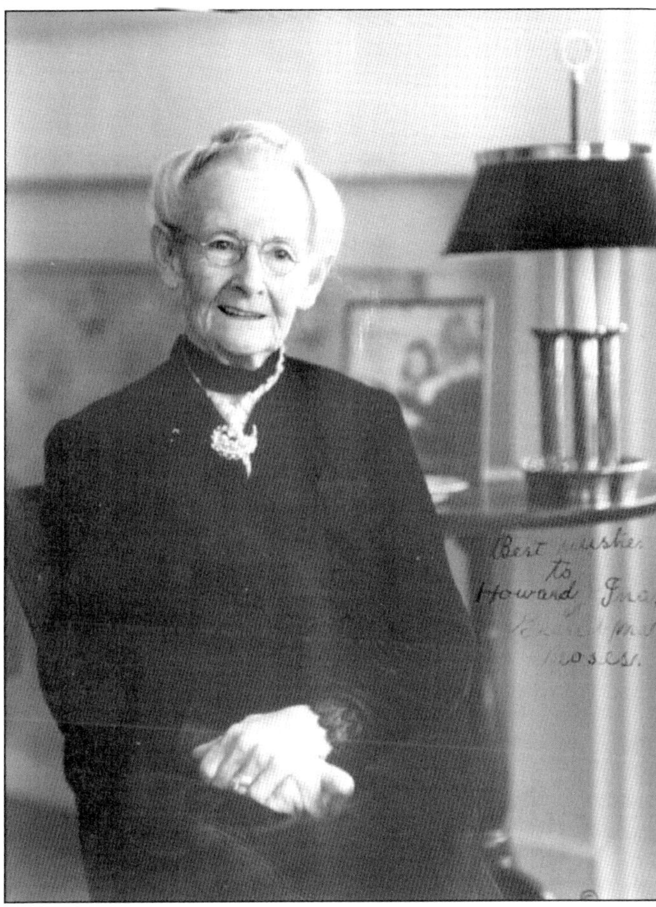

Anna Mary Robertson Moses, known to the world as Grandma Moses, lived in Eagle Bridge until her death in 1961 at the age of 101. Her great-grandson now runs a vegetable business on her farm, and her great-granddaughter now lives in her house. This photograph is made out to her grandson's in-laws, Howard and Ina Harrison of Hoosick Falls. (Courtesy of Grandma Moses Properties.)

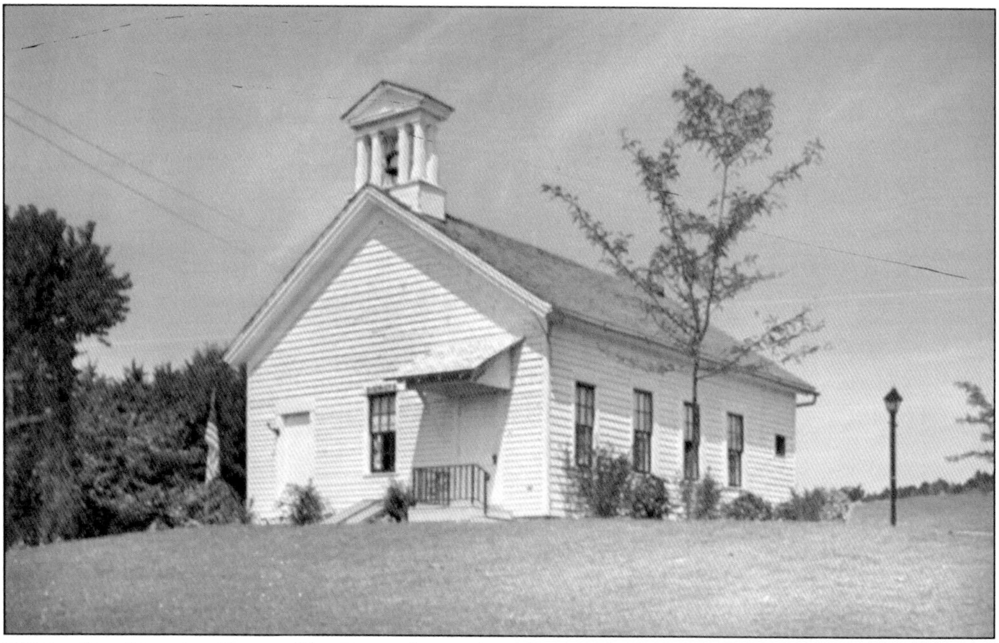

White Creek's schoolhouse No. 3 was located at the southern end of Turnpike Road. Situated halfway between the villages of Cambridge and Hoosick Falls, the residents of Eagle Bridge voted in 1959 to join the Cambridge School District. In 1968, the schoolhouse was moved and became a museum on Grandma Moses Road. Later it was moved to its current location at the Bennington Museum.

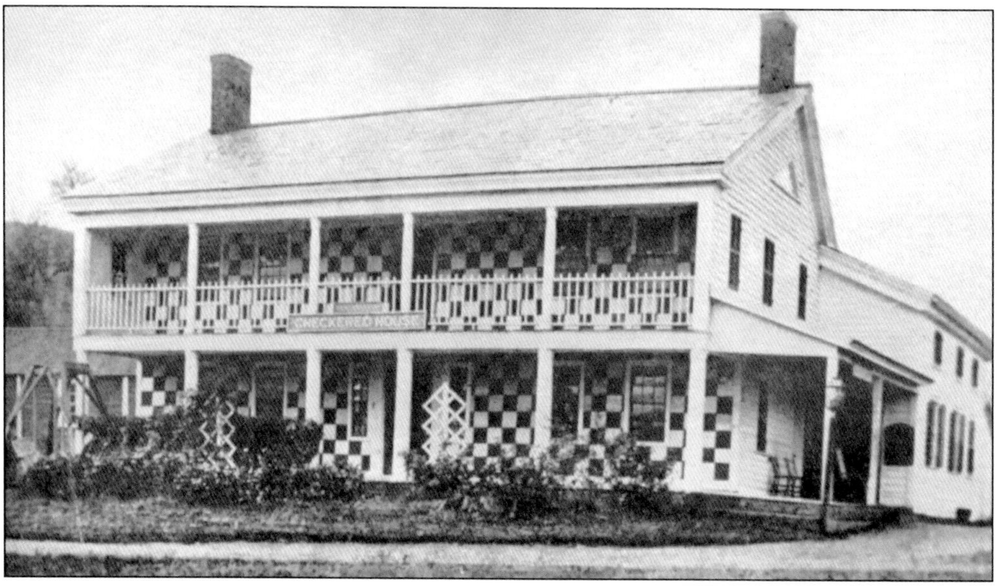

In 1765, James Cowden, one of 30 Scotch–Irish settlers in White Creek, built a tavern. It became a popular hostelry on the Northern Turnpike. After the Revolutionary War, Major Cowden painted all sides in large squares of red and white, prompting the name "Checkered House." The house was repainted in 1853 with only the front in red and white checkers. The house was destroyed by fire on February 10, 1907.

Thomas Comstock died a heroic death at the Battle of Bennington. For years, his wife, Sarah, was a celebrity at annual celebrations. Later Sarah married Capt. Edward Long. After Long's death, she married Maj. James Cowden and lived in the Checkered House. After Cowden's death, she married Burgess Hall. On May 9, 1811, she was laid to rest beside Major Cowden in the graveyard north of the Checkered House. (Courtesy CVA.)

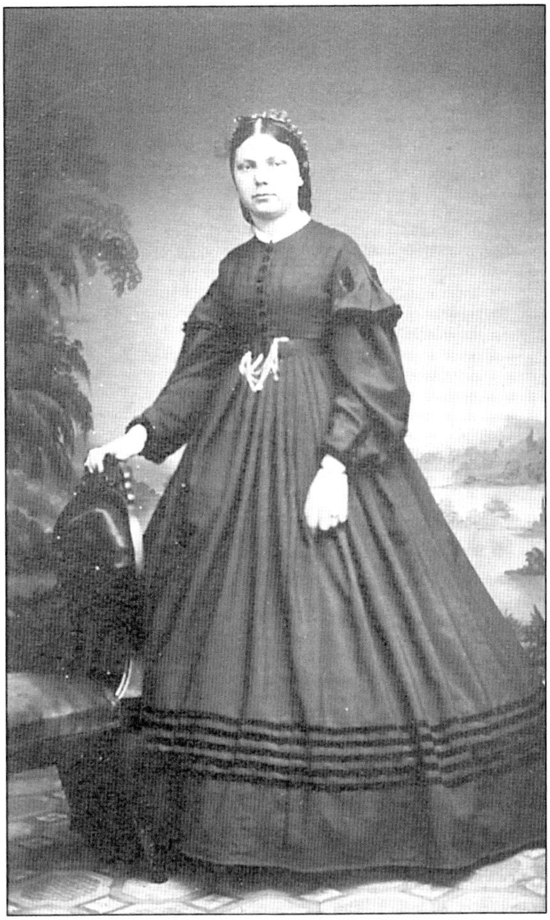

The New York State Central School Act of 1927 provided money to consolidate rural schools into centralized systems. At that time, there were 276 rural schools throughout the county, with about 40 located in Cambridge, White Creek, and Jackson. Many schools survived until the late 1950s. Local folklore tells of one rural school that refused to close, the issue being forced when the central school hired the rural school's only teacher.

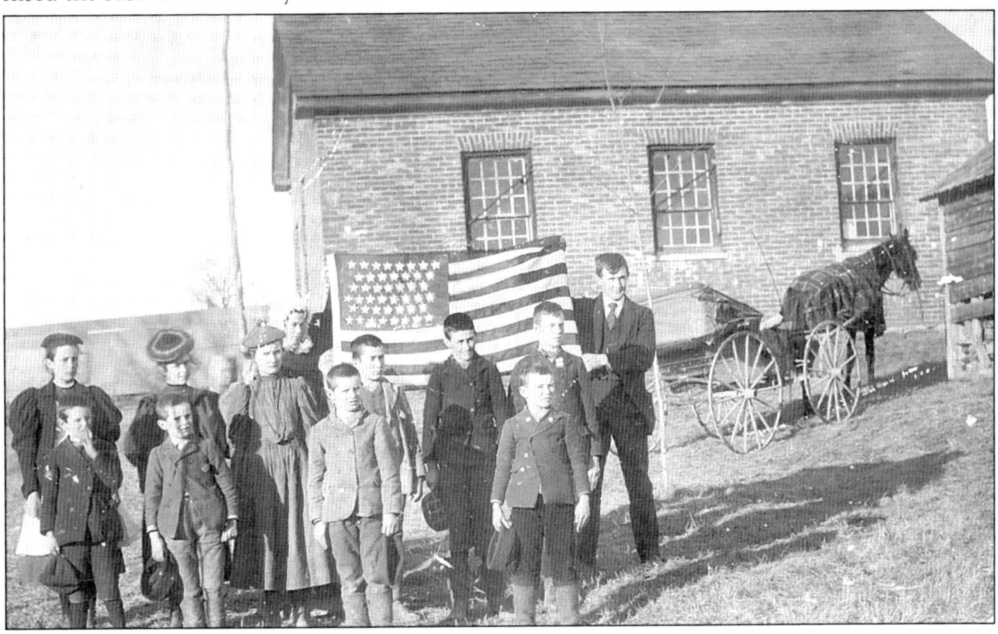

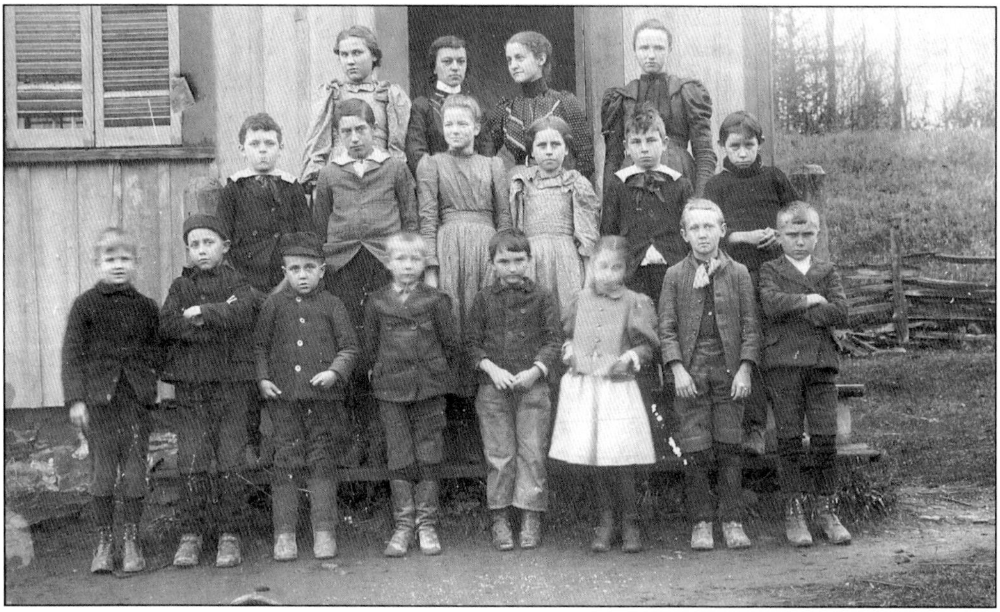

The older boys in the one-room schoolhouses were responsible for arriving early on winter mornings to fire up the woodstove. After completing the eighth grade, students moved from their rural schoolhouse to the Cambridge Union School.

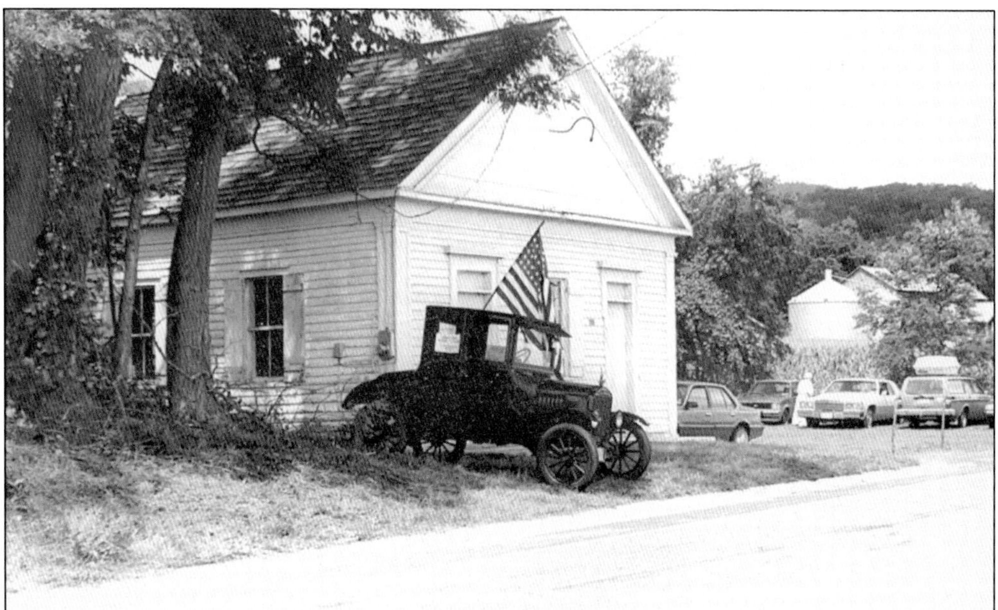

Two miles north of the village of Cambridge, on New York Route 22 in the town of Jackson, is District No. 6 schoolhouse. Today the building serves as the town offices. One of town supervisor John Rich's antique cars is in front of the Town of Jackson office during the 1976 bicentennial celebration.

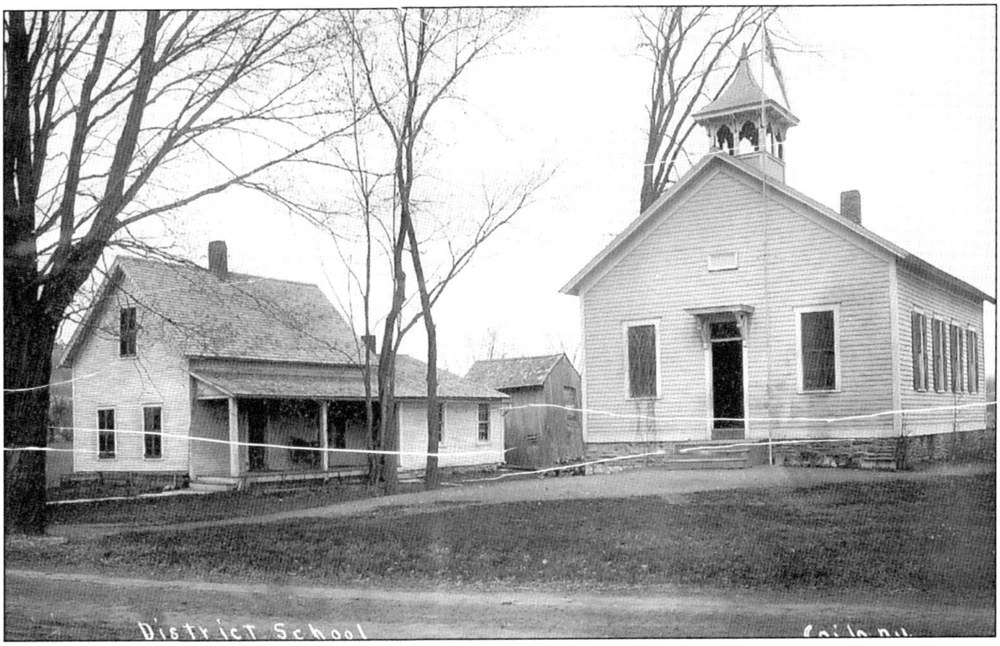

Cambridge has a long history of moving buildings. The Coila schoolhouse was dragged across New York Route 372 to become the addition to the Coila Presbyterian Church. In the early 1900s, the original railroad depot was moved to become a private residence on Pleasant Street. William Hitchcock moved a house from South Park Street to Mitchell Avenue to make more open space on the north end of his farm.

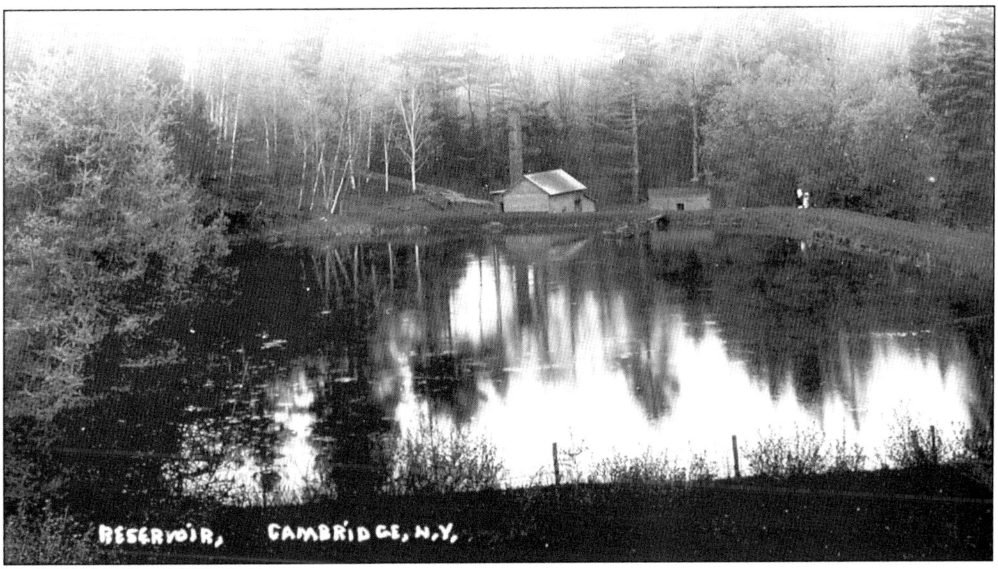

In 1885, the Cambridge Water Works (CWW) company built its lower reservoir at the northwest corner of Route 313 and Fish Hatchery Road. Water from Simpson Springs was pumped south 1 mile to the upper reservoir on Bowen Hill. Gravity fed water the remaining 2 miles to the village. George McKie was the first president of CWW. The Hitchcock-Gottry family ran the CWW for over 80 years.

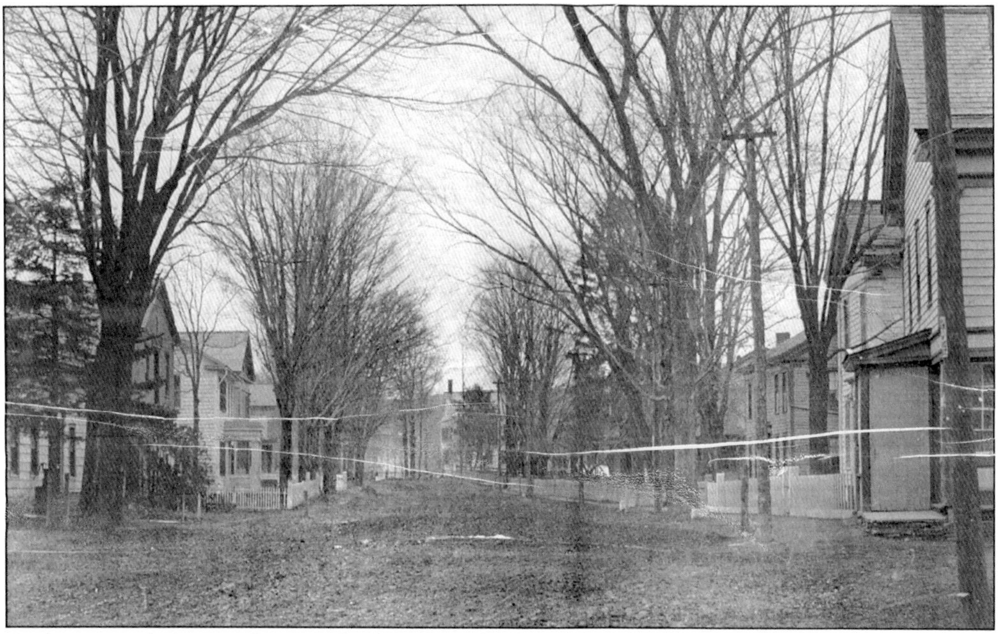

Coila was settled around 1763. The first store, built by James McGill around 1781, is the building closest and on the far right. The area was first known as Green Settlement and later Stephenson's Corner. The name Coila first appeared around 1850, when a post office opened there. The Scottish ancestry of the residents probably led to their naming their community Coila, after a muse in a Robert Burns poem. (Courtesy of Linda Lufkin Taylor.)

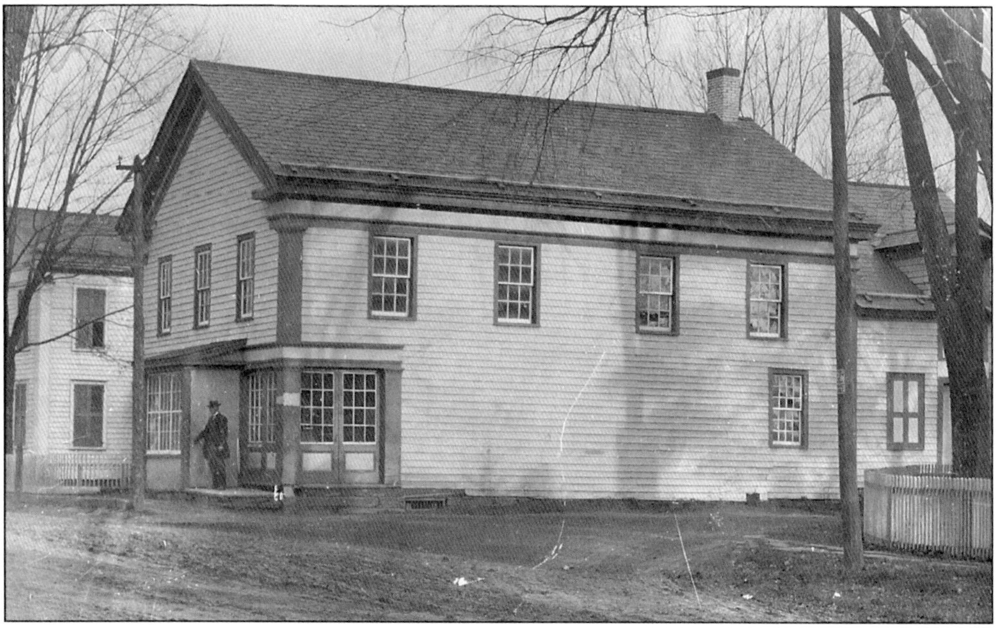

The Coila Store, once Stephenson's and later McNaughton and McNeill, still stands on the corner of Content Farms Road and New York Route 372. In 1852, Coila had two general stores, two blacksmith shops, a wagon shop, a harness and shoe shop, two schools, and a church. In 1866, Coila voted to remain independent and not join the Village of Cambridge. (Courtesy of Linda Lufkin Taylor.)

Katherine (Kitty) Hopkins, from Old Cambridge, was a devoted music educator and talented composer. She spent her life challenging barriers. She was the first woman in Saratoga County to earn an electrician's card. She was also the first female bugler hired at the tradition-rich Saratoga Race Course.

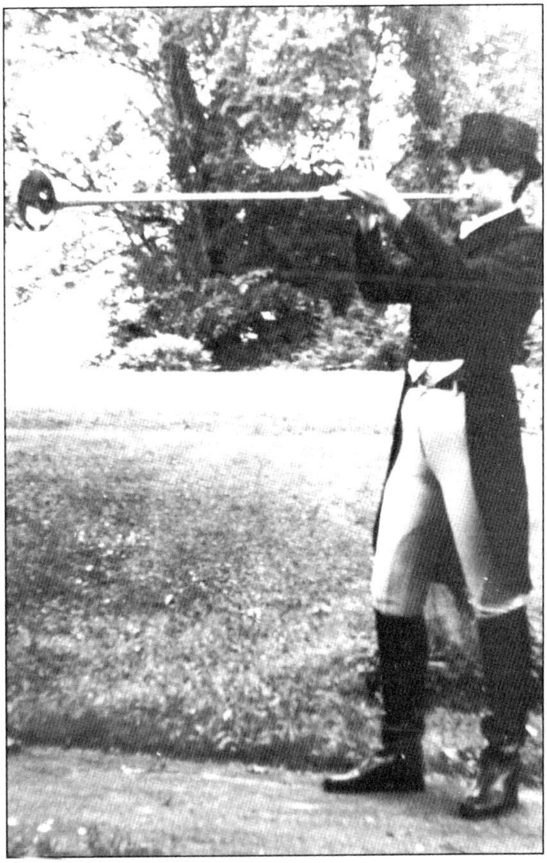

The 1940 Town of Jackson crew included, from left to right, McMorris, Beaty, Driggis, Green, Carney, and unidentified. One year earlier, Supt. Roland Lufkin left the town crew for his state job. (Courtesy of Linda Lufkin Taylor.)

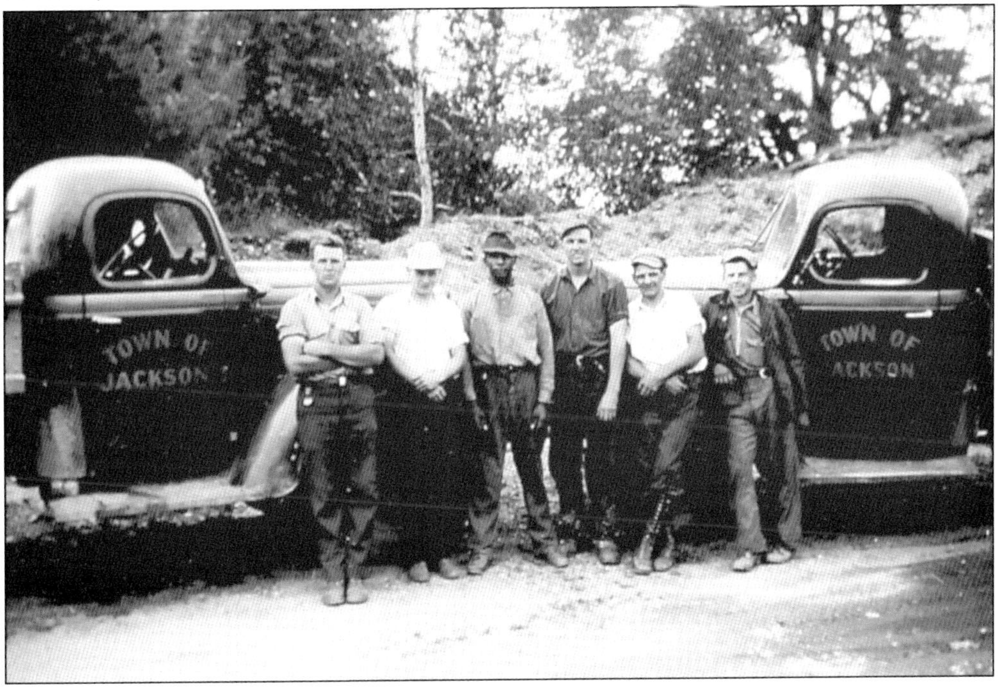

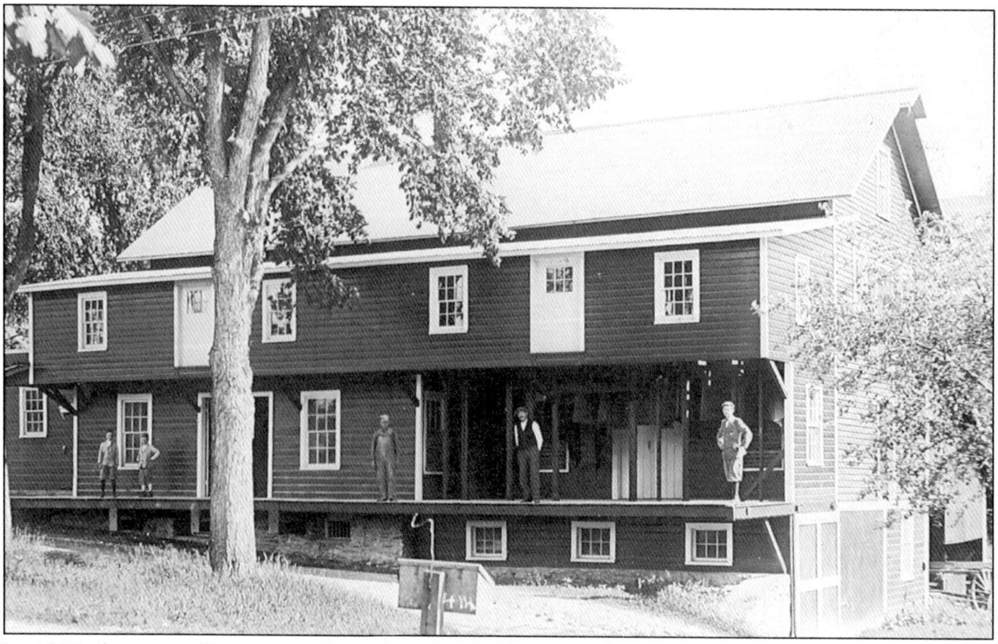

In 1910, the upper floor was enlarged at the Collamer Mill on Ash Grove Road. Woodworking continued in the mill until it burned in October 1929. The one-story building that replaced the mill continued operation until the late 1970s.

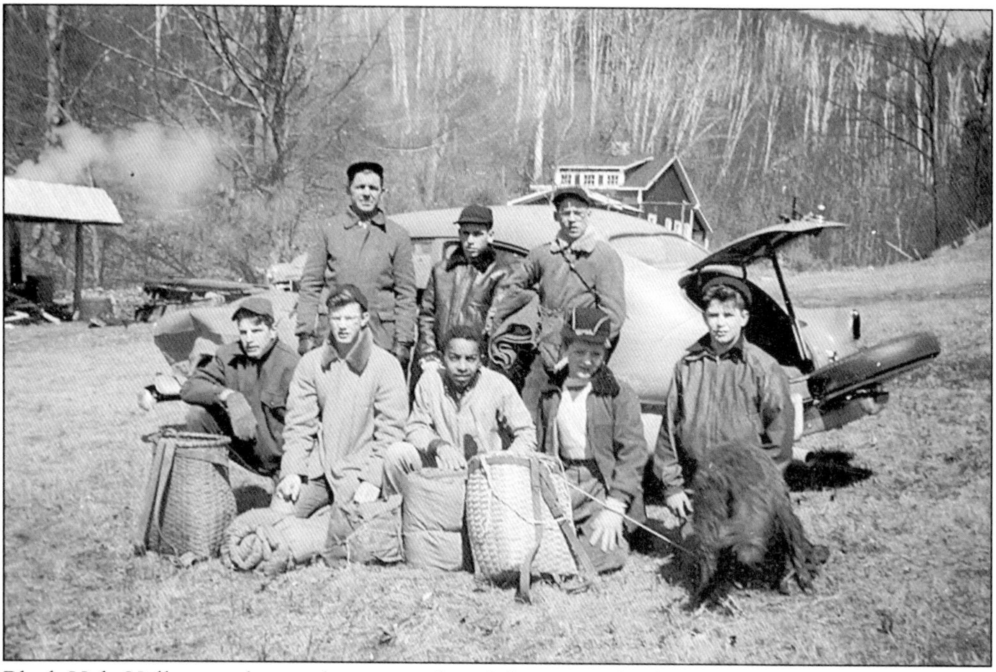

Black Hole Hollow, at the northeastern edge of the town of White Creek, lies in Vermont. It is serviced by the Cambridge Post Office since only mountain trails connect it to Vermont. In 1781, the Cambridge Valley voted to merge with Vermont. One year later, the Cambridge representatives left the Vermont Legislature, asking to be reinstated to Charlotte County (later Washington County) in New York State. (Courtesy CVA.)

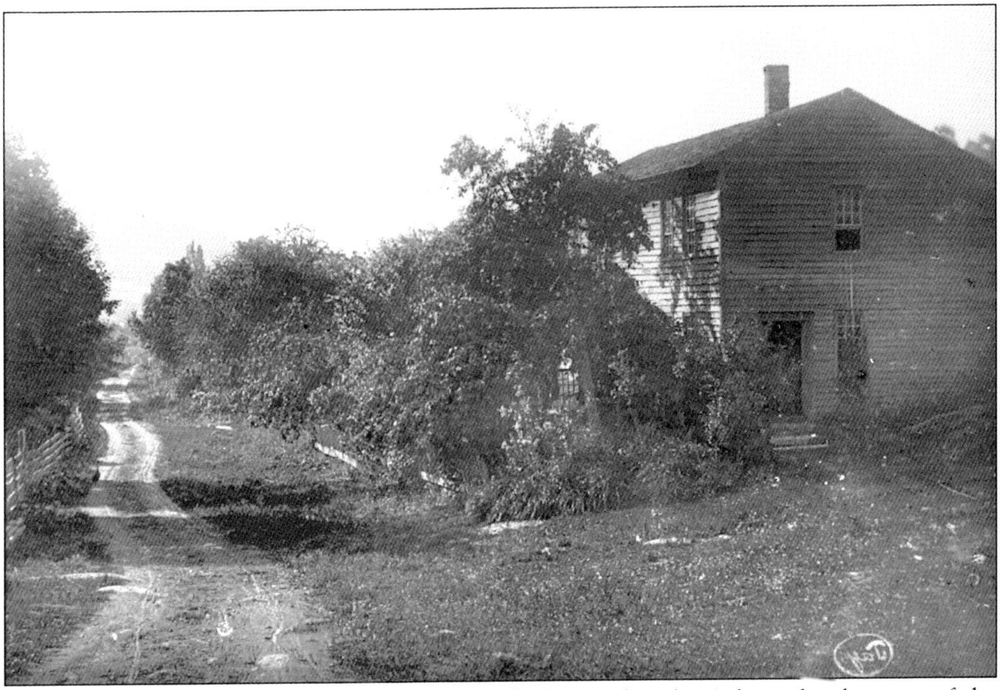

A portion of the Embury patent was named Ash Grove after the Ashton family, some of the original settlers. This early inn was on the coach route through Pumpkin Hook in Ashgrove to Bennington and points east. The trail was used by the Algonquian raiders in the French and Indian War. (Courtesy CVA.)

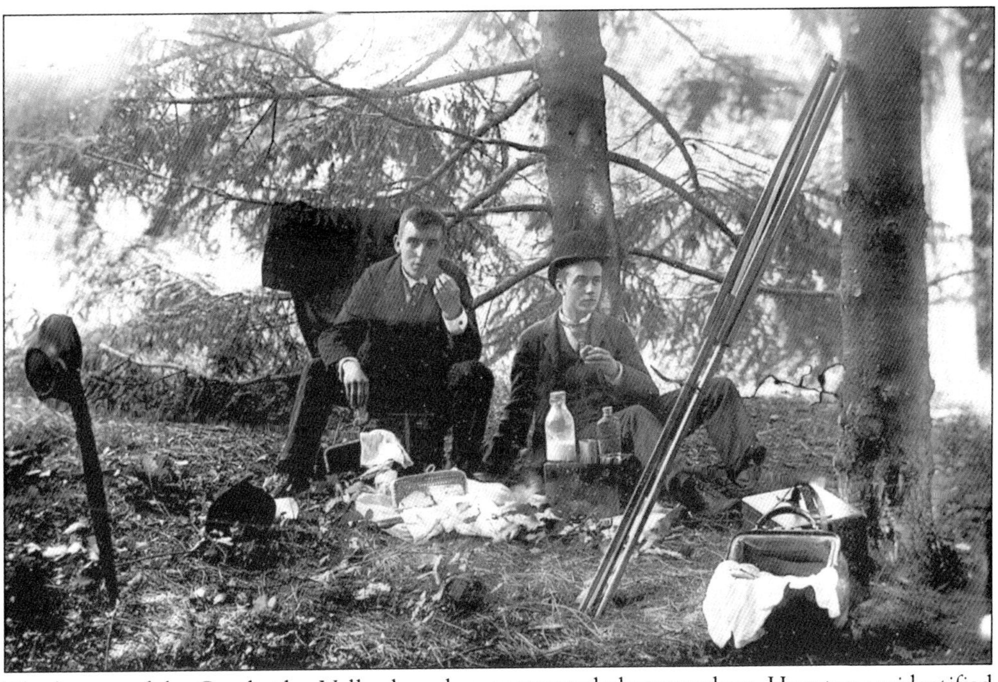

The beauty of the Cambridge Valley has always attracted photographers. Here two unidentified men set their equipment aside to enjoy a lunch in White Creek. (Courtesy CVA.)

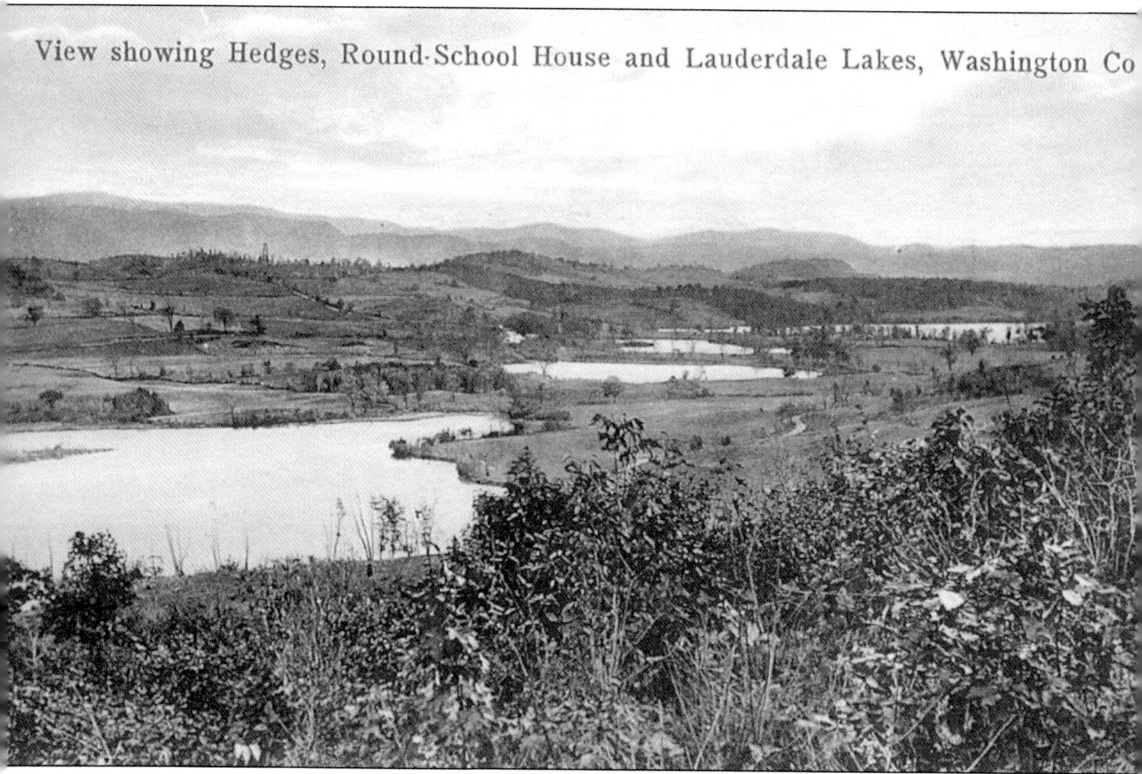

A portion of the town of Jackson was long referred to as Pond Valley. Looking southeastward, Hedges Lake (Big Pond) is in the foreground, and Lake Lauderdale (Long Pond) is in the distance. In between are Dead Pond and Schoolhouse Pond. The beautiful hills of the Annaquasacoke patent are in the background. The Owl Kill River runs out of the south end of Lake Lauderdale.

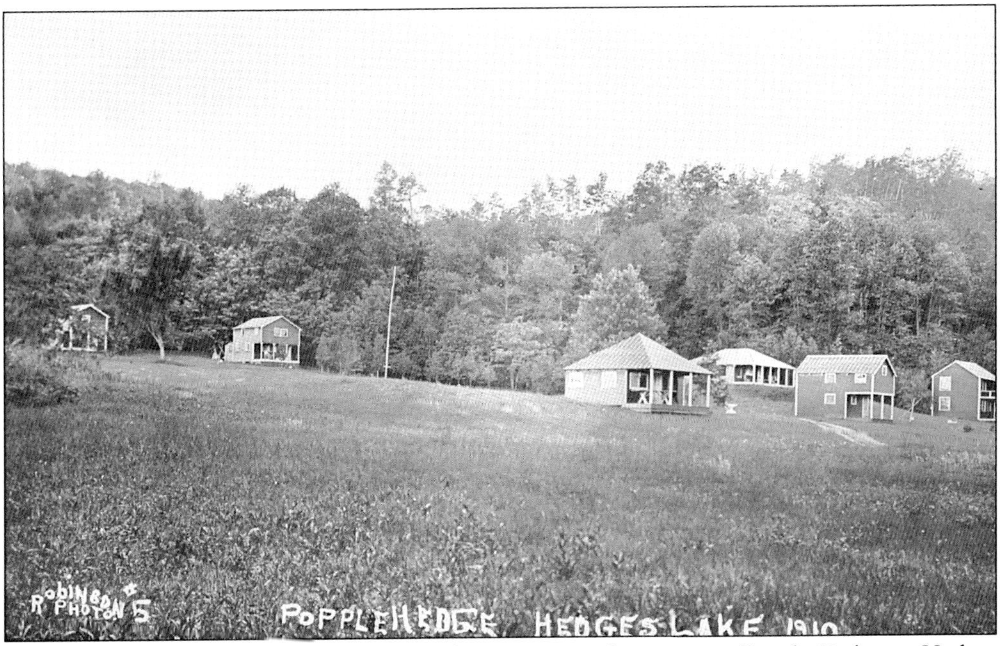

In the early 1900s, O. B. Cleveland supplied ice cream to the camps at Popple Hedge on Hedges Lake. The ice cream traveled to Shushan by railroad, from where Cleveland would take it to the lake in his buggy.

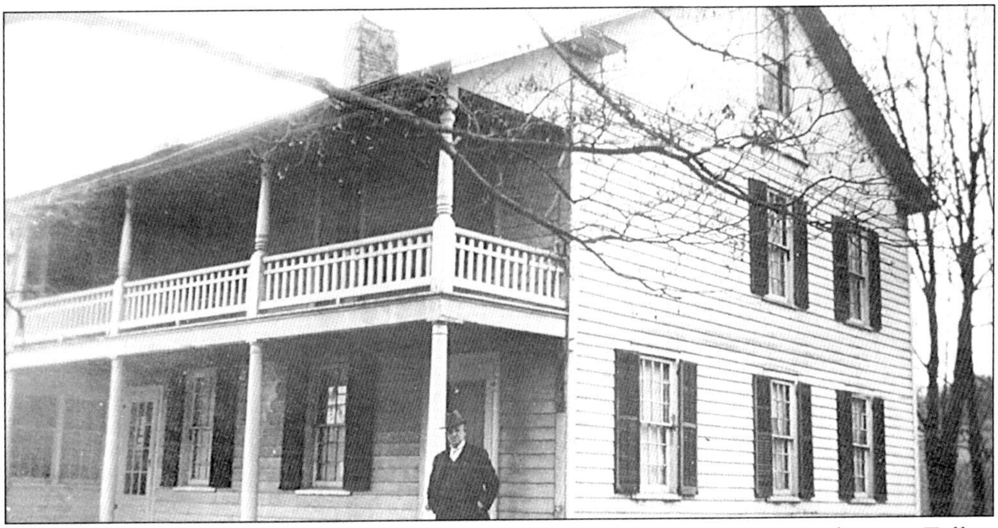

A. Jay Tefft poses by the house on the north end of Hedges Lake. Tefft, the son of Martin Tefft, a Cambridge dentist, published the *Cambridge Enterprise* newspaper in the 1870s. At one time, the newspaper office was above the post office at the northwest corner of Main and Broad Streets. (Courtesy of Katherine Wilkinson.)

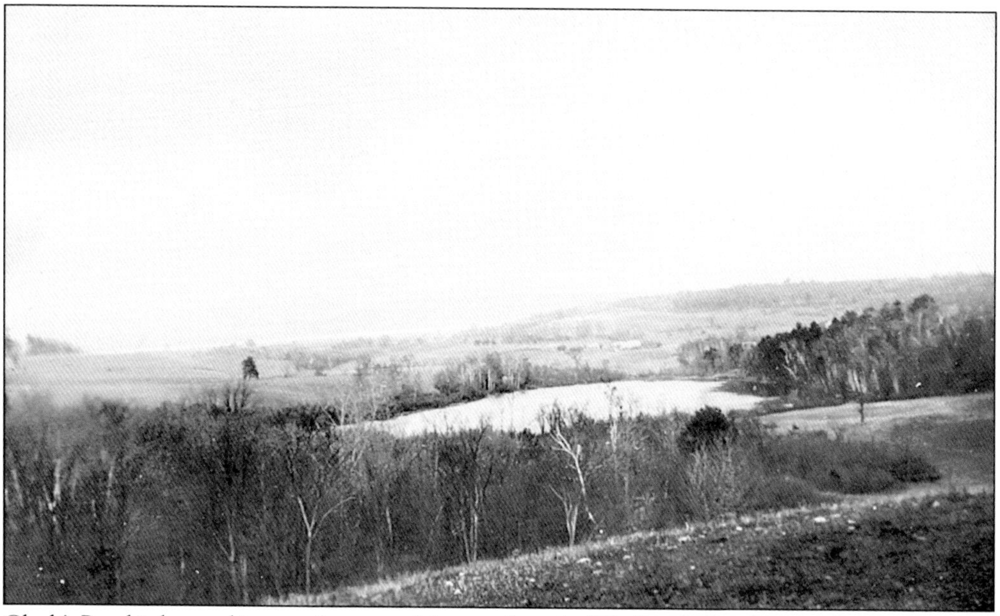

Clark's Pond is located just to the east of the north end of Hedges Lake. Once called Little Pond, it was originally connected to Hedges Lake. When the flax mill on Scotch Hill dammed the brook, Hedges Lake dropped 40 to 60 feet, creating the new pond.

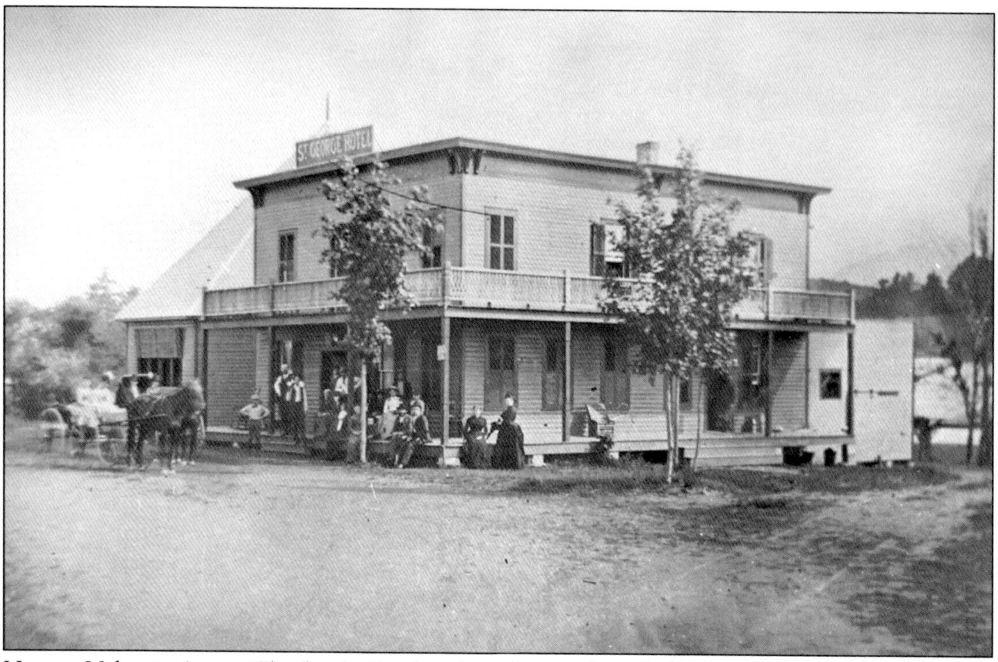

Harvey Valentine's son, Charles, built a hotel on the south end of Lake Lauderdale around 1880. When it was destroyed by fire in 1890, it was rebuilt as the St. George Hotel. A portion of the octagonal dance hall can be seen on the left. (Courtesy CVA.)

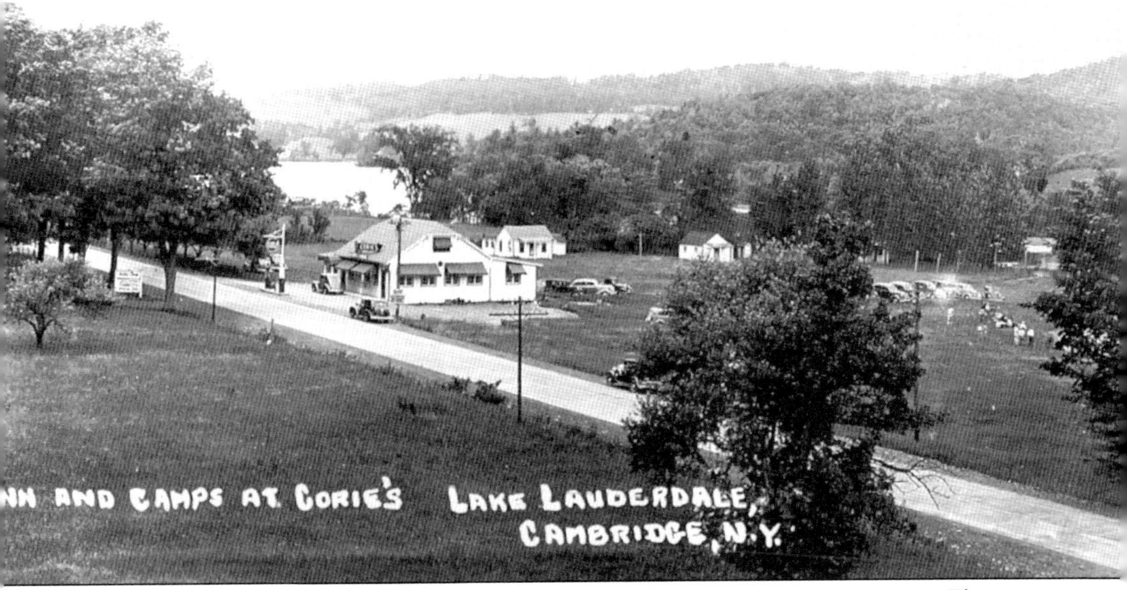

The southern end of Lake Lauderdale has always attracted many summertime visitors. This area was the home of the Lauderdale Fair in the 1880s. The fair was purchased and moved to the north edge of Cambridge village in 1891, where it was renamed the Cambridge Fair. The Valentine family operated a side-wheel steamboat on the lake.

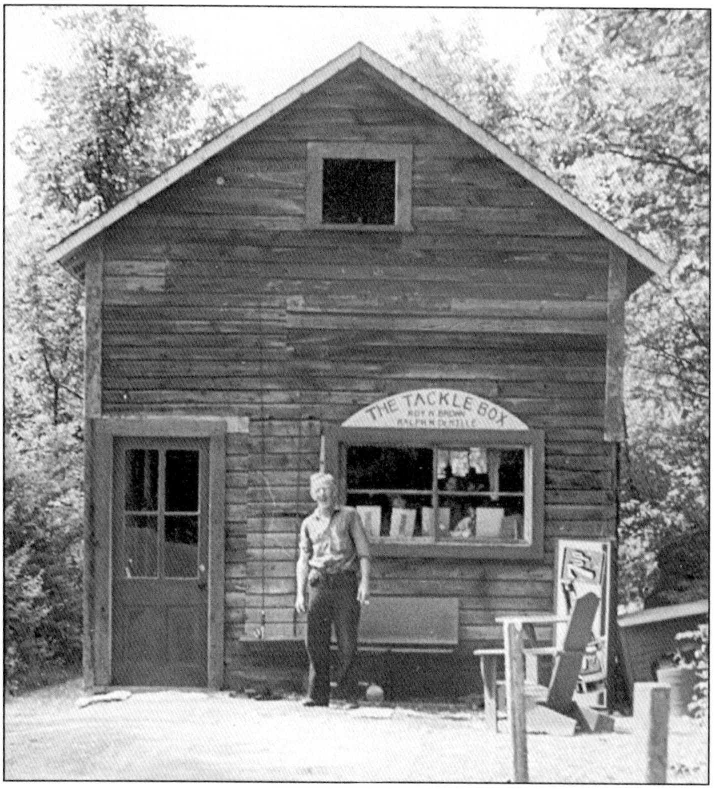

No visit to Cambridge would be complete without a fishing trip on the Battenkill, and no fishing trip in the 1960s would be complete without a visit with Roy Brown. After a morning's fish, a cheeseburger at the Tackle Box was a perfect lunchtime treat. Over the door, Roy proudly displayed what he called the largest fish ever taken from the Battenkill.

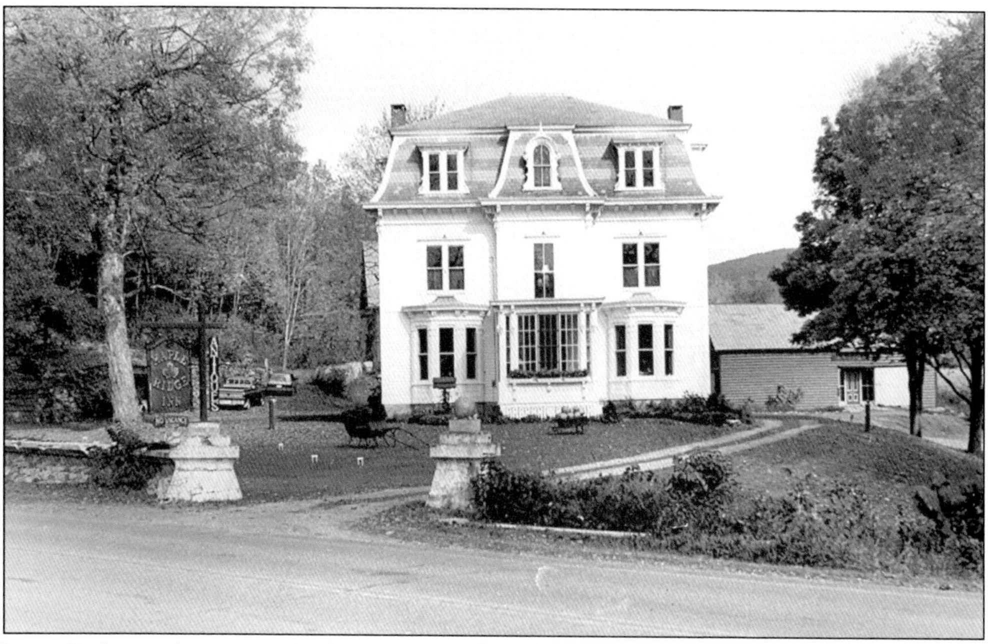

James Robertson's estate, today known as Maple Ridge, was at the northern edge of Coila across from his tannery pond. A second tannery pond was at the southern edge of Coila where Cambridge Creek flows into the village. Animal remains were dumped in the creek, eventually getting trapped at Blakeley's dam behind the old school and creating foul orders throughout the village.

The Northern Turnpike Company was incorporated in 1799 to build a road from Lansingburgh to Granville. A marble mileage marker was placed every mile along the 53-mile route. The markers in the Cambridge Valley were encased in a stone frame. Three such markers like the one shown here are still present. The daily stage traffic on the turnpike helped the financial development of Cambridge.

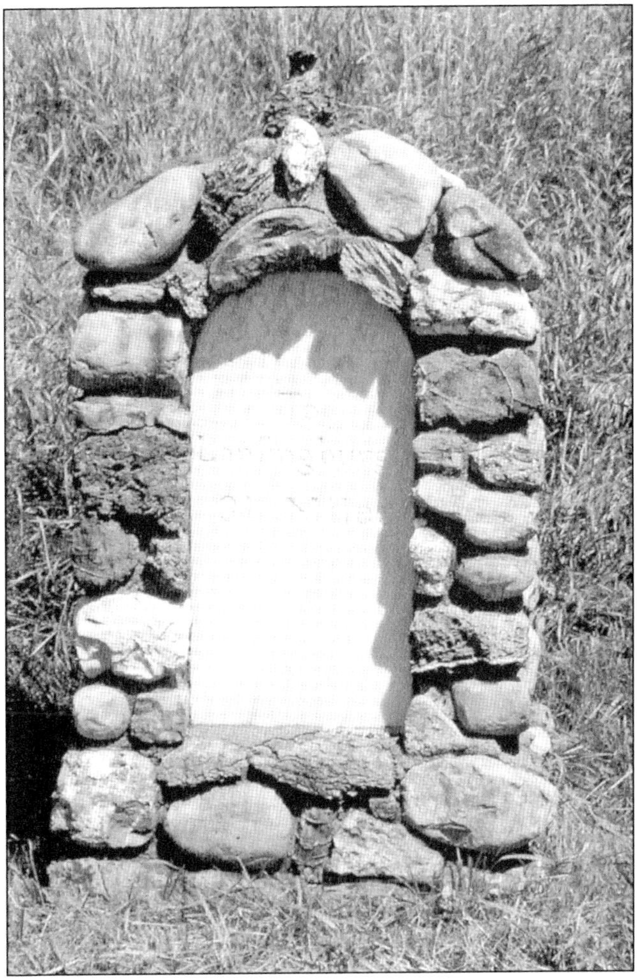

The town of White Creek had 16 one-room schoolhouses in 1866. Several stand today, most as private residences. School district No. 14 at the junction of Turnpike Road and Duell Hollow serves as the house of worship for the Gospel Lighthouse congregation. (Courtesy CVA.)

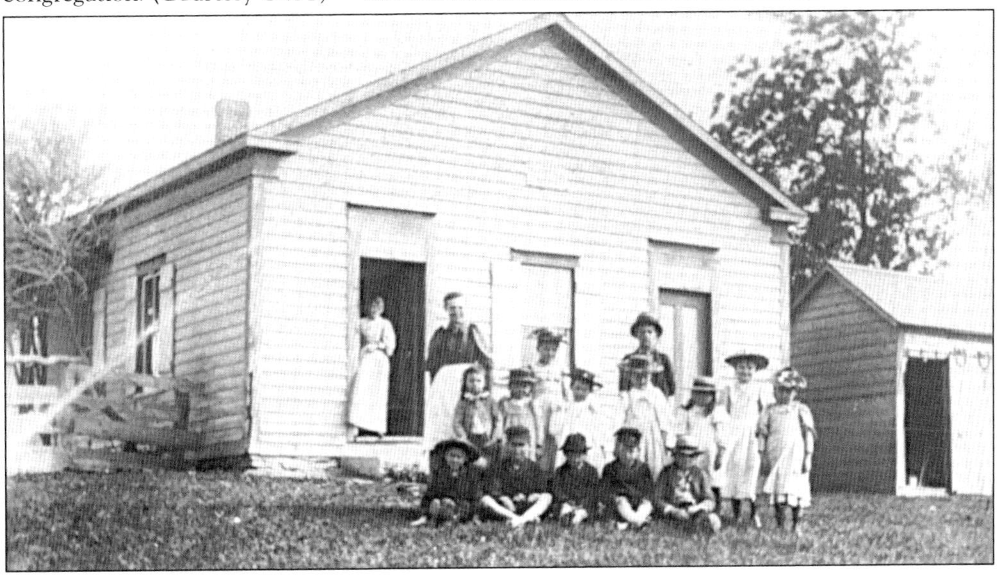

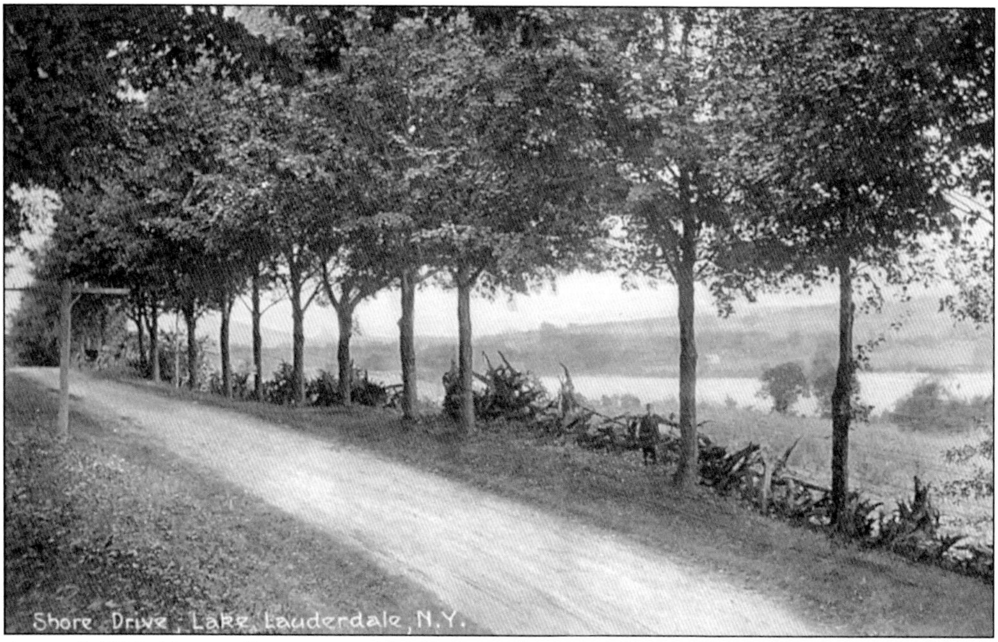

Around 1900, Horace Bump owned land along the west side of Lake Lauderdale, an area still referred to by old-timers as Bump's Hill. He sold some land to Mr. Rockwell, who later sold to Edwin Cornell. On this land, Cornell built the first camp on the lake. Cornell's daughter, Elsa, married Malcolm Parrish in 1917. They took over the camps, which remain in the Parrish family today.

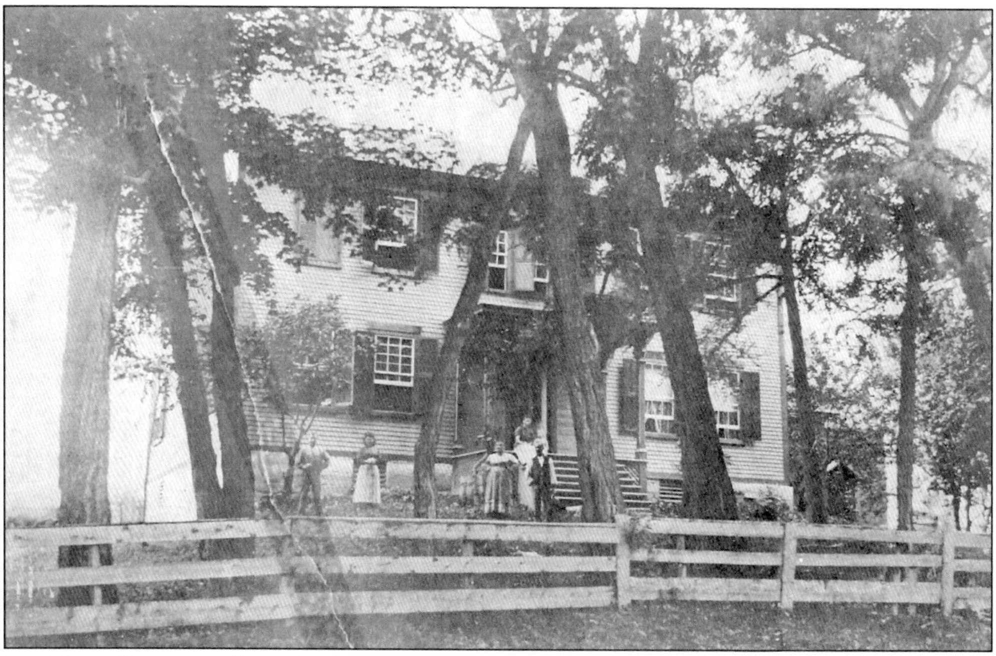

Paul Cornell was a nephew of White Creek pioneer John Allen. They built a gristmill near White Creek village that Cornell later converted to the Washington Company factory. Cornell was a Master Mason, allocating one room in his house as their meeting hall. (Courtesy CPL.)

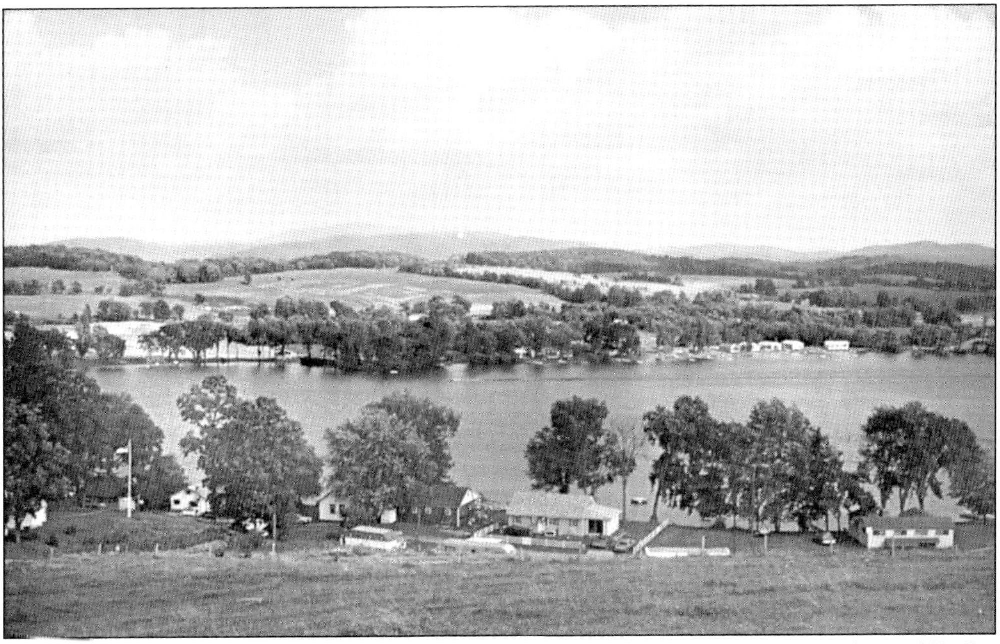

In the 1960s, Gordon Nesbitt's pavilion on Hedges Lake had record hops on Tuesday and Friday from 8:30 p.m. to midnight and roller-skating the other nights. The pavilion was open from May 25 until October 1 and served as home for the community swimming lessons program.

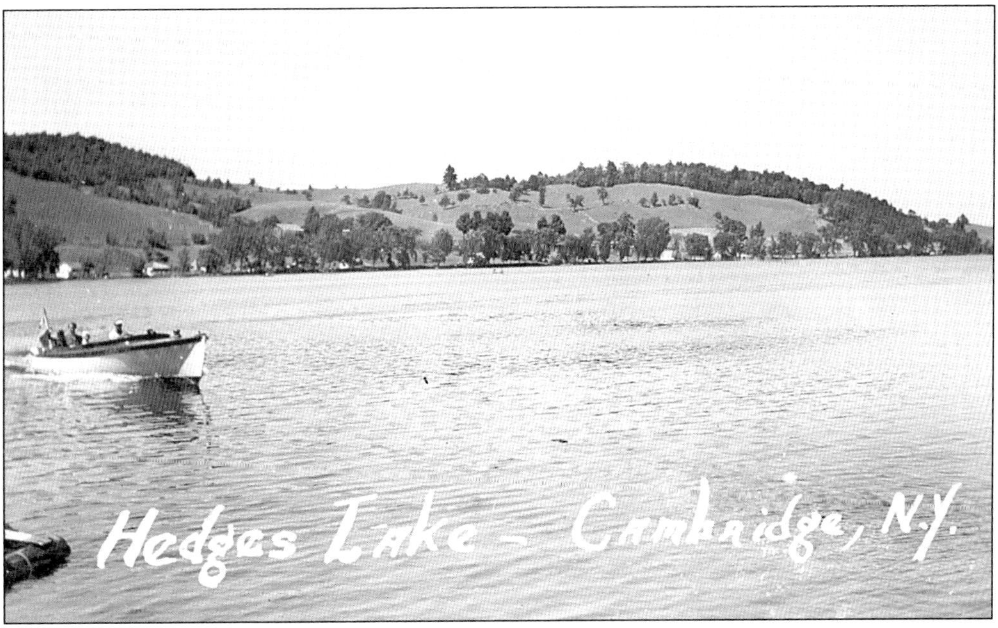

The tree-bare hills of the town of Jackson in the background were the result of vast sheep farming. Jackson was the largest wool producer in the county, and one of the largest in the state. Shortly after the Declaration of Independence was signed, a contest was held to identify the best woolen cloth made in the new nation. Scott Woodward of Cambridge won the $40 first prize.

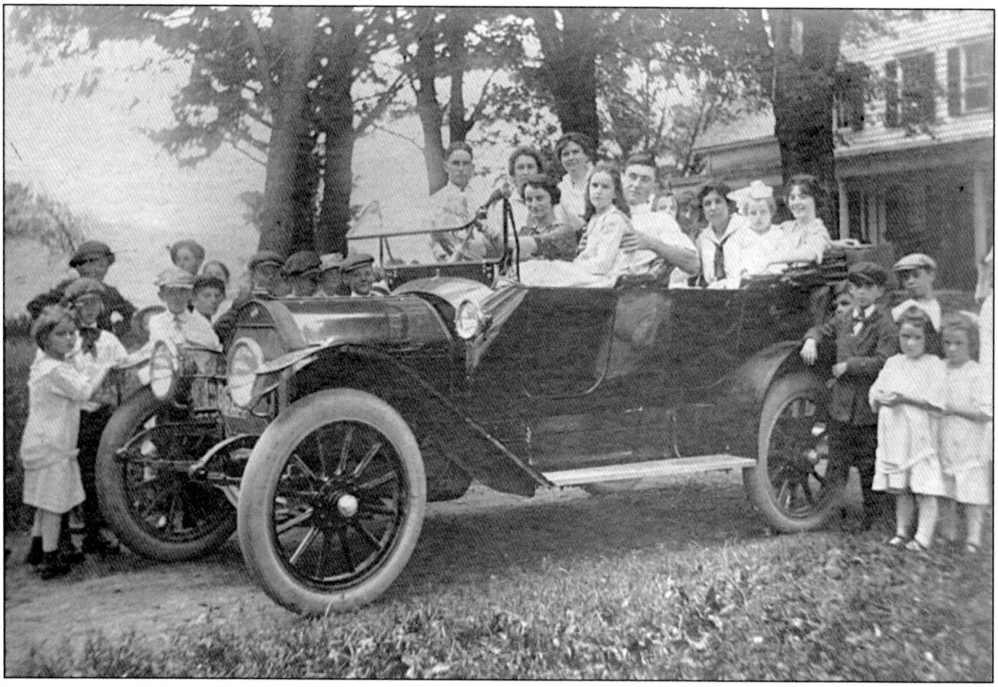

In the early 1900s, the St. Patrick's Church picnic was held at the Geary farm in Ash Grove. The farm was originally the McKie farm, leading to multiple names for the same road: Geary Hill Road and McKie Hollow Road. (Courtesy CVA.)

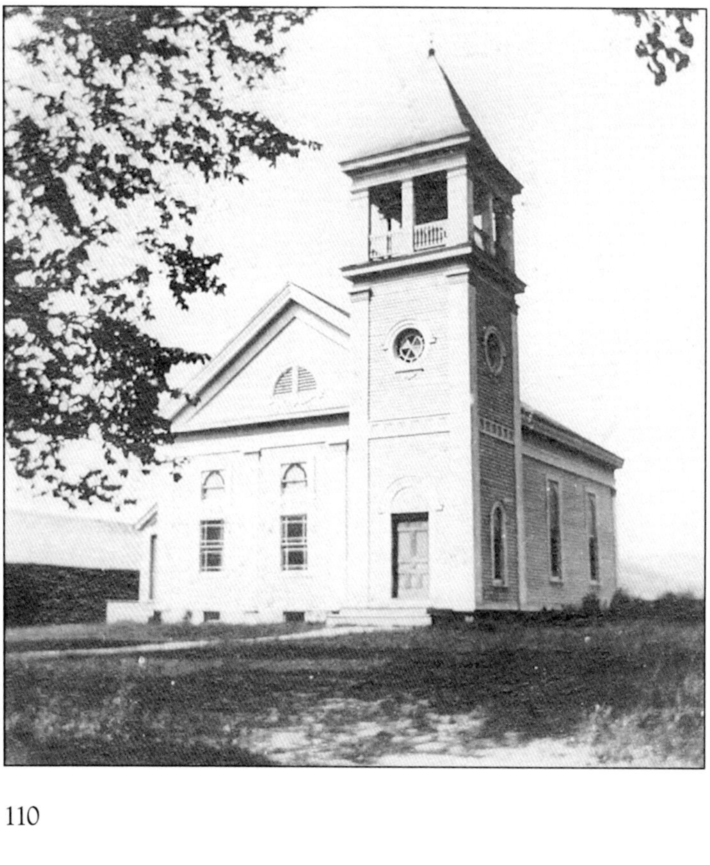

In 1796, the village of White Creek began the Cambridge Church, or Union House. Completed in 1807, the church was used by many denominations. The Baptists were the first, as Elder Waite had moved the original congregation to Waite's Corners after the war. Other co-occupants of Jermain Hall, as the building was also called, were the Methodists, who organized in White Creek in 1831 rather than remain associated with the Methodists in Ash Grove.

Five

PARADES

Cambridge loves its parades. People from the three towns and the numerous small communities always come together when it is time for a parade. The firemen and the bands can always be counted on to march, as can the local government, sports, and social organizations.

In 1916, Cambridge's Old Home Week celebrated the alignment of three special anniversaries: the 100th anniversary of the creation of the towns of White Creek and Jackson, the 50th anniversary of the creation of the village of Cambridge, and the 25th anniversary of the creation of the Cambridge Union School. The celebration included one of Cambridge's finest parades, rivaling the Floral Parades held during the initial years of the great Cambridge Fair.

Parades serve to document the community since everyone takes photographs of their friends and family marching. The buildings in the background of the photographs are often the only reminders of places long-ago destroyed by fire or progress.

Today a Santa Parade kicks off the December holiday season. The "kids from 1 to 92" line Main Street to rush to collect the candy being tossed by Santa and his number one helper, the mayor. Future generations will learn much about the community from the photographs of today's parades.

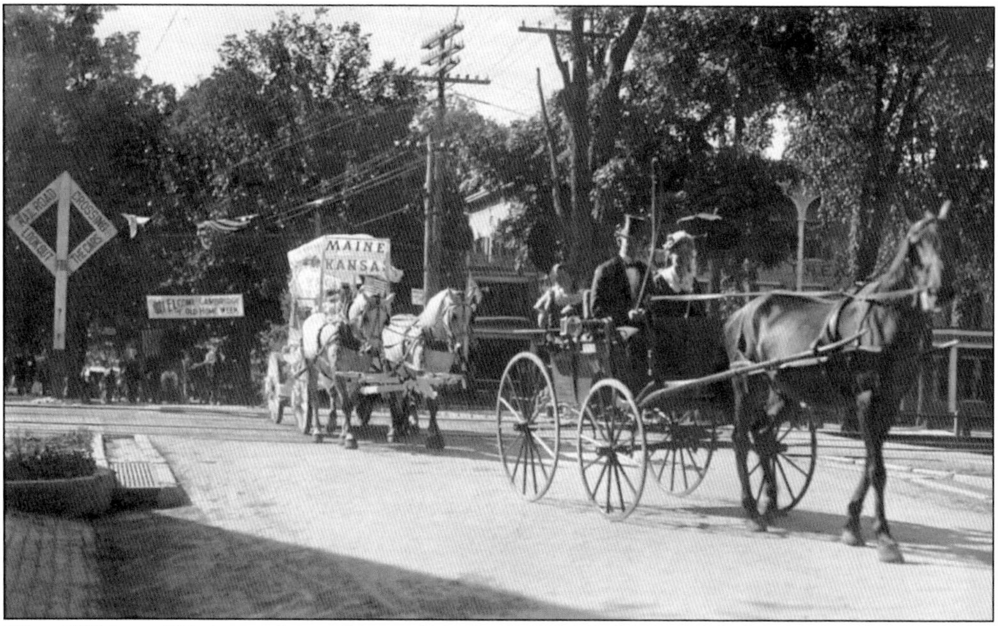

The Old Home Week parade, on September 12, 1916, started at Academy Street and ended at the Cambridge Fairgrounds. The order of entries in the parade matched the time line of Cambridge's history: the Native Americans, a Puritan minister, the Checkered House, George Washington and the DAR, stagecoaches, carriages, Abraham Lincoln, fire department, Cambridge Valley band, and finally, motorcars. (Courtesy CPL.)

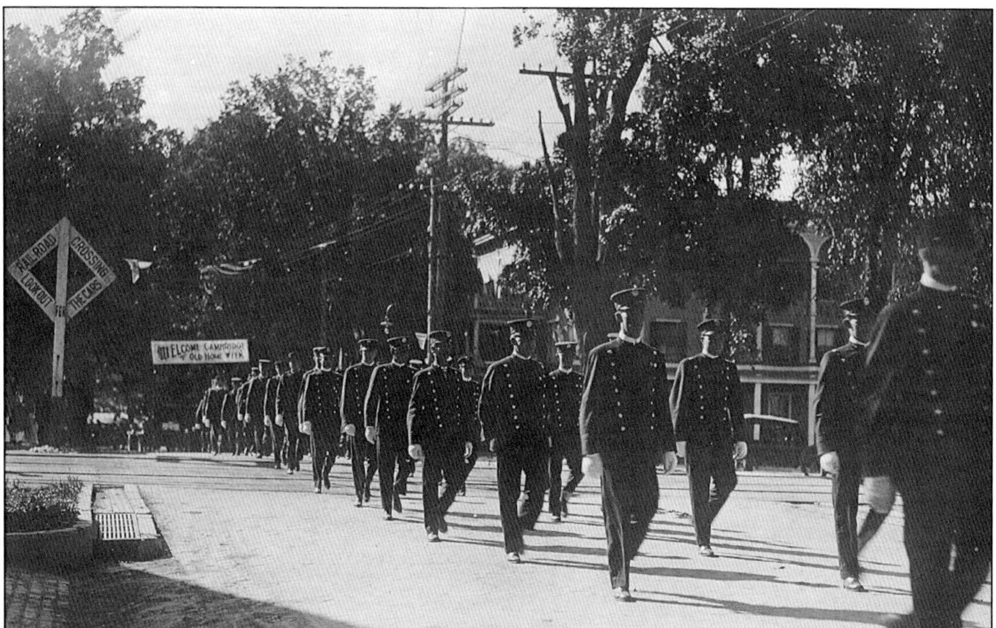

The idea of Old Home Week was conceived by Rev. John R. Fisher. He served on the executive committee with Robert Law, George McFarland, David Sheridan, and Frank Richardson. The trees lining Main Street were planted 40 years before, during the 1876 centennial celebration. (Courtesy CPL.)

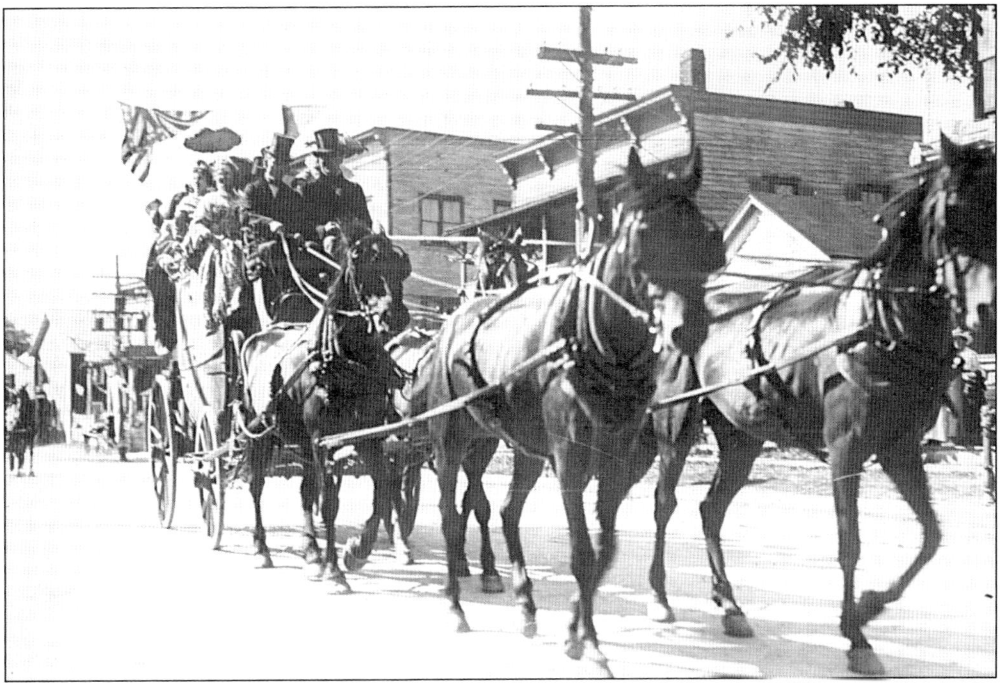

This stage passes through the West End during the 1916 Old Home Week parade. This entry in the parade represented the early 1800s, when stagecoach traffic along the Northern Turnpike passed through Cambridge Corners. This traffic gave rise to hotels and livery stables, helping Cambridge prosper. (Courtesy CPL.)

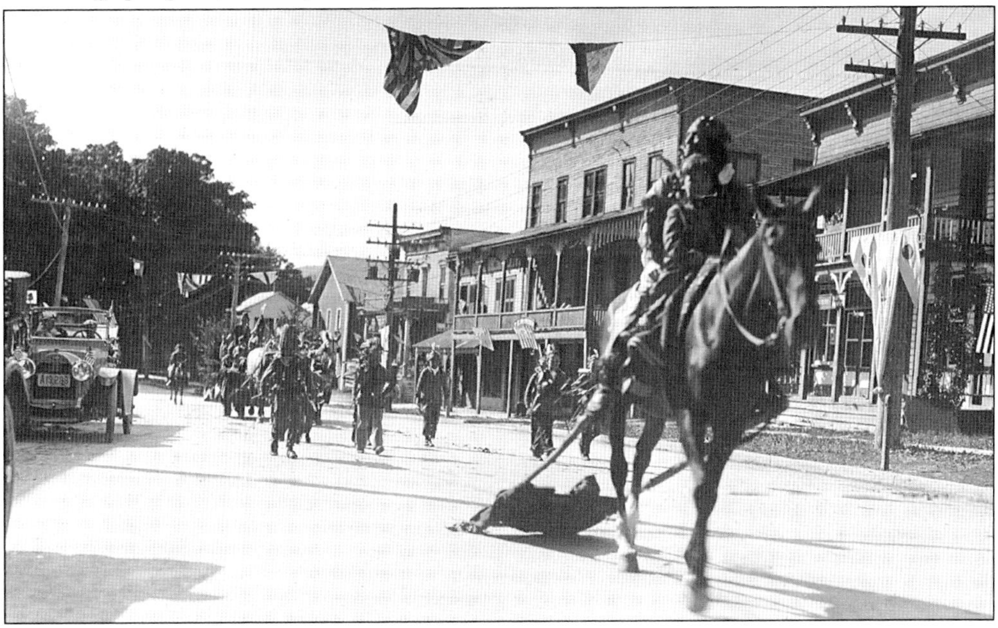

Parade photographs serve to document buildings. The tall building in the center shows how the West End Market looked in 1916. The building to the left strides the Cambridge Creek and housed the Larmon Hose Company No. 2 in 1910. The three buildings to the left of the market and the one to the right no longer adorn the West End. (Courtesy CPL.)

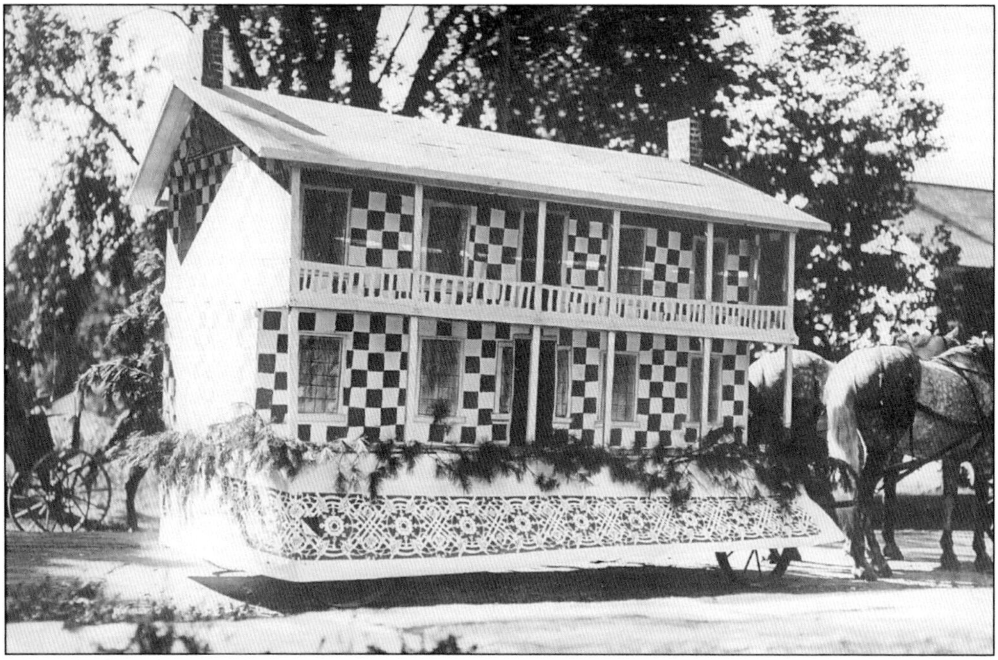

The Checkered House float was near the front of the 1916 Old Home Week parade, celebrating its honor as one of the oldest local landmarks. The Cowden Tavern, built around 1765, was used by General Baum as his headquarters on August 15, 1777, the eve of the Battle of Bennington. After the war, the clapboards on all sides were painted in large squares of red and white. (Courtesy CPL.)

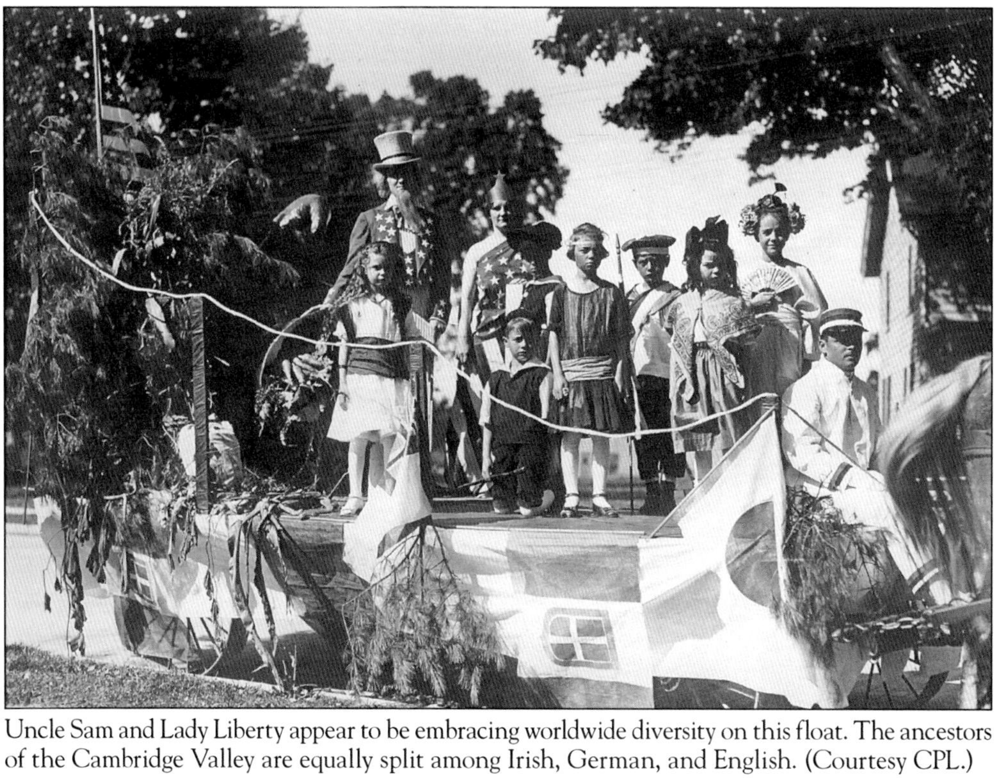

Uncle Sam and Lady Liberty appear to be embracing worldwide diversity on this float. The ancestors of the Cambridge Valley are equally split among Irish, German, and English. (Courtesy CPL.)

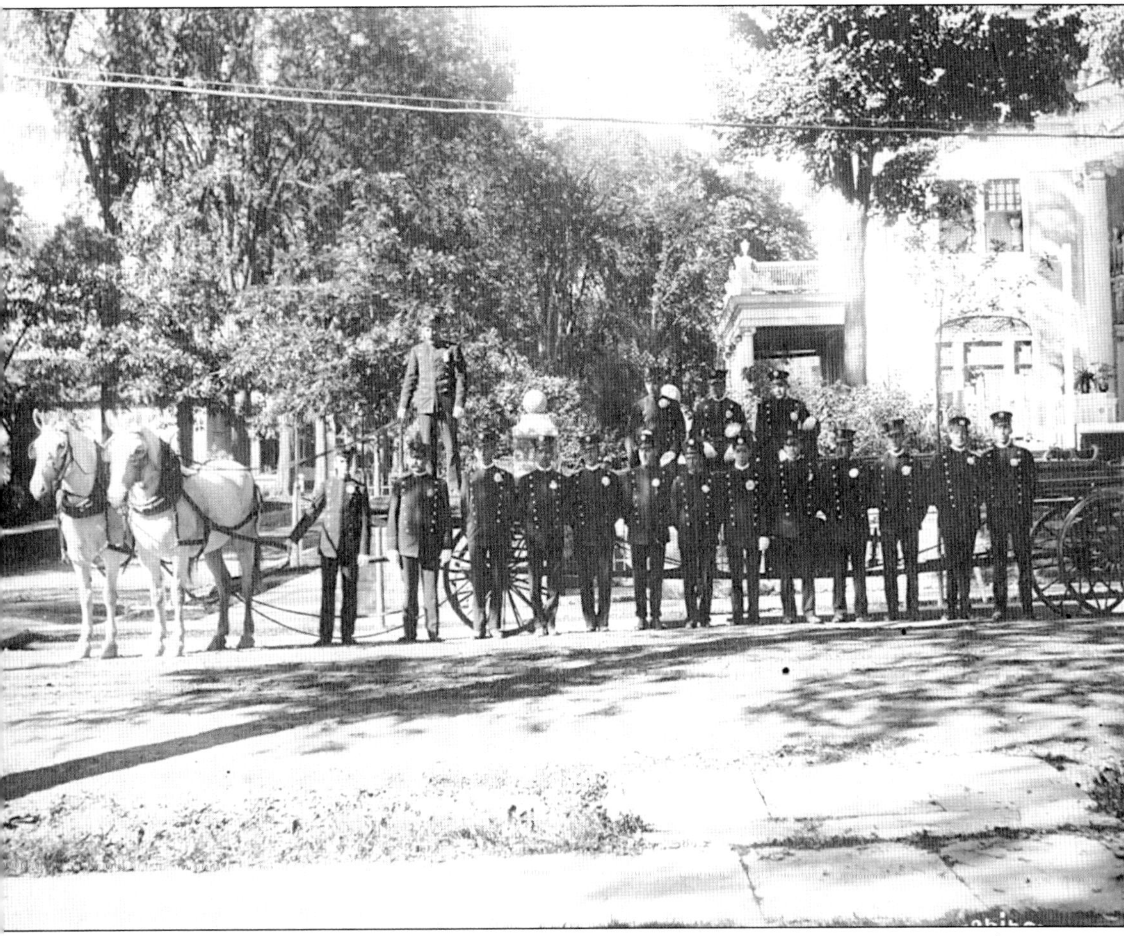

The Cambridge Hook and Ladder Company No. 1, organized in the 1870s, is shown around 1910 in parade uniform with its equipment, a hand-drawn ladder truck. The Hooks were famous for their annual minstrel shows of nostalgic recollection. Although disbanded around 1931 when the Cambridge Fire Department was formed, the Hooks continued as a social group. When they finally ceased in 1954, their last act was to donate their treasury to the United Presbyterian Church for its Carillon Fund. How fitting that the Hooks helped finance the replacement of the old church bells, which for many years called them to the fire station. When the Cambridge Water Works was completed in 1886, the Hooks helped certify each hydrant capable of pumping 50 feet in the air. The testing began at Dorr's Corners. When testing reached Park Street, cheers erupted as water sailed over the Irving House (brick hotel). On South Union Street, the last hydrant tested failed. Sabotage was discovered, wood and stone was removed, and the hydrant passed.

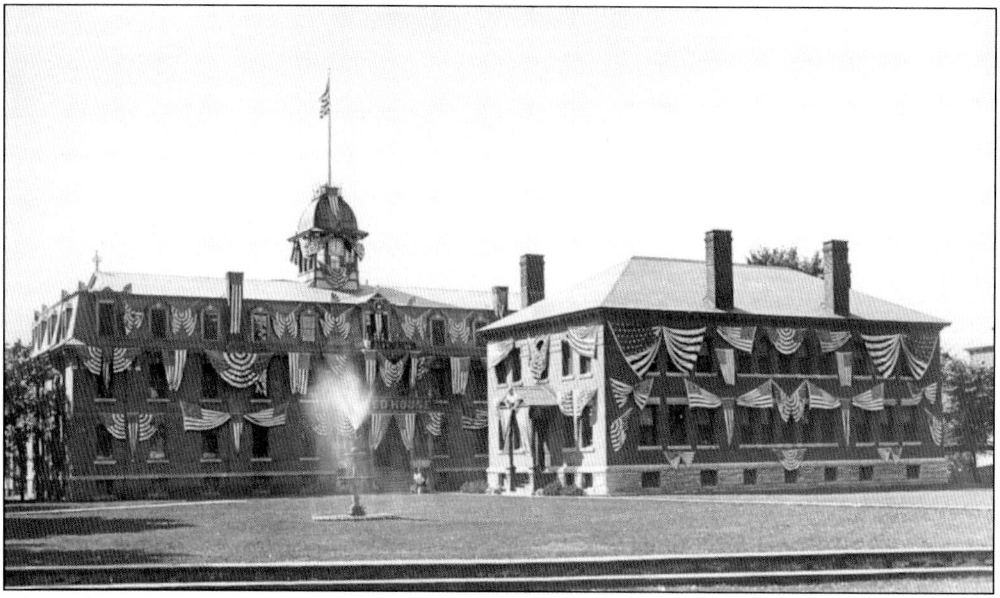

The Old Home Week celebration kicked off with historical sermons in each of the local churches. A Sunday afternoon ceremony on the lawn of the Rice Seed Company featured New York State congressman William Bennett. The *Washington County Post* described the scene as such: "A day more beautiful, air more bracing, a view over the hill and valley more charming Cambridge never saw." (Courtesy CPL.)

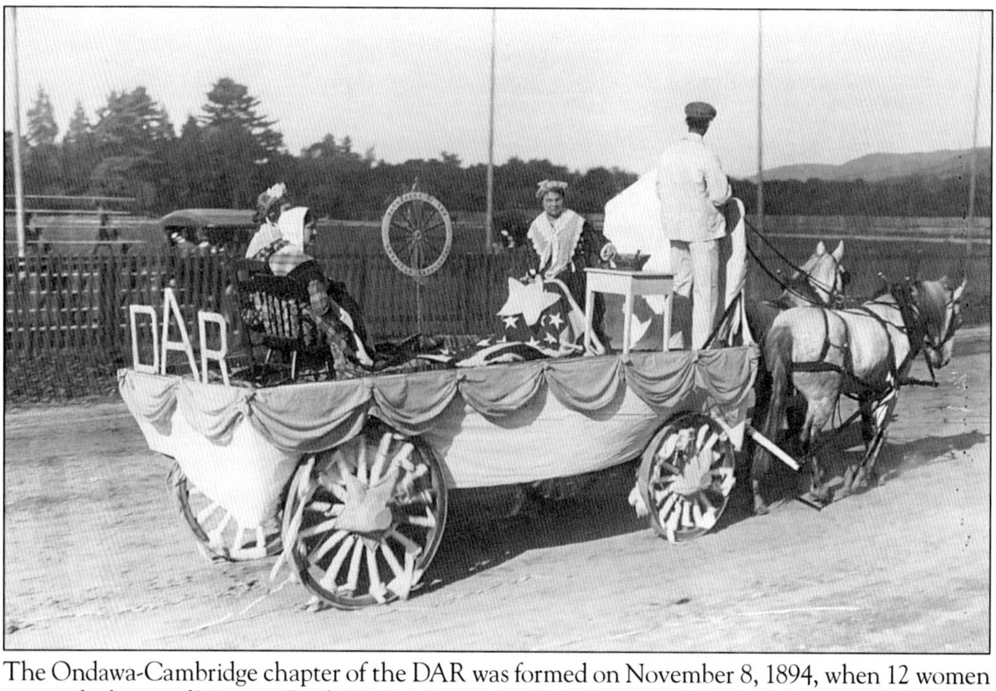

The Ondawa-Cambridge chapter of the DAR was formed on November 8, 1894, when 12 women met at the home of Minerva Buck McKie. It was the 12th chapter in New York State and the 125th in the nation. Their entry in the 1916 Old Home Week parade, shown navigating the racetrack at the Cambridge Fairgrounds, followed the George Washington float, as entries appeared in chronological order. (Courtesy CPL.)

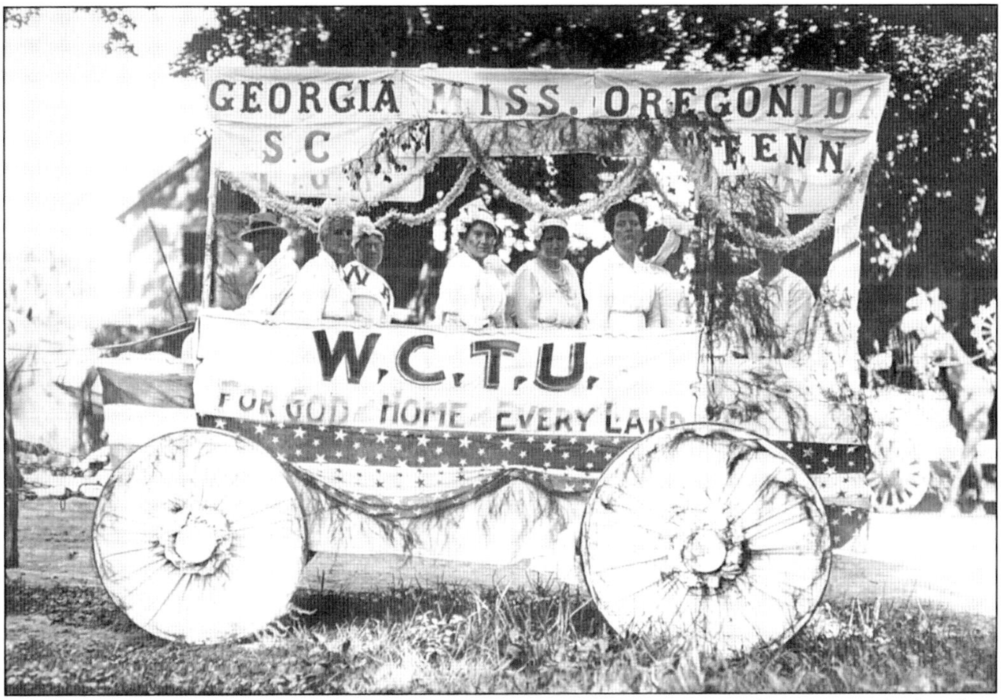

The Women's Christian Temperance Union (WCTU) celebrated the 19 dry states with this float in the 1916 Old Home Week parade. The WCTU in Cambridge was organized on May 25, 1879, six years after the national foundation in Evanston, Illinois. Initially there were 56 members in the Cambridge chapter, with Mrs. Frances Gray Blinn serving as president. Key members in 1916 included Mrs. J. J. Gray and Mrs. J. B. Rice Jr. (Courtesy CPL.)

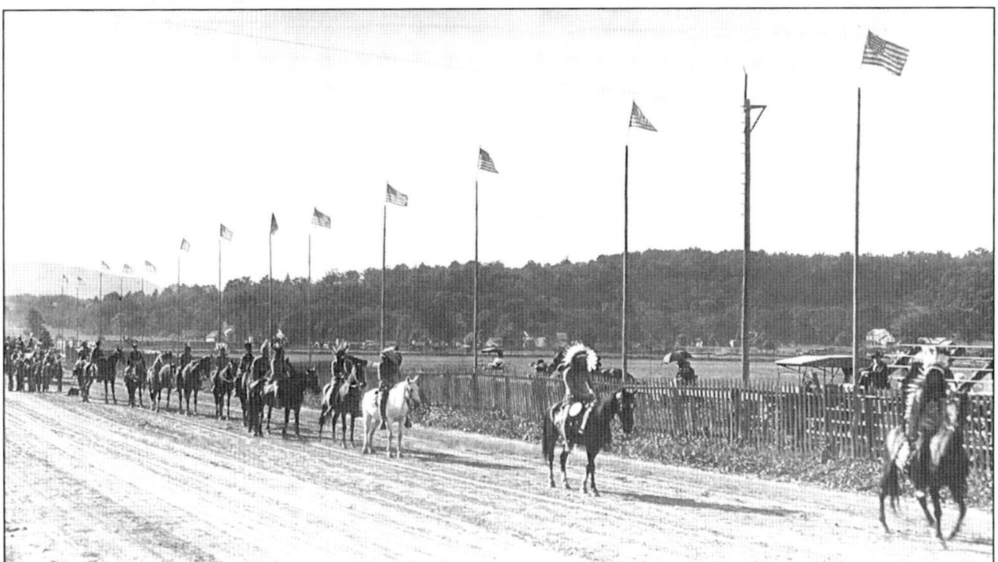

This book focuses on the Cambridge Valley, from the Revolution War forward. However, much has been recorded elsewhere about prewar history, including the Native Americans. Because of their impact on the early development of Cambridge, the Native Americans led the Old Home Week parade. (Courtesy CPL.)

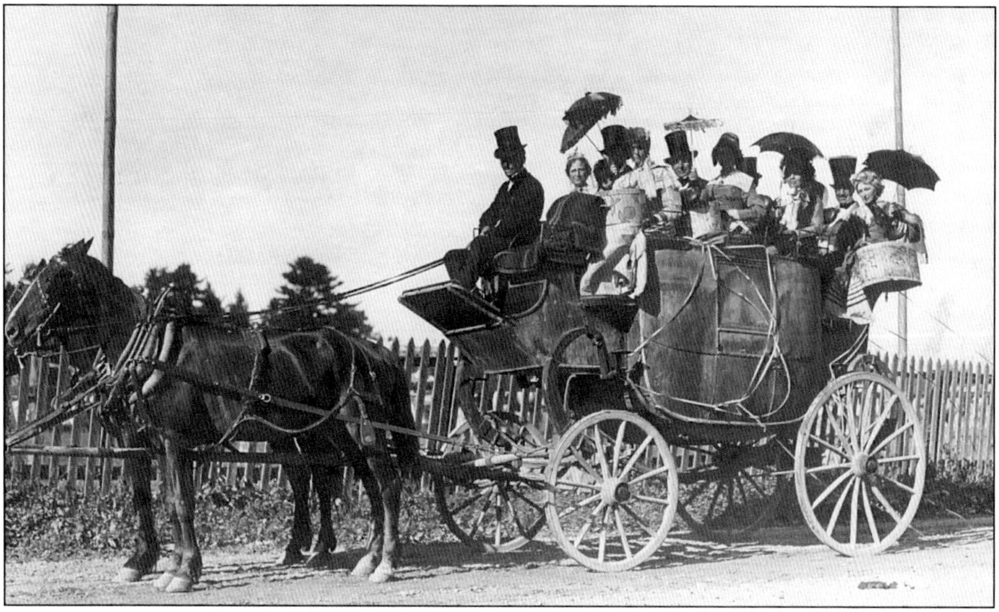

Distinguished local men and women probably raided their parents' and grandparents' attics as they donned vintage attire for the 1916 Old Home Week parade. Over 8,000 people attended the ceremonies in Fuller's Grove on the west side of South Park Street. Originally, a Children's Parade had been scheduled also. This was cancelled due to widespread fear caused by an outbreak of infantile paralysis in Brooklyn in early summer. (Courtesy CPL.)

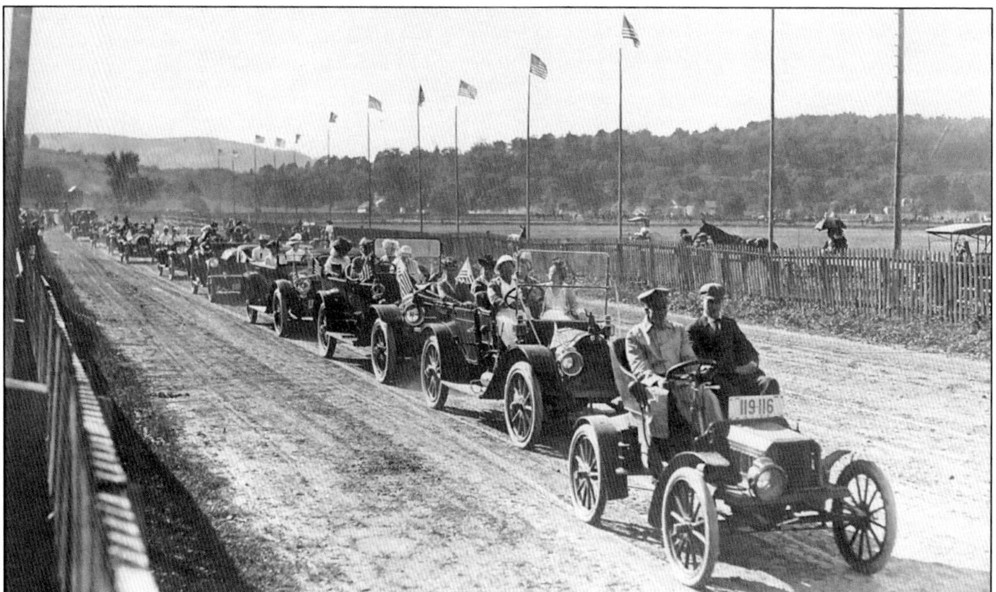

The entries in the 1916 Old Home Week parade appeared in chronological order, beginning with Native Americans and ending with motorcars. Even the motorcars appeared to line up by age. In the distance on the right, Woodlands Cemetery can be seen. In the distance on the left is Academy Hill, where Robert McClellan had recently announced plans to build a hospital in honor of his mother, Mary. (Courtesy CPL.)

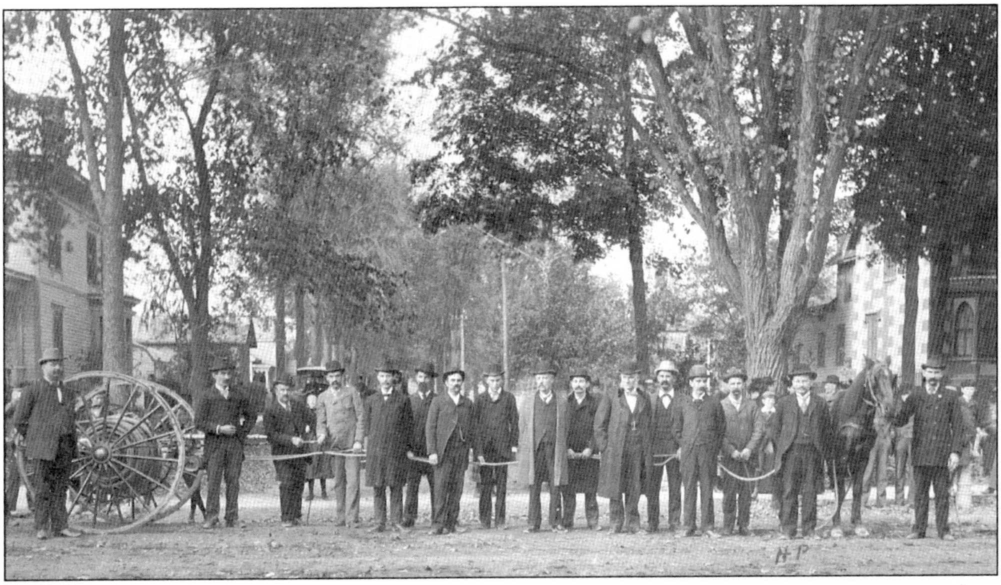

Hiram Parrish stands second from the right with the Hallelujah Hose Company No. 3. When the fire company was formed in 1887, the name was left blank on the form. The company soon garnered its nickname since many of the local clergy were charter members. In the background on the right is John Crocker's house, which was later torn down by J. B. Rice to build his mansion. (Courtesy CVA.)

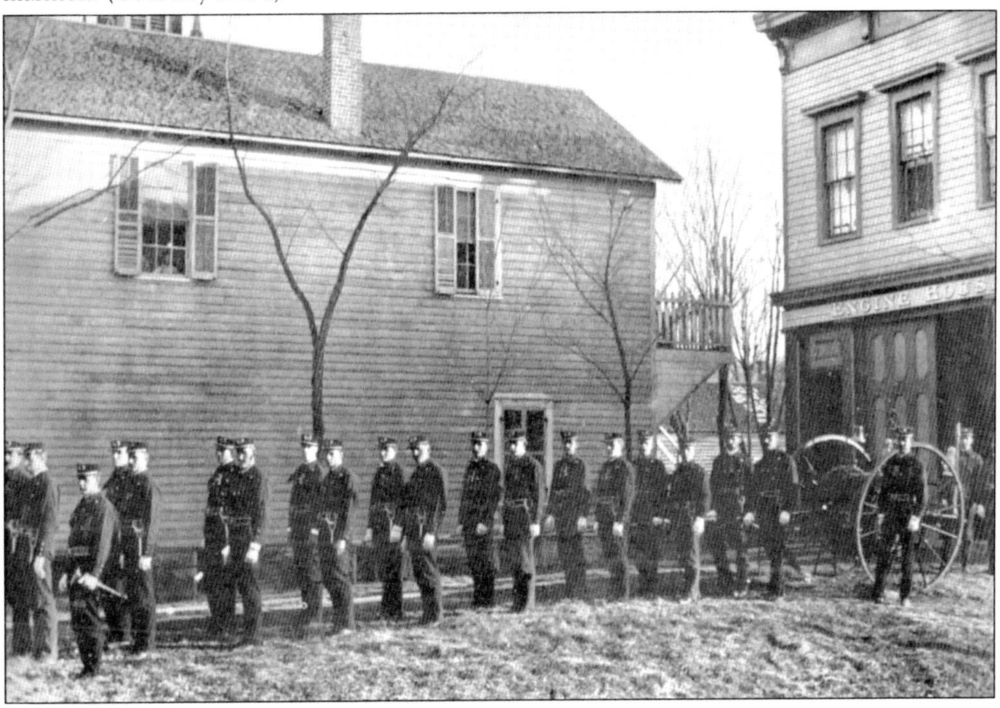

The J. B. Rice Hose Company No. 1 stands with its hose cart in front of the J. J. Gray Engine House. The hose cart was pulled by a team of people, not horses. The Russell Hose No. 1 disbanded in the early 1890s to be revived two years later under a new name. The new unit was named for Rice, a local business leader and chief engineer of the department.

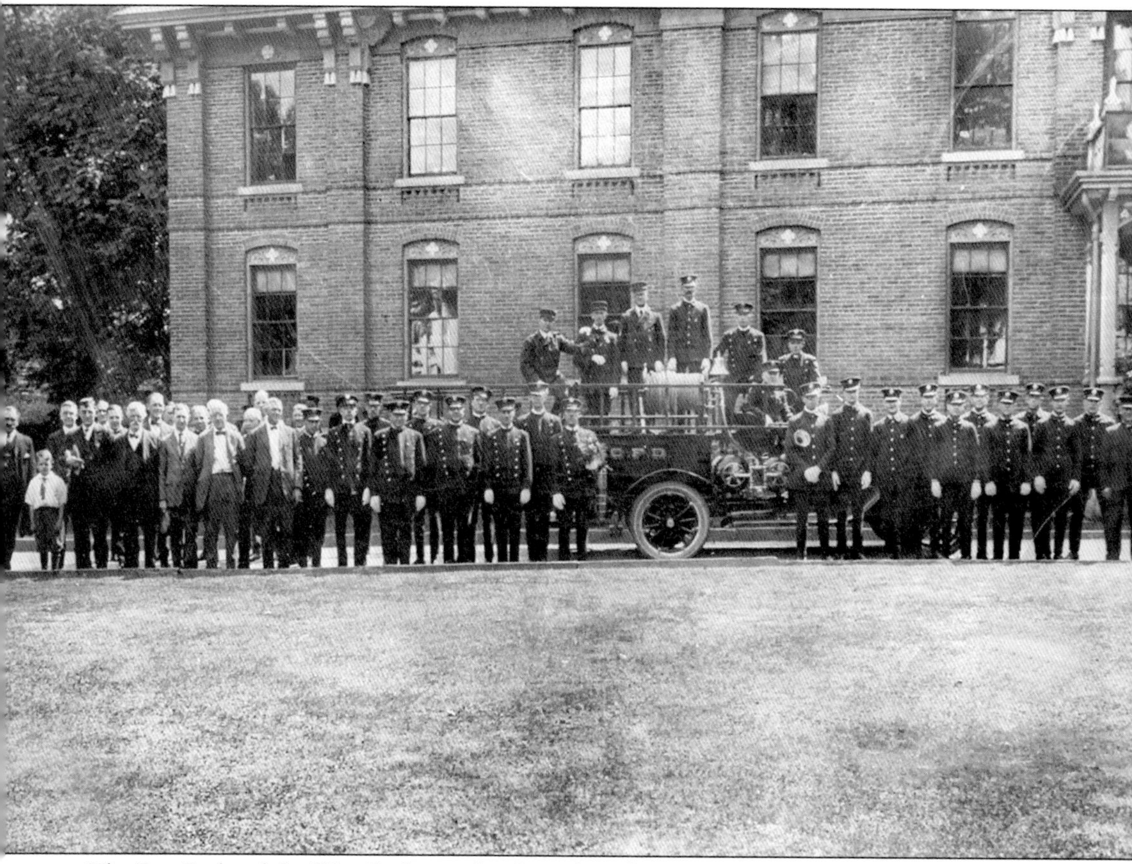

The East End and the West End united to form the village of Cambridge in 1866, but four separate fire companies existed until 1931. They were J. B. Rice Hose No. 1, John Larmon Hose No. 2, Hallelujah Hose No. 3, and the Cambridge Hooks. In this photograph, each company can be identified by a different uniform. On the left is the Hallelujah Hose Company, who never had official uniforms. According to local folklore, once when asked to dress in uniform, they appeared adorned in Prince Albert coats and straw hats.

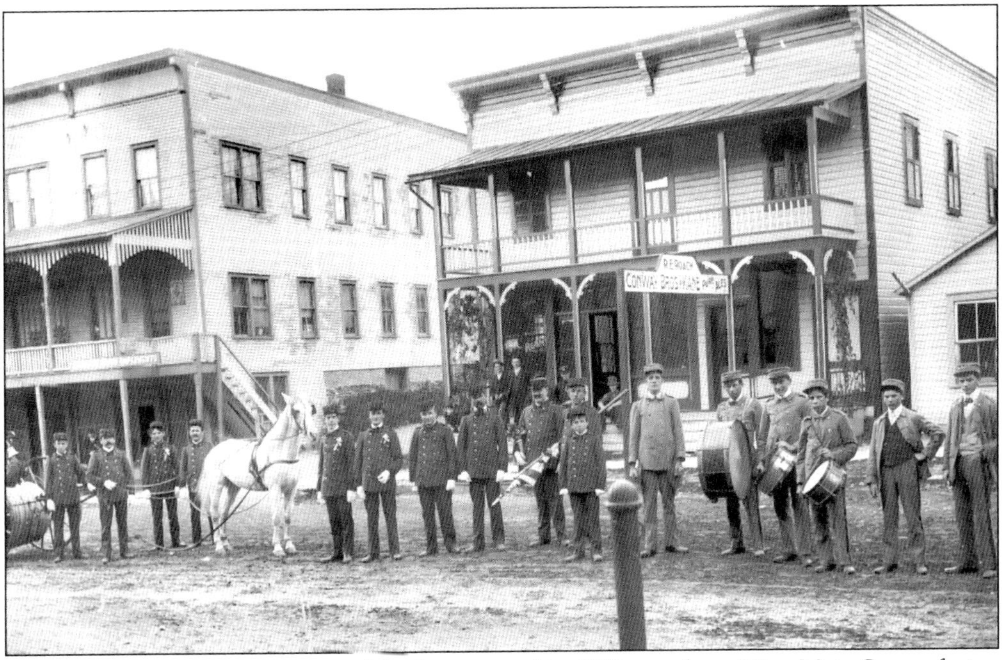

The John Larmon Hose Company No. 2, organized in 1887, stands on West Main Street, facing south. In the back on the left is the West End Market, then housing Osborne Farm Implements. To the right is the Hazlem building that burned in February 1961. In 1910, the Larmon fire station was on the north side of West Main Street, moving to the south side by 1925.

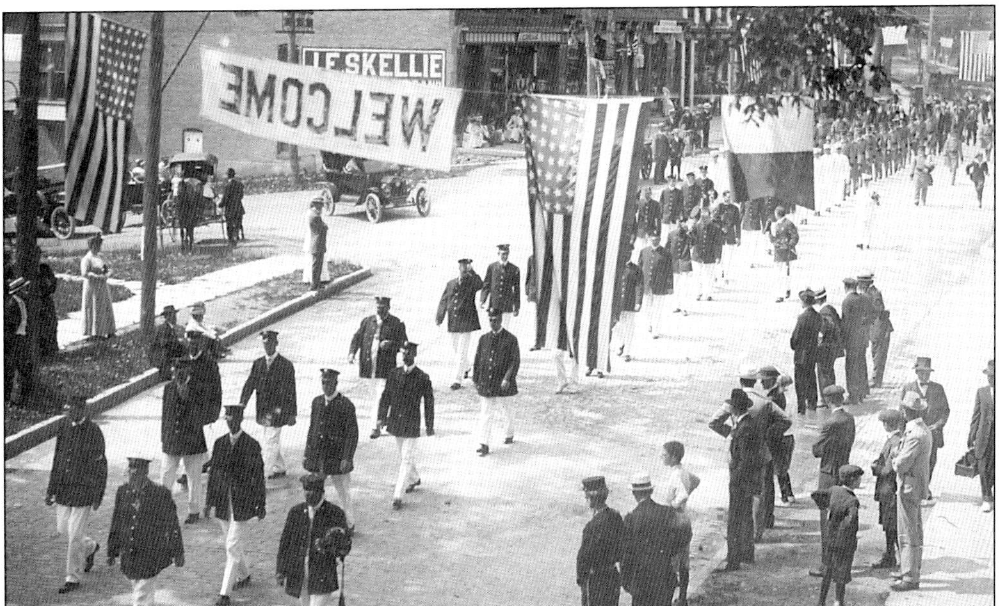

The 1915 Firemen's Muster parade marched on Main Street, which had been paved with yellow bricks two years earlier. Prior to the paving, Main Street became a mud bath after storms. Local folklore tells of a parade marching on the sidewalks while spectators stood in the muddy street. In April 1914, following a late spring storm, residents celebrated their newly paved and dry Main Street with an impromptu street dance. (Courtesy CVA.)

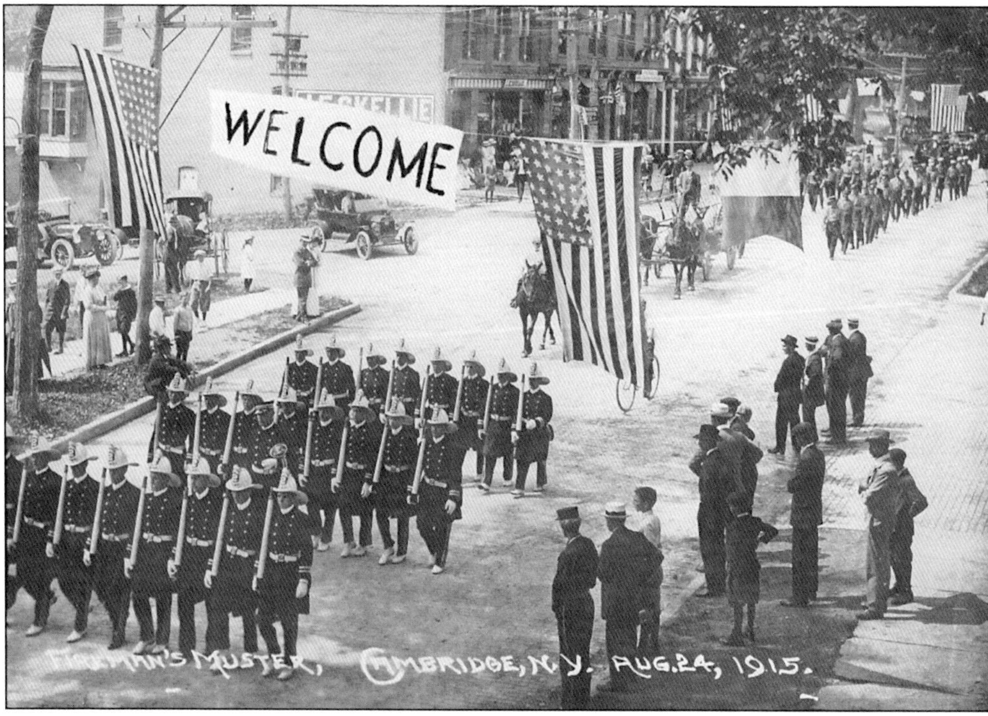

Early on parade day, kids hoping to ride on the fire engine in the parade rushed to the firehouse to find a spot. The village banned this in the early 1960s.

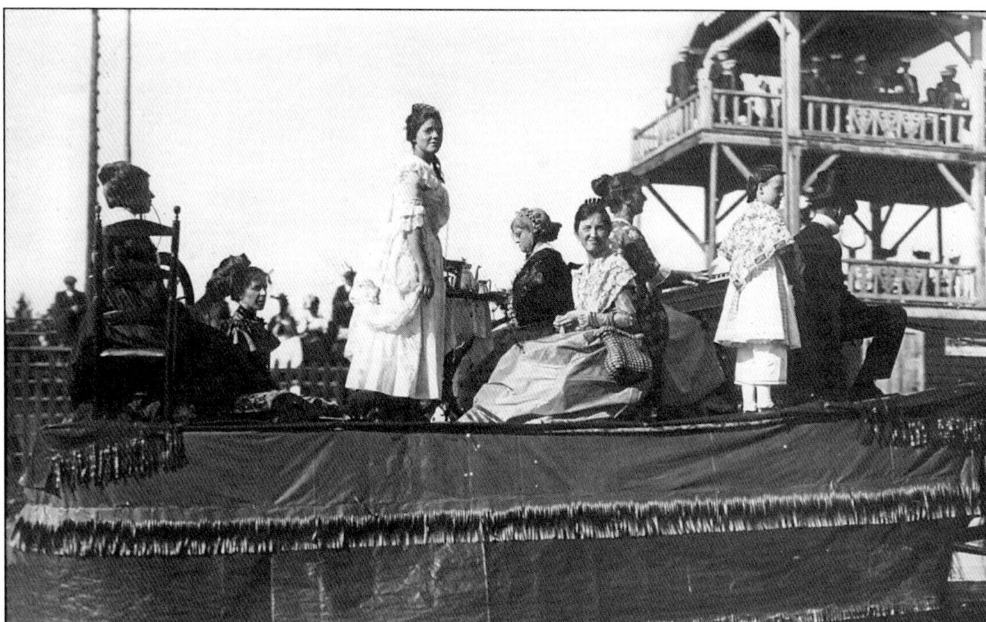

As this float parades around the racetrack at the Cambridge Fairgrounds, the bandstand can be seen in the background (right). The Cambridge Band, one of the oldest continuous village bands in America, can be seen on the upper level. (Courtesy CPL.)

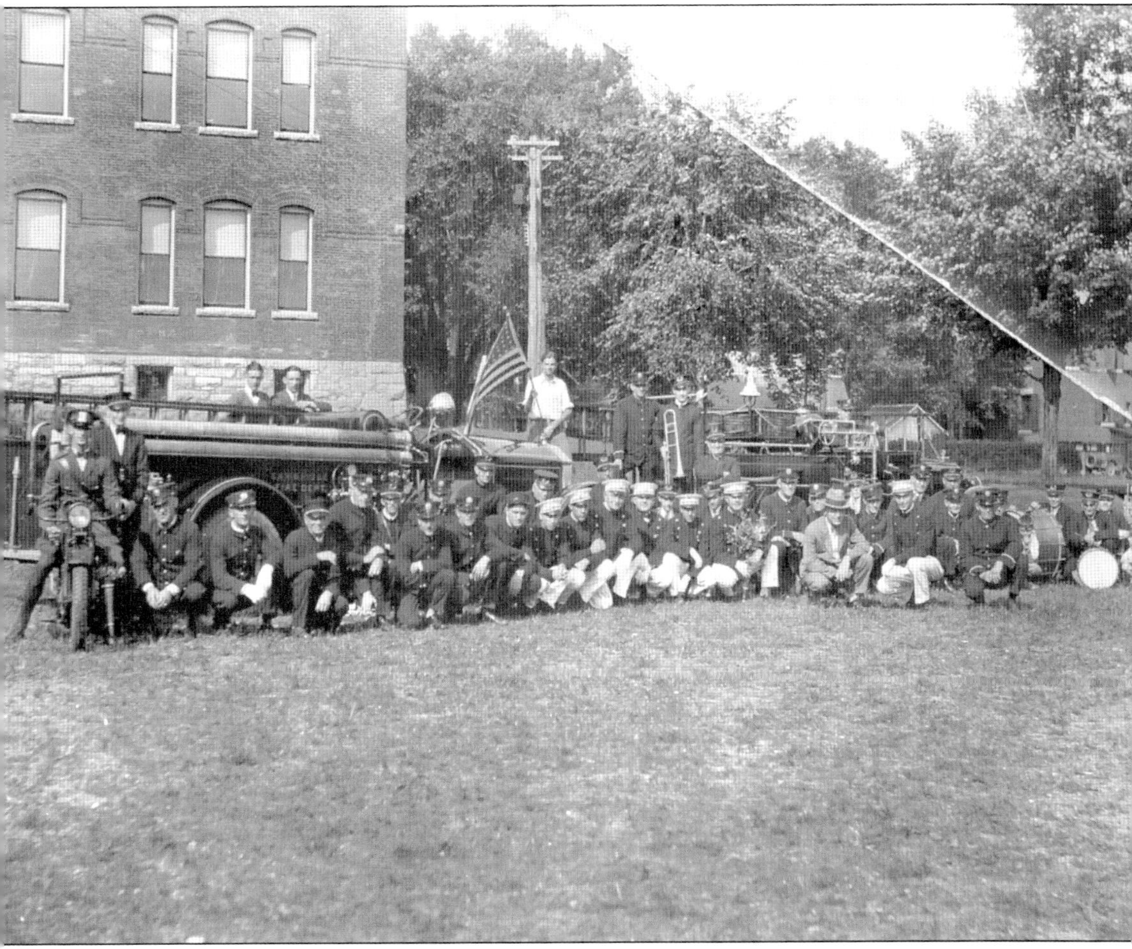

Even though the fire truck reads Cambridge Fire Department, the uniforms show that there were still several separate departments. This led to an interesting circumstance when, in 1921, the village purchased a mechanical fire engine to be shared by the four fire companies. The firemen wanted a parade to show off the new engine, and each company wanted to drive. The parade started in the middle of the village at the J. J. Gray Engine House. The Hooks drove the fire engine from the firehouse heading eastward toward Dorr's Corners. When the parade reached its most easterly point, they descended, and the J. B. Rice Hose Company hopped aboard to drive the engine westward back to the railroad tracks. There the John Larmon Hose Company took to the driver's seat, taking the fire engine to the most westerly point. Finally the Hallelujah Hose Company had its turn, driving the engine back to the firehouse. (Courtesy CVA.)

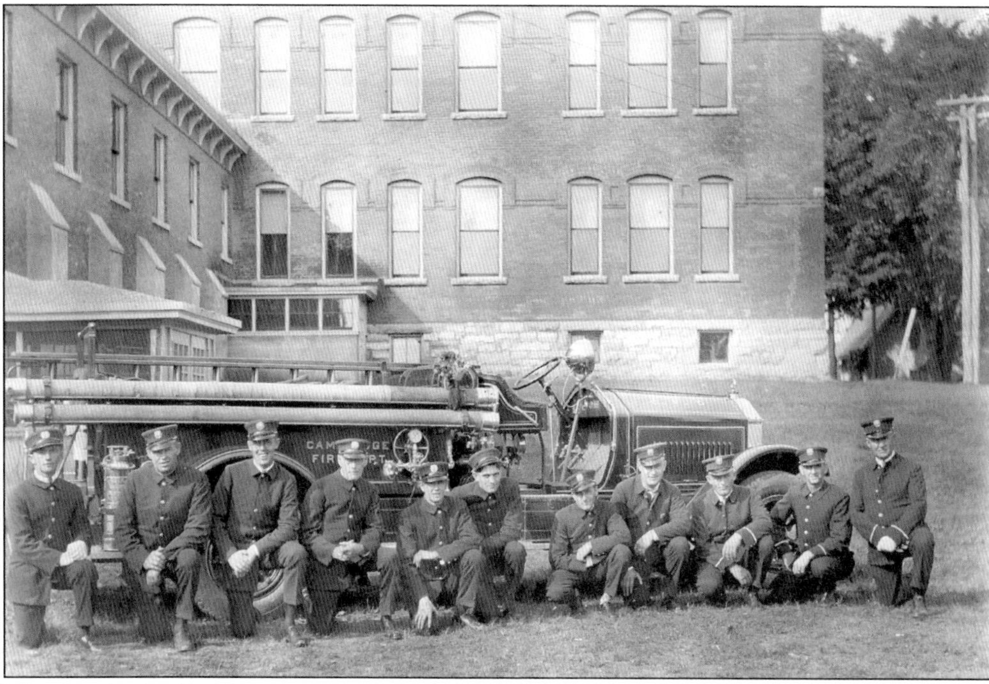

The Cambridge Fire Department poses behind the Union School following a Memorial Day parade in the mid-1940s. In 1931, the four smaller fire companies had consolidated into one unit. The 1926 American LaFrance fire engine was replaced in 1961. (Courtesy CVA.)

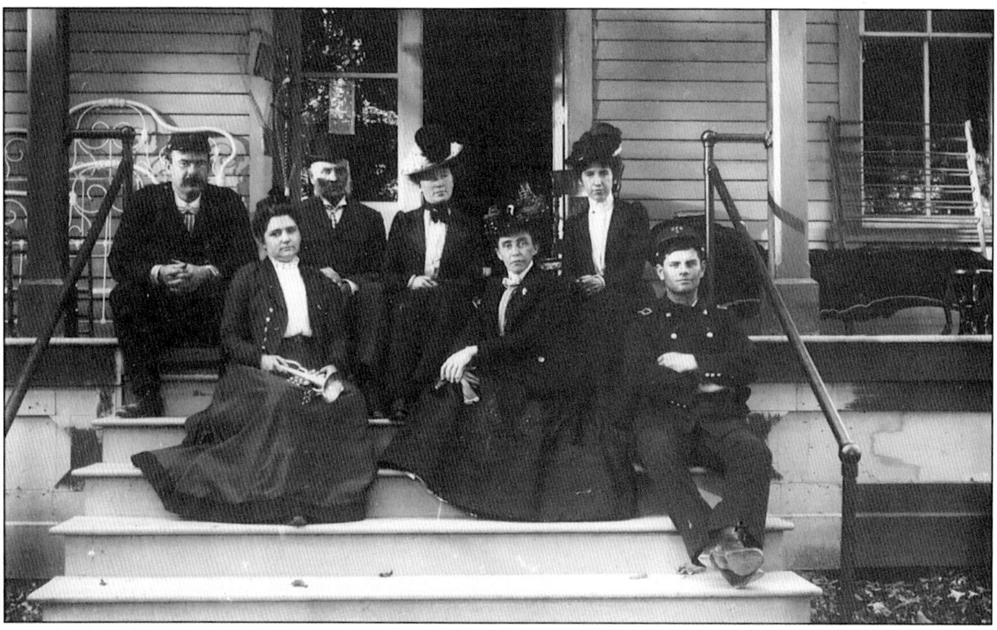

Parade days have always been a great time for families to gather and to record the moment with photographs. This photograph may have been taken following a parade, as the man in the lower right is wearing the uniform of J. B. Rice Hose No. 1. The building could be the E. C. Oatman furniture store, later the Charles Ackley furniture store, and today Cambridge Antiques. (Courtesy CVA.)

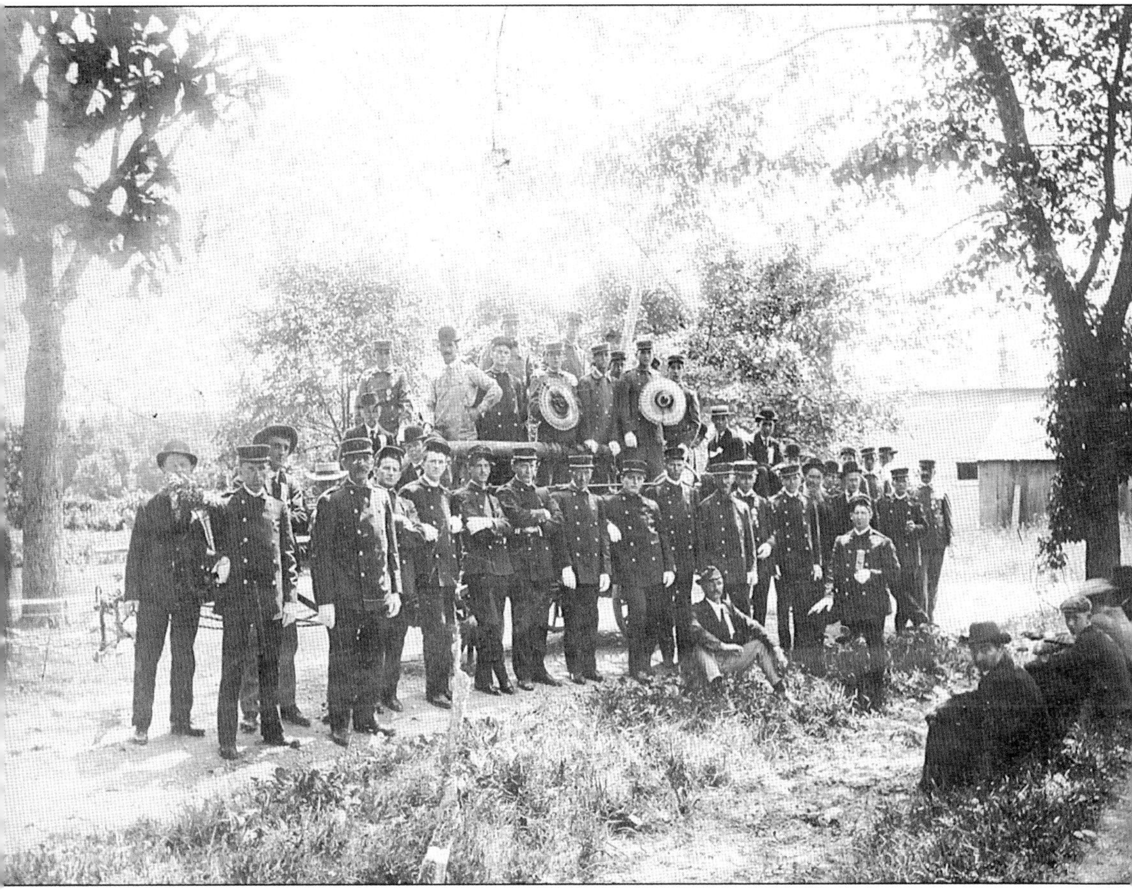

The Cambridge firemen relax after a Fireman's Muster competition. They appear to be standing in front of and aboard the J. J. Gray pumper. In 1868, shortly after the village had incorporated, J. J. Gray was given the task to find a suitable firefighting apparatus. The pumper bore his name thereafter. In 1921, in preparation for the Firemen's Muster in Bennington, the pumper was brought out of retirement. It was completely dismantled and reassembled, tight as a drum, by Tom Ryan, a local plumber. Soon the pumper was ready to be tested at Blair's Brook (Owl Kill) behind the McGhee Lumber Company. To the cheers of hundreds of onlookers, the J. J. Gray spit the water 308 feet. From then until the muster, members of the fire department stood guard at the engine house to prevent sabotage by a rival fire company. Finally at the firemen's muster, the J. J. Gray barely outshot the pumper of the Rough and Readies from Greenwich to win the annual competition.

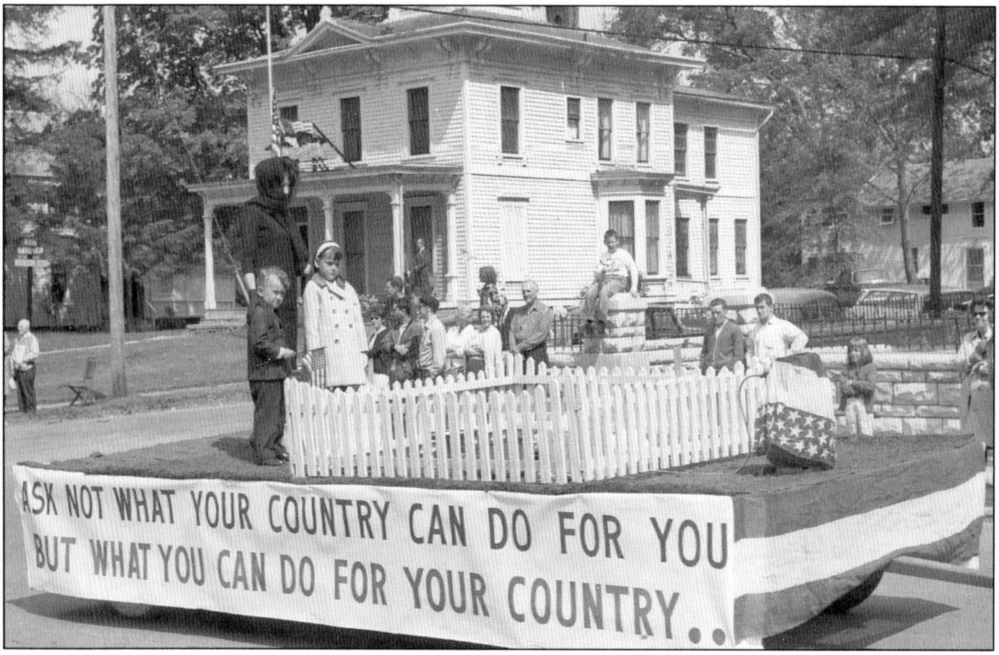

The Memorial Day parade, probably 1964, shows Cambridge mourning its fallen president, John Kennedy. The building in the background, the former residence of A. B. McNish on the northwest corner of West Main and St. Lukes Streets, served as the Maxson American Legion Post before the construction of the current post on Route 22 north of the village. (Courtesy CVA.)

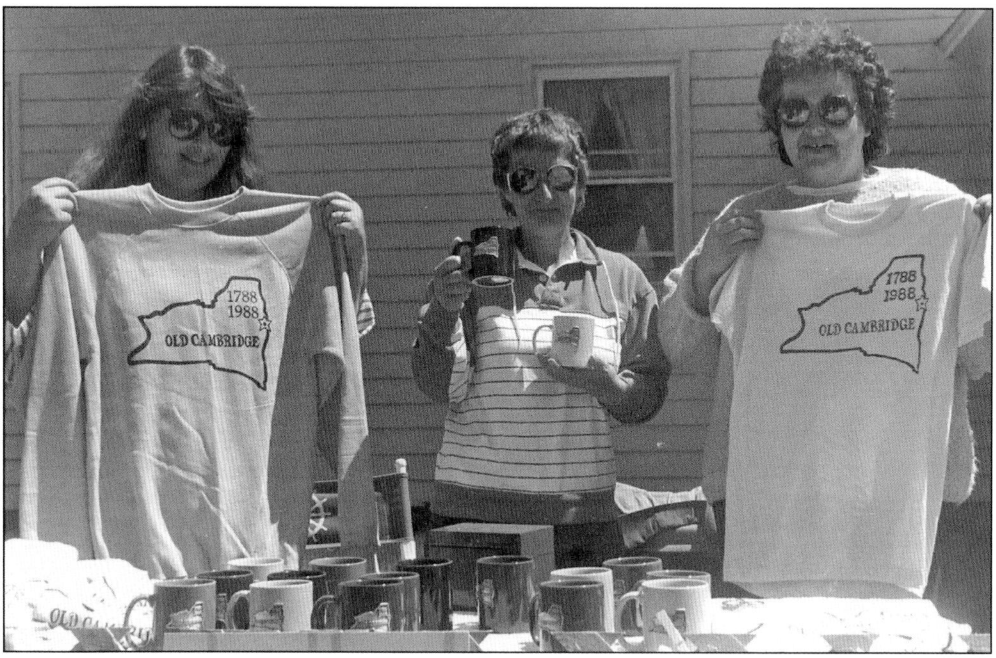

In 1988, Cambridge celebrated one of its many anniversaries, the 200 years since the formation of the town of Cambridge in Albany County. The community banded together to produce a 300-page history of old Cambridge, including genealogy of many distinguished families. (Courtesy CVA.)

BIBLIOGRAPHY

Clay, Bob, Carlton Foster, Bob Raymond, Tom Shiland, and Dave Thornton. *Old Cambridge 1788–1988*. Cambridge, NY: A and M Printers, 1988.

Everts and Ensign. *History of Washington County 1737–1878*. Philadelphia, PA: Lippincott and Company, 1878.

Gottry, Ken. *1866–1875 Historical Sketch of the Village of Cambridge*. Cambridge, NY: *Washington County Post*, 1976.

Moscrip, Amos. *Old Cambridge District*. Granville, NY: Grastorf Press, 1941.

Sanborn Map Company. *Cambridge Insurance Maps*. New York, NY: Sanborn Printers, 1904, 1910, 1925.

Smart, James, and Henry Noble. *Centennial of Old Cambridge 1773–1873*. Cambridge, NY: *Washington County Post*, 1874.

By Committee. *Old Home Week 1916*. Cambridge, NY: *Washington County Post*, 1916.